Rome Spreads Her Wings

To my wonderful wife Alex and my gorgeous two children,
Thomas and Caitlin.
Thank you for making my life so enjoyable.

Rome Spreads Her Wings

Territorial Expansion Between the Punic Wars

Gareth C. Sampson

Pen & Sword
MILITARY

First published in Great Britain in 2016 by
Pen & Sword Military
an imprint of
Pen & Sword Books Ltd
47 Church Street
Barnsley
South Yorkshire
S70 2AS

ISBN 978 1 78303 055 2

A CIP catalogue record for this book is available from the British
Library

Typeset in Ehrhardt by
Mac Style Ltd, Bridlington, East Yorkshire
Printed and bound in the UK by CPI Group (UK) Ltd,
Croydon, CRO 4YY

Pen & Sword Books Ltd incorporates the imprints of Pen & Sword
Archaeology, Atlas, Aviation, Battleground, Discovery, Family
History, History, Maritime, Military, Naval, Politics, Railways, Select,
Transport, True Crime, and Fiction, Frontline Books, Leo Cooper,
Praetorian Press, Seaforth Publishing and Wharncliffe.

For a complete list of Pen & Sword titles please contact
PEN & SWORD BOOKS LIMITED
47 Church Street, Barnsley, South Yorkshire, S70 2AS, England
E-mail: enquiries@pen-and-sword.co.uk
Website: www.pen-and-sword.co.uk

Contents

Acknowledgements   vii
Maps and Diagrams   viii
Introduction – In the Shadow of the Punic Wars   xvi
Timeline of Key Conflicts – 241–218 BC   xviii

Part I: Rome Before and After the First Punic War (338–218 BC)   1

Chapter 1   Roman Expansion in Italy and Beyond (338–241 BC)   3

Chapter 2   Roman Expansion in the Mediterranean – Sicily,
                  Sardinia and Corsica (241–218 BC)   17

Part II: Roman Expansion in Italy and the East (238–228 BC)   33

Chapter 3   Roman Expansion in Italy – The Gallic and Ligurian
                  Wars (238–230 BC)   35

Chapter 4   Roman Expansion in the East – The First Illyrian War
                  (230–228 BC)   62

Chapter 5   Carthaginian Expansion in Spain and the Roman
                  Response (237–226 BC)   90

**Part III: Roman Expansion in Italy and the Gallic War
(228–218 BC)**   111

Chapter 6   The Gallic War I – The Road to Telamon   113

Chapter 7   The Gallic War II – The Battle of Telamon (225 BC)   132

Chapter 8   The Gallic War III – The Roman Invasion of
                  Northern Italy (224–223 BC)   148

Chapter 9   The Gallic War IV – The Battle of Clastidium (222 BC)
                  and Subsequent Campaigns (222–218 BC)   164

Part IV: The Consequences of Expansion (225–218 BC)   183

Chapter 10   Roman Expansion in the East – The Second Illyrian
                 War (219 BC)   185

Chapter 11   Carthaginian Expansion in Spain and the Roman
                 Response (225–218 BC)   201

Conclusion: The Grand Strategy of the Roman Republic?   218
Appendix I: The Sources   224
Appendix II: Kings, Consuls and Triumphs   231
Appendix III: The Re-emergence of the Tribunate of the Plebs?   234
Appendix IV: Polybius and Roman Manpower – An Overview   240
Appendix V: Consequences   243
Bibliography   248
Notes and References   257
Index   274

Acknowledgements

As always, the greatest acknowledgement goes out to my wife Alex, without whose support this book (nor any of them) would never have been written. Supporting a husband writing a book, whilst writing one of your own and looking after a young baby and a toddler, is a truly Herculean effort.

Notable mentions go out to our son Thomas, who is growing up splendidly, and our new daughter Caitlin, whose arrival led to another delay in finishing a book. Being a daddy and a historian is a challenge, but the children make it more than worthwhile.

A lifelong debt of gratitude goes out to my parents, who have always supported me and encouraged my love of learning.

As always, a debt of gratitude goes out to my editor Phil Sidnell, whose patience is legendary and usually sorely tested when I'm writing a book.

There are a number of individuals who through the years have inspired the love of Roman history in me and mentored me along the way; Michael Gracey at William Hulme, David Shotter at Lancaster and Tim Cornell at Manchester. My heartfelt thanks go out to them all.

Thanks go out to the Manchester Diaspora, now reduced to Ian, James, Gary, Greg and Jason. As always big hugs go out to Pete and Nicki back in the US.

On a more practical note, thanks go out to the Central Library at Plymouth for their truly excellent interlibrary service, which frankly continues to put most university libraries to shame. Also thanks go to the Alumni Society at Manchester for organising JSTOR access for alumni, which has been a lifesaver.

Maps and Diagrams

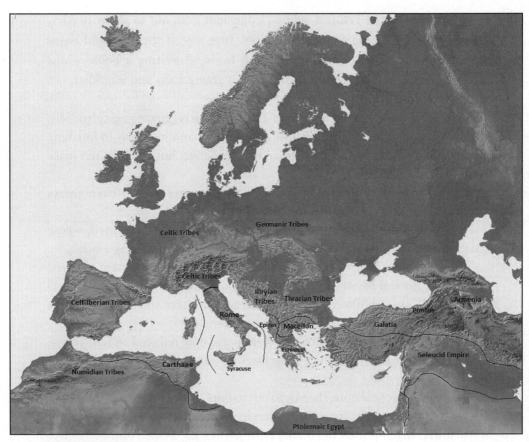

Map 1: The Mediterranean World in 241 BC.

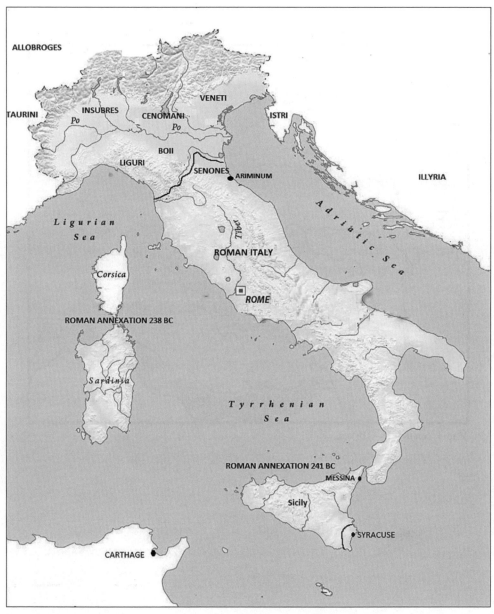

Map 2: Italy (241–218 BC).

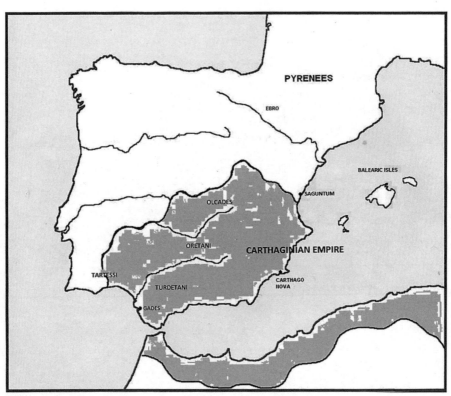

Map 3: Spain (237–218 BC).

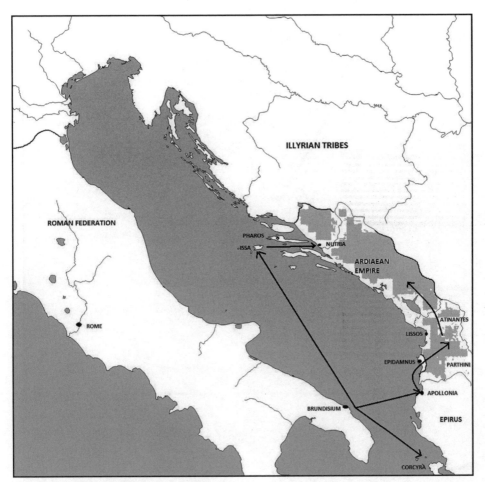

Map 4: First Illyrian War (229–228 BC)

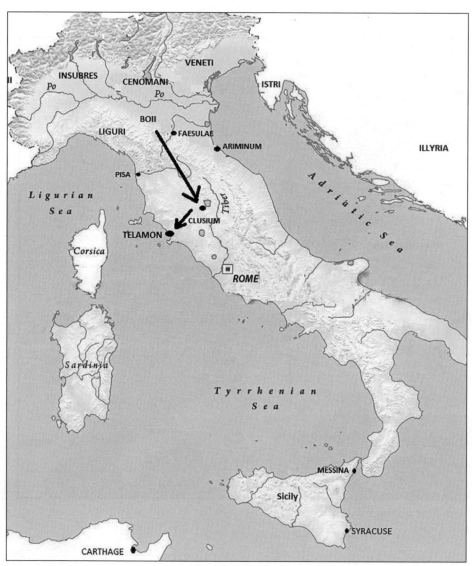

Map 5: Gallic War (225 BC)

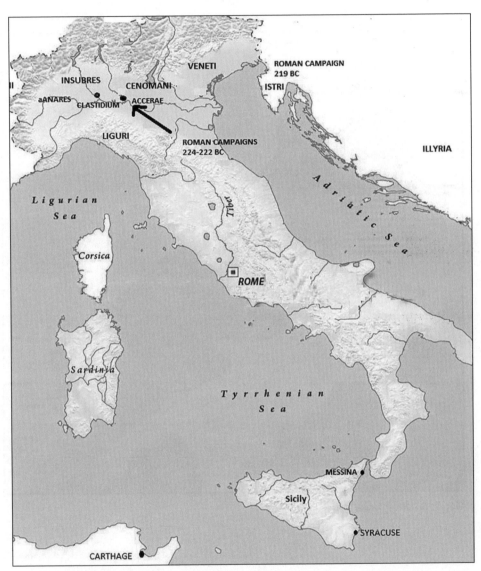

Map 6: Gallic War (224–222 BC)

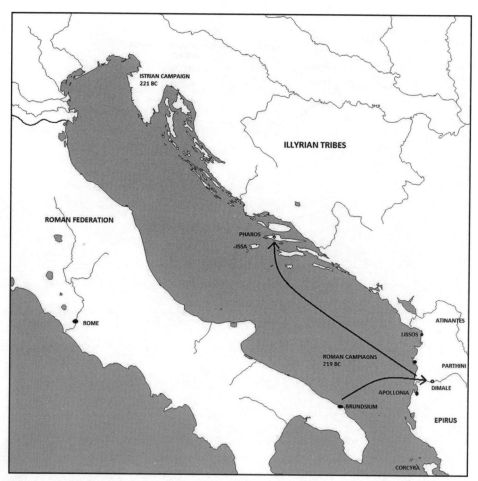

Map 7: Second Illyrian War (219 BC)

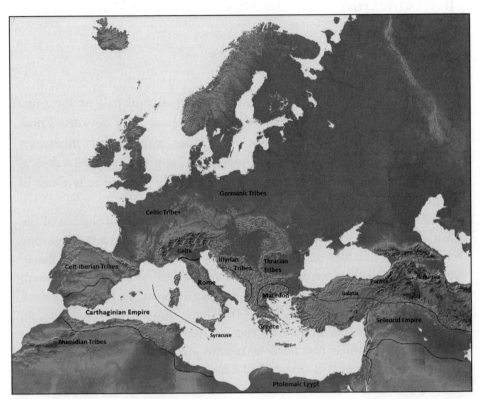

Map 8: The Mediterranean World in 218 BC

Introduction – In the Shadow of the Punic Wars

The period which is now known as the second half of the third century BC is dominated by the two great wars between Rome and Carthage, known as the Punic Wars, with the years inbetween (241–218 BC) usually passed over. However, this approach ignores a critical period in Roman military history and overlooks three major milestones in the history of the Republic and its military expansion.

The first major factor is that it was during this period that the last of the great Gallic invasions of Roman territory occurred. Modern historiography tends to view Carthage as Rome's major rival in this period and the power that represented the greatest threat to Rome's expansion and very survival. Yet this view overlooks the fact that Rome had a potentially far greater rival, far closer to home: the Gauls. It was the Gauls who had achieved what no other rival power had in Rome's history: successfully attacking the city of Rome itself, which had been sacked by the Gauls in the early fourth century. Furthermore, in this period Gaul extended beyond the Alps and encompassed northern Italy. Thus Rome faced a numerically superior rival right on its doorstep and one which could march on the city within weeks. It was in this period that the centuries' – long war between Rome and the Gauls, for control of the territory which is now Italy, reached its conclusion, culminating in the Battle of Telamon, one of the most important battles that the Republic fought.

The two other factors relate to military expansion outside of Italy. The first of these concerns the fact that it was in this period that Rome acquired its first overseas provinces. Although these first provinces were limited in terms of their size and distance from Italy (Sicily, Sardinia and Corsica), they were nevertheless a major step on Rome's overseas expansion, setting the foundation for what was to come. Furthermore, Rome's experiences in this period set the tone for the shape of overseas expansion for the next 100 years.

The third factor found in this period is that Rome took another major step in its military expansion outside of Italy by crossing the Adriatic for the first time in its history and fighting wars on the Greek mainland. The two wars which Rome fought in Illyria in this period established the foundation which was to set Rome on a path drawing them inexorably further into the world of Hellenistic great power politics and warfare, which would ultimately end 100 years later in the Roman conquest of Greece, a conquest which in one form or another would last for the next 1,600 years.

Therefore, these two decades provided the building blocks upon which the later Roman Empire was founded; control of Italy, overseas provinces and military intervention in Greece. For these reasons, this period needs to be studied and analysed in its own right and brought out of the shadow of the Punic Wars. For too long the events of this period have been seen through the lens of the Punic Wars, with every event viewed in terms of the relationship between Rome and Carthage. Yet until late in this period, Carthage was not the issue at the forefront of Roman minds; this study hopes to redresses this.

Timeline of Key Conflicts – 241–218 BC

BC

241	End of the First Punic War
	Roman annexation of Sicily
241–237	Mercenary (Truceless) War in North Africa
238	Roman annexation of Sardinia and Corsica
238–236	Boian War
238–233	Ligurian War
237	Carthaginian invasion of Spain
232	Tribunate of C. Flaminius
231	Senatorial Delegation sent to Spain
229–228	First Illyrian War
228	Roman Embassies sent to Greece
	Human Sacrifice in Rome
227	Number of Praetors raised to four (Sicily and Sardinia/Corsica)
226	Ebro Treaty between Rome and Carthage
225–222	Gallic War
225	Gallic invasion of Roman Italy
	Battle of Telamon
	Roman invasion of Cisalpine Gaul
222	Battle of Clastidium
221	Istrian War
220	Alpine Campaign
219	Second Illyrian War
	Carthaginian attack on Saguntum
218	Fall of Saguntum
	Roman Declaration of war begins the Second Punic War
	Gallic War

Notes on Roman Names

All Roman names in the text are given in their traditional form, including the abbreviated first name. Below is a list of the Roman first names referred to in the text and their abbreviations.

A.	Aulus.
Ap.	Appius
C.	Caius
Cn.	Cnaeus
D.	Decimus
K.	Kaeso
L.	Lucius
M.	Marcus
Mam.	Mamercus
P.	Publius
Q.	Quintus
Ser.	Servius
Sex.	Sextus
Sp.	Spurius
T.	Titus
Ti.	Tiberius

Part I

Rome Before and After the First Punic War
(338–218 BC)

Chapter One

Roman Expansion in Italy and Beyond
(338–241 BC)

B efore we can examine the period in question (241–218 BC) we must
first understand how this period fits in with the wider expansion of
the Roman state and the events which took place prior to 241 BC. It
is tempting to view Rome of the third century BC through the lens of the
later, more famous period; a Rome which was unquestioned master of Italy,
able to defeat any other Mediterranean power and on an inevitable course
to mastery of the Mediterranean world. However, this was not the Rome
of the third century BC. By 241 BC, Rome had only recently taken control
of central and southern Italy, the latter of which had seen recent attempts
made to annex it to being either a part of a Syracusan empire to the south
or an Epirote empire to the east. Furthermore, it is important to note that
Rome's control of Italy did not extend to the north of the peninsula, which
was occupied by a collection of Gallic tribes and formed part of a wider
civilisation, which stretched from Spain to the Balkans and beyond.

We must also not forget that Italy did not exist in isolation, but was
part of a Mediterranean world which was undergoing a major upheaval in
terms of the established world order. Less than 100 years before 241 BC, the
ancient superpower of Persia had been destroyed within a decade by one
man: Alexander III (the Great) of Macedon. His death in 323 BC unleashed
a generation of warfare across Greece and the Near East, which by the
280s had stabilised into an uneasy balance of power between three new
superpowers: Antigonid Macedon, the Seleucid Empire and Ptolemaic
Egypt (see Map 1). Italy sat on the edges of this new world order, but
within striking distance of mainland Greece, dominated by the Antigonid
Dynasty of Macedon.

The Roman Federation therefore must be placed in this context. To the
north lay the vast and seemingly endless expanses of mainland Europe

and the tribes that dwelt within, which encompassed northern Italy itself. To the east lay the far more culturally advanced civilisation of Greece, dominated by the great power of Macedon. To the south and the east lay the Carthaginian Empire, centred on North Africa, but extending across the western Mediterranean. Compared to these great civilisations, Rome was the emerging, and in some ways upstart power, and by 241 BC had announced itself on the wider world stage by an extraordinary period of expansion.

Roman Expansion in Italy (338–264 BC)

The year 338 BC marks a decisive point in the history of Italy, as coincidently it did in Greece, albeit for different reasons. In Greece, King Philip II of Macedon was victorious at the Battle of Chaeronea, which established Macedonian suzerainty over the Greek states for the next 200 years. In Italy, another war was also ending; this time between Rome and her former allies in the Latin League, with Rome emerging victorious. Rome's victory in this war did not give her suzerainty over Italy (akin to that of Macedon in Greece), merely mastery of the region of Latium, but the political settlement that followed this victory did provide the foundation for Rome's domination of Italy, and ultimately the wider Mediterranean world.

Prior to the Latin War, Rome had been at war with her near neighbours for over four centuries (if we are to believe the traditional chronology) and yet barely controlled any territory beyond the coastal plains of Latium itself, in western central Italy. Furthermore, Rome faced an equally powerful neighbour in terms of the Samnite Federation and the ever-constant threat of the Gallic tribes of northern Italy (who had sacked Rome itself just fifty years earlier, c.390–386 BC). Therefore, to put Rome's efforts in perspective, they had only conquered the neighbouring city of Veii (roughly ten miles from Rome) in 396 BC after intermittent warfare lasting 300 years. Yet despite this, within sixty years of the peace settlement of 338 BC Rome had established an unprecedented control of all central and southern Italy. It is to this political settlement (which accompanied the end of the Latin War) which we must turn our focus, when looking of the reasons behind this extraordinary wave of military expansion.[1]

Prior to this war, fought by Rome against their rebellious allies, Rome's power ostensibly lay through being head of the Latin League, a defensive alliance of supposedly equal states. However, over the centuries this federation had evolved into being dominated by Rome and, as many of her allies saw it, seemed to exist solely for Rome's benefit. It was this resentment of Roman dominance of the League which saw Rome's allies attempt to break free from the League and thus brought about the Roman–Latin War of 341–338 BC. Unfortunately for the other Latin cities, the war merely confirmed Roman military dominance and her enemies were comprehensively defeated.

Having been freed from the need to preserve the pretence of an alliance of equals, the Romans dissolved the Latin League and in its place stood a new unofficial federation, that of Rome. Livy provides a detailed description of these reforms, which he ascribes to the Consul L. Furius Camillus.[2] Instead of common ties between all the participants, each of the Latin cities was tied to Rome individually by treaty. Rome secured their treaties by means of carrot and stick policies. The 'stick' came in the form of Roman veteran colonies planted at strategic points within the territories of the defeated Latin states, accompanied by land confiscations. The 'carrot', however, was two-fold. Firstly, the various cities were able to maintain their own internal political and social structures and the local elites were left free from Roman interference to pursue their own internal policies. What was sacrificed was an independent foreign policy, which was now slaved to that of Rome. However, aside from this, they were left to their own devices, speaking their own language, continuing with the own culture and carrying on business as usual.

Furthermore, the Romans introduced a new graduated series of citizenship levels. At the peak was Roman citizenship, which gave full political and judicial rights, followed by partial citizenship (*civitas cine suffragio*), which had no rights of political participation in Rome, and only limited legal protection from Romans.[3] This system of differentiating levels of citizenship allowed Rome the ability to incorporate new peoples without diluting the original core of the Roman citizens or jeopardizing the Roman elite's control of its institutions, especially as voting had to take place in person in Rome itself. Despite the different grades of citizenship, this was not a closed system, nor was it one restricted to race.[4] This meant that there were opportunities for advancement within the system, to both communities and in particular their elites, giving them a stake in the Roman system and buying their loyalty.

However, at the heart of this settlement lay the obligation on all citizens (whether full or partial) to be called upon for military service in Rome's armies. It was not only those with citizenship (full and partial) who could be conscripted into the Roman Army, but Rome's Italian allies were duty bound to send their citizens to serve in Rome's armies. This created a massive supply of potential manpower for Rome, which was to be the central pillar of all future Roman expansion. In the ancient world, city states were limited by the availability of citizen manpower and one heavy defeat could set a state back a generation.

The years that followed this settlement saw a series of wars against Rome's neighbours, most prominently the Samnite Federation. Starting in 326 BC, the Second Samnite War[5] lasted for twenty years (until 304 BC), and saw Rome's fortunes swing between victories and humiliating defeats, such as the Battle of Caudine Forks in 321 BC, which forever ranked as one of Rome's most humiliating military reversals. Nevertheless, by 304 BC Rome had the upper hand and the Samnites were forced to sue for peace, albeit maintaining their independence.

The period saw two major reforms to the Roman military system. In 312 BC, one of the Censors, Ap. Claudius Caecus, ordered the construction of the Via Appia, the first major paved road in Italy, connecting Rome and Capua (crossing the Alban Hills and the Pontine Marshes). This allowed Rome to move her armies far more swiftly to the south to support the war against the Samnites.

The following year saw a Tribune of the Plebs (C. Marcius) pass a law allowing for the sixteen Tribunes of the Soldiers to be elected by the people, rather than appointed by the commanders. It has long been argued that this law came at the same time as the Romans doubled their legions from two to four (having four Tribunes per legion) and that this also coincided with the abandonment of the phalanx and the development of the more flexible Roman maniple.[6] This year also saw the outbreak of war between Rome and various Etruscan cities. The years that followed saw Rome advance into central Italy and up into Umbria, conquering a number of peoples, such as the Herenici and Aequi and allying with others, such as the Marsi. The result of this was that by the late 300s BC Roman power extended throughout central Italy.

This massive extension of Roman power naturally led to a reaction from the peoples who were not yet under Roman rule, resulting in the formation of an alliance between the Samnites, Etruscans, Umbrians and Gauls (of northern Italy). This resulted in the war that is most commonly referred to as the Third Samnite War (298–290 BC), but was far wider in scale than the name suggests. This conflict was Rome's greatest victory to date and resulted in Rome defeating each of the opposing alliance and gaining control of all of central and much of southern Italy, stretching to the Adriatic coast. The year 295 BC saw the Battle of Sentinum, in which Rome was able to field an army of 36,000, a huge figure for the time, and defeat a combined force of Gauls and Samnites. By 290 BC the surrender of the Samnites meant that the only regions of Italy which now lay outside of Roman control were the Gallic tribes of northern Italy and the Greek city states of the south.

A further war with the Gallic tribes of northern Italy soon followed (against the Boii and Senones), which ultimately saw further Roman success, culminating in a victory at the Battle of Lake Vadimon in 283 BC. A large section of the northern Adriatic coastline of Italy was thus added to Rome's Italian empire. This war was soon followed by the more famous war for southern Italy, where Rome faced one of the Hellenistic world's most celebrated generals: Pyrrhus, King of Epirus. Thus, for the first time, Rome faced a Hellenistic army from mainland Greece and famously at the battles of Heraclea and Ausculum (280 and 279 BC) were comprehensively defeated. These battles, however, gave rise to the modern concept of a 'Pyrrhic victory' as the Romans, thanks to their system of treaties and obligations to provide manpower, were able to replace their losses and return to full strength within the year, whilst Pyrrhus found his numbers steadily declining. Following a number of unsuccessful campaigns in Sicily, Pyrrhus returned to Italy and was finally defeated at the Battle of Beneventum in 275 BC. Following his withdrawal back to Greece, Rome advanced into southern Italy and conquered the Greek city states therein.

Rome and the First Punic War (264–241 BC)

The conquest of southern Italy brought Roman territory into proximity with the perpetual warzone that was the island of Sicily. For centuries the island had seen warfare between native peoples and various external powers, who coveted the island for its natural resources and strategic position. Perhaps the longest period of fighting had been between the North African power of Carthage and the native Sicilian power of Syracuse, with neither side managing to achieve a lasting dominance.[7]

In the 270s, however, this balance of power had been disrupted by the arrival of King Pyrrhus of Epirus. Having defeated the Romans twice in battle, but unable to conclude the war, Pyrrhus accepted an offer from the Sicilian peoples, led by Syracuse, to take command of native Sicily and drive out the Carthaginians. Unable to resist the dream of a Sicilian, and possible African, empire to add to his hopes of an Italian one, Pyrrhus accepted and crossed into Sicily with his army in 278 BC.[8] Ironically, this invasion brought the traditional allies of Carthage and Rome closer together, as they concluded a fresh (anti-Pyrrhic) alliance. However, Pyrrhus's Sicilian campaign followed a similar course to his Italian one, being unable to convert military victory on the battlefield into a lasting settlement. Having alienated his Sicilian allies, he quit Sicily to return to his original ambition of carving out an Italian empire in 276 BC, leaving behind a shattered island.

This chaos was exploited by a group known as the Mamertines;[9] these were Campanian mercenaries who made a bid to seize control of large swathes of Sicily for themselves. In response to this new threat, a Syracusan general named Hiero (II) formed an alliance of native forces and drove the Mamertines back into the north-eastern tip of Sicily, and the city of Messana, which controlled the strategic crossing from Sicily to Italy (see Map 2).[10] Faced with defeat at the hands of Hiero in c.265/264 BC the Mamertines appealed to both Carthage and Rome to assist them. Seeing a chance to restore their Sicilian empire, the Carthaginians agreed and installed a garrison at Messina, thwarting their old Syracusan rivals.

Unfortunately for all three sides already involved in the war in Sicily, the Roman Senate continued to debate the Mamertine request, understandably, as they had never operated in Sicily before, and they and the Carthaginians were long-standing allies. Ultimately, however, it was a vote of the Roman people which determined that Rome would send aid to Sicily and the Mamertines, and the Senate thus dispatched the Consul Ap. Claudius Caudex to Messina with a Roman Army.[11] Thus the situation in Sicily saw the entry of a fourth military force. Given the Roman vote of support, the Mamertines threw their lot in with Rome and were able to expel the Carthaginian garrison, allowing the Romans to seize control of the city. Faced with the expansion of Roman power into Sicily, the Carthaginians and Syracusans – traditionally old enemies – found common cause against

Rome and thus the First Punic War began. Thus the war started as Rome and the Mamertines versus Carthage and the Syracusans (and their allies).

Ever since 264 BC, historians have been examining the question as to why Rome intervened in the interminable struggles in Sicily, and ultimately it must be acknowledged that we will never know for sure. Certainly the stated cause of the Roman intervention itself seems weak; defending rogue mercenaries who had seized a native city. This is especially the case given that a few years earlier, in 270 BC, the Romans had expelled a similar group of Campanian mercenaries who had seized the city of Rhegium, in southern Italy.

Yet, as detailed above, Rome was undergoing a major period of expansion and had just seized control of southern Italy. As history had shown, southern Italy was open to attack from both mainland Greece (Epirus), but also from Sicily. In the period 390–386 BC Dionysius, the Tyrant of Syracuse, had invaded and conquered much of southern Italy, adding it to his greater Syracusan empire.[12] Having conquered southern Italy, Dionysius then used it as a launch pad to invade Epirus itself, to place a puppet on the throne. Therefore, strategically, no control of southern Italy would be secure without securing its eastern and western flanks (Epirus and Sicily). The Mamertine appeal thus gave Rome the excuse they needed to intervene and the prospect of Carthaginian control of Messina provided the motivation. Thus, for the first time, Rome embarked upon an overseas war.

During the early years of the war, Rome experienced a number of successes. They moved swiftly from the conquest of Messina to a siege of Syracuse itself, but fared no better than either the Athenians or the Carthaginians had over the centuries. However, what they could not achieve through force of arms they achieved through diplomacy when Hiero, now Tyrant of Syracuse, was persuaded to break his alliance with Carthage and conclude a treaty with Rome instead. Thus, within a year of the war's outbreak Rome had secured both Messina and Syracuse and had isolated Carthage.

The Romans built on this success and 262 BC saw Rome storm the city of Agrigentum, a key Carthaginian base on the southern Sicilian coast. From this high point, however, the war in Sicily became one of attrition, with the Carthaginians wisely avoiding open battle on land. In an attempt to gain the initiative in the war, Rome invested heavily in building its first wartime navy in order to tackle Carthaginian naval dominance and cut Sicily off from Carthage itself. At first the Romans proved victorious, as seen in 260 BC at the Battle of Mylae, which saw a Roman Consul, C. Duilius, celebrate the city's first naval triumph. This was in great part due to the Roman tactic of engaging ships at close quarters, using grappling irons to tie the two ships together and then sending marines across to secure the other ship; thus turning a naval engagement into an infantry one.

Unfortunately for Rome, the war in Sicily had descended into a series of prolonged sieges, with the Carthaginian withdrawing to their key bases and allowing Roman forces free reign across the island's interior. To end this stalemate in 256 BC, the Roman Consuls undertook their boldest military manoeuvre to date when L. Manlius Vulso Longus and M. Atilius Regulus led an invasion of Africa itself, in an attempt to knock Carthage out of the war. Another naval victory, at the Battle of Ecnomus, allowed the Romans to land their army in Africa. Unfortunately the Roman Army was then comprehensively defeated in the Battle of Bagradas the following year, at the hands of a Spartan mercenary commander named Xanthippus. With this bold invasion defeated, the war dragged on for another decade of Roman sieges in Sicily and naval encounters in Sicilian waters.

Ultimately, the First Punic War became one of attrition, with the resources of both empires being stretched to the limit. In the end, Rome was able to make the most of its fiscal and human resources and by 242 BC was able to finally reduce the last key Carthaginian strongholds of Drepana and Lilybaeum. With Sicily lost and Rome vying for control of the seas, the Carthaginian Senate had no choice but to seek terms. Thus Rome had won its first overseas war, but only through attrition. For Carthage, the terms of the peace treaty were the evacuation of all its forces from Sicily and twenty years of war reparations.[13]

The Aftermath of the First Punic War – Rebellion in Italy

At the conclusion of the war, both sides were faced with rebellions amongst their own allies. In Rome's case, this rebellion broke out in 241 BC and centred on the Falisci. The Falisci were an Italic people who lived in Etruria, some thirty miles north of Rome. Regretably, there are no detailed surviving accounts of this revolt, which is unfortunate given the oddness of its timing; just as Rome emerged victorious from twenty years of warfare and had large numbers of battle-hardened soldiers already mobilised. Of the surviving accounts which do mention the revolt and ensuing war, Zonaras and Eutropius provide the most detail:

'At the time under discussion the Romans made war upon the Faliscans and Manlius Torquatus ravaged their country. In a battle with them his heavy infantry was worsted, but his cavalry conquered. In a second engagement with them he was victorious and took possession of their arms, their cavalry, their goods, their slaves, and half their country. Later on, the original city, which was set upon a steep mountain, was torn down and another one was built, which was easier of access.'[14]

'Quintus Lutatius and Aulius Manlius, being created Consuls, made war upon the Falisci, formerly a powerful people of Italy, which war the Consuls in conjunction brought to a termination within six days after they took the field; fifteen thousand of the enemy were slain, and peace was granted to the rest, but half their land was taken from them.'[15]

'For at Rome there followed civil war against the Falisci, but this they brought to a speedy and favourable conclusion, taking Falerii in a few days.'[16]

'When the Faliscans revolted, they were subdued on the sixth day and their surrender was accepted.'[17]

'The Roman waged war on the Faliscans, of whom 15,000 fell in the ensuing battle.'[18]

As can be seen, we have no details as to why the Falisci chose this moment to revolt. Given the close proximity of the Falisci to Rome, the history of the conflict between these two tribes stretched back to the fifth century BC, when the Falisci allied to Rome's ancient enemy, the Veii, and went to war with Rome. Following the defeat of the Veii, the Falisci were soon defeated themselves (in 394 BC). A generation later they joined another rebellion against Roman rule (in 357 BC), but were again defeated, signing a forty-year truce with Rome. After this we hear of no further encounters with them.

Despite the lack of any immediate motive for the revolt, the Romans clearly took the matter seriously, dispatching both Consuls to crush the rebellion. Given the casualties involved, this was clearly a large-scale rebellion, but of far greater danger to Rome was the precedent it would set and the danger of revolt spreading to the other subjugated races of Italy, especially in the freshly conquered south.

As detailed in our surviving sources, the proximity of the Falisci to Rome meant that the Consuls mobilised and marched to the Falisci within six days. The Consuls, led by A. Manlius Torquatus Atticus, seemingly fought two battles, both of which were Roman victories, though interestingly Zonaras does report that the Roman maniple was defeated by the Faliscan infantry during the first encounter.

Nevertheless, the end result was a six-day war which apparently saw 15,000 Falisci killed and their capital city (Falerii) destroyed, with the population deported to a new, and less defendable, site in Etruria. Both Consuls returned to Rome and were awarded Triumphs for their swift action. Despite the seemingly inevitable conclusion to this revolt, Rome acted swiftly and brutally to ensure that this example did not spread and made a clear statement to the other tribes, over whom it was the dominant power in Italy.

The Aftermath of the First Punic War – Rebellion in Africa

Throughout the Punic War the bulk of the Carthaginian forces were composed of mercenaries from a number of different peoples. Having evacuated them from Sicily to Africa, following the end of the war, a dispute arose over the pay they were owed, which given the losses of the war and the Roman indemnity, Carthage was in no position to pay. With no Carthaginian forces between them and the capital, the mercenaries were able to march against Carthage itself, sparking off what has become known as the Mercenary or Truceless War; a war which lasted from 240–237 BC and which nearly destroyed the Carthaginian Empire.[19] For Carthage the danger did not only lie in the revolt of their mercenaries, but in this revolt spreading. Whilst Rome was able to stamp on the initial rebellion before it could spread, the Carthaginians were not so fortunate and the revolt soon spread to the native African tribes which had been subdued by Carthage, who were encouraged by the mercenaries to rise up against its Carthaginian overlords. Soon Carthage lost control of the interior of their African territory, with the city of Tunis falling into rebel hands and those of Utica and Hippo Acra finding themselves under siege.

As the year progressed the rebellion spread beyond Africa, with Carthage losing control of its remaining Mediterranean possessions of Sardinia and possibly Corsica, when the mercenary forces acting as garrisons also joined the rebellion. We are not told if this rebellion spread to Carthage's Spanish possessions.[20] Worse was to come in the war in Africa. The Carthaginians were able to muster a fresh army, which must have been a mixture of existing loyalist mercenaries, with perhaps some freshly hired ones and any loyalist African or Spanish tribesmen. Bolstered by a contingent of elephants and under the command of the Carthaginian general Hanno, the Carthaginians moved to relieve the siege of Utica. Utilising his elephants, Hanno was able to smash through the besieging army and relieve the city. Hanno then entered Utica, leaving his army camped outside the city walls. Unfortunately for him, however, the mercenaries regrouped and attacked the Carthaginians, catching them unawares and slaughtering them.

From this low point, the Carthaginians were able to reverse their fortunes, a turnaround which was principally down to the actions of one man: Hamilcar Barca, a veteran of the Punic War in Sicily. He was appointed joint commander in Africa, along with Hanno, and made a lightning assault on the mercenary army at Utica. Despite being outnumbered, he was able to defeat the mercenaries at the Battle of Bagradas River. Hamilcar then marched into the Libyan interior, retaking rebellious cities or reaffirming the loyalty of those that were wavering. He was also able to utilise his family connections and split the native tribes; thanks to his daughter's marriage to a Numidian prince, who brought over a force of Numidians. The two forces combined to defeat a mercenary/native force in battle, allowing Carthage to end the year with a victory and place the war on a more even footing.

Having achieved a measure of stability, the Carthaginians were able to build upon this the following year (239 BC), but faced a number of potential hazards. The first of these came through disagreements between Carthage's two leading generals, Hanno and Hamilcar, which threatened to undermine the Carthaginian war effort. The second came from the revolt of a number of previously loyal African cities, including the freshly relieved Utica. The third came from the war descending into a new level of brutality, with the torture and execution of Carthaginian prisoners by the mercenaries.

Yet the Carthaginians were able to overcome each of these factors. In terms of the joint command, Hamilcar emerged as the victor, with Hanno being removed from his role. He was able to take to the field and scored a notable victory over the mercenary army at the Battle of the Saw. Having first trapped the mercenary army in a valley, he was able to capture their leaders and force the rest into battle. In terms of brutality, Hamilcar matched the mercenaries in his execution of prisoners, making it clear to both sides that there would be no quarter given. Hamilcar then laid siege to the rebel stronghold of Tunis, but the mercenaries were able to defeat a Carthaginian general, Hannibal (no relation). Despite this reverse, Hamilcar, now aided by his former rival Hanno, put another army into the field and defeated the mercenaries in 237 BC in open battle, bringing the war to a successful conclusion.

With the mercenaries defeated, attention could be turned to the rebellious African cities and the Numidian tribes. Isolated and clearly on the losing side, Utica and the others accepted terms and were brought back under Carthaginian domination. Unlike the cities, the Numidian tribes continued to fight on. In response, Hamilcar was dispatched and swiftly defeated them in battle, forcing them to come to terms. Thus by 237 BC a rebellion which at one point threatened to destroy the Carthaginian civilisation in Africa, was comprehensively defeated, and control of Africa was restored. Outside of Africa it was another matter. Sicily remained lost to them, the fate of Carthaginian possessions in Spain remains unknown, but those in Sardinia and Corsica were lost to them, first to rebellious mercenary garrisons, then to troublesome natives and finally to Rome itself (see Chapter Two).

Rome and Carthage at Peace – Rome and Carthage at War (241–237 BC)

Yet for the Carthaginians, no matter how serious the war against the mercenaries and Africans tribes became, there was always the potential for matters to spiral completely out of their control, and for defeat to become a certainty through Roman intervention. Although Carthage lost the First Punic War, this was more due to military exhaustion and the inability to be able to defend, or reinforce, their Sicilian territories. There had been no 'knockout' blow, mainly due to their long avoidance of open battle in Sicily, following the opening years of the war. In fact one of the most decisive encounters of the war had been the Carthaginian victory at the Battle of Bagradas, which destroyed the Roman invasion of Africa.

Yet with the bulk of its army composed of African natives and mercenaries, large elements of which were now in open revolt, Carthage was clearly in no position to resist a Roman military intervention. Furthermore, as the war progressed there were two clear flashpoints. First came the capture of a number of Italian traders, who had been supplying the rebels in Africa. Given the appalling treatment of prisoners from both sides in the war, the fate of these men could easily have roused the Senate and People of Rome into action. Second (in 239 BC) was the far more serious appeal by the rebellious Africa city of Utica directly to Rome to intervene. Having established a precedent in 264 BC for overseas intervention, with the acceptance of the request for aid from the rebellious former mercenaries in control of Messina, clearly there was a danger that Rome would accept this request and invade Africa.

Yet in Rome there seemed little appetite for further intervention and the request was not only turned down, but Roman mediators were sent by the Senate to reconcile the warring parties and when this failed, Rome put in place several measures to actively help the Carthaginians. This goodwill had in great part been facilitated by the release of the Italian traders unharmed. Nevertheless, Rome responded by releasing all remaining Carthaginian prisoners of war without ransom, boosting Carthage's military resources. Shipments of grain were sent to Carthage to feed its citizens and Rome facilitated Carthage hiring fresh mercenaries. Syracuse too rendered assistance to its former enemy, something that would not have been possible without tacit Roman approval. Therefore, far from seizing the opportunity to finish Carthage off when she was weakest, Rome actively supported Carthage and aided them in their struggles against their rebellious allies.

As in all of the cases, without any contemporary sources, we will never understand why Rome chose not to intervene on this occasion. Perhaps it was a case of Africa being a step too far at this point and of limited strategic value, unlike Sicily. Involvement in North Africa would have exposed Rome to fighting both Carthage and the Numidian tribes of the African hinterland, for little apparent gain. Rome herself had just finished an exhausting twenty years of warfare and there may have been little appetite in the popular assemblies (the ultimate decision-makers on matters of Roman warfare) for another overseas adventure, when Carthage clearly posed no threat. There is also the disastrous example of Rome's first intervention in African with the destruction of the invasion force at the Battle of Bagradas in 255 BC Furthermore, Rome herself had suffered rebellion at home and despite the recent war, Carthage had always been an ally in the region (allegedly since the founding of the Republic),[21] with the two most recently finding common cause against Pyrrhus.

In 238 BC, however, this positive relationship changed and saw the outbreak of the Second Punic War between Rome and Carthage, again over Roman intervention on a Mediterranean island, this time the island of Sardinia. As will be outlined in the following chapter, Rome took the strategic decision to annex the islands of Sardinia and Corsica, and when Carthage objected Rome declared war; meaning that the Second Punic War actually broke out in 238 BC. Naturally, faced with the prospect of a war with Rome, having not recovered from the first war and with the war in Africa still raging, Carthage backed down. Thus this Second Punic War actually passed without a single military exchange and Carthage gave up any hope of recovering Sardinia and Corsica, at least in the short term. These additional losses, added to that of Sicily, erased Carthage's presence from the Mediterranean itself, restricting its empire to North Africa and possibly some possessions on the coast of Spain.

Given the severe danger to the continued existence of Carthage during this period, the loss of Sardinia and Corsica (first to rebellion and then to Roman annexation) may have seemed light given what could have happened had Rome shown the appetite to intervene in North Africa. Nevertheless, Carthage emerged from the Mercenary War with the core of its empire intact, providing it with a solid base on which to rebuild its strength. During this period Rome had shown itself to be at best an unreliable ally, rather than outright enemies. However, the annexation of Sardinia and Corsica, followed by the declaration of war; which was only averted thanks to Carthage's acquiescence, accompanied by the payment of an additional indemnity, only stoked the fires of resentment that the First Punic War had created.

Chapter Two

Roman Expansion in the Mediterranean – Sicily, Sardinia and Corsica (241–218 BC)

T he first region which saw Roman expansion in this period lay to the south and the west of Italy and focused on the islands of Sicily, Sardinia and Corsica. It was with these territories that Rome first expanded its empire beyond the shores of Italy.

To the Winner the Spoils – Rome and Sicily (241–228 BC)

It was the Roman intervention in Sicily which sparked off the First Punic War (see Chapter One) and it was Sicily which represented Rome's major gain at the end of the war. Sicily had been fought over for centuries, with a range of external foes invading and attempting to carve out a Mediterranean empire on the island.[1] The most notable of these foes were perhaps the Athenians, who launched an ill-judged and ultimately disastrous attack on Syracuse in 415–413 BC, now referred to as the Sicilian Expedition.[2] The most persistent overseas enemy, however, had been the Carthaginians, who were keen to expand their empire into the western Mediterranean, annexing Sardinia and large areas of northern and western Sicily. Although the fortunes of the Sicilian cities fluctuated over the years, Carthage was never able to secure the whole island, with the native resistance most commonly being spearheaded by Syracuse, most commonly ruled by a tyranny.[3] Most recently the Syracusans had invited Pyrrhus, King of Epirus, to rule over them and take command of the war against the Carthaginians. This campaign, however, ended with a Pyrrhic withdrawal back to Italy in 276 BC (see Chapter Four).

Ironically it was Pyrrhus' most famous opponents, the Romans, who were able to succeed where he had failed and overturn centuries of Carthaginian domination of Sicily. During the First Punic War, the Romans were able to defeat the Carthaginian forces and force them to evacuate the island completely, leaving vast swathes of Sicily under their de-facto control. In 241 BC the Romans took the fateful, and some would say inevitable, step and sent a Consul, Q. Lutatius Cero, to establish Rome's permanent control of the island, in what would become Rome's first overseas province.

Lutatius established Roman control by a mixture of diplomacy and force. The peace treaty with Carthage which formally ended the First Punic War contained clauses enshrining the Carthaginian evacuation of the island and securing peaceful relations between Carthage and Syracuse. Diplomatic relations of friendship were also established between Rome and Hiero II, Tyrant of Syracuse, securing the independence of the Syracusan territories (which occupied the south east of the island), albeit under Roman protection. In terms of the use of force, Zonaras provides the following description:

> Quintus Lutatius became consul and departed for Sicily, where with his brother Catulus he established order throughout the island; he also deprived the inhabitants of their arms. Thus Sicily, with the exception of Hiero's domain, was enslaved by the Romans; and thenceforth they were on friendly terms with the Carthaginians. [4]

Although we have no surviving descriptions of the debates that occurred in the Roman Senate in making this decision, the logic behind the move to secure control of Sicily is clear to see, for two particular reasons. The first is based on a matter of Italian security. Whoever controlled Sicily had a springboard from which to invade southern Italy, a short distance across the straits of Messina, which shared a common Greek-flavoured civilisation with Sicily and had long-standing ties. In fact it was the Syracusans, not the Carthaginians, who were the first to take this step and carve out a southern Italy empire using Sicily as a base, during the early fourth century BC (390–385 BC) under the Tyrant Dionysius. Clearly the Senate believed that they could no longer afford Carthage to have a presence on Sicily; the danger, whether real or imagined, of an invasion of southern Italy was too great. The second obvious advantage Sicily offered was its abundance of natural resources, in particular its role as a surplus producer of grain and a breadbasket for the region. Thus control of Sicily would lead to greater food security for Italy.

However, despite all this talk of provinces, it is unclear exactly what sort of rule the Romans exerted over Sicily in the period 241–228 BC. All the sources that provide details on this time are from far later periods of Roman history, when Roman rule over Sicily and its status as Rome's first overseas province was an established fact. It is clear that Lutatius brought order to the island and entrenched Roman dominance, with Zonaras stating that he disarmed the other cities and territories. However, this does not mean that Rome took the decision to turn this territory into a formalised Roman province, with the political infrastructure that entailed. Roman aims for security and resources could be secured by expelling the Carthaginians and ensuring no native ruler filled the vacuum.

It is clear that Sicily represented something new for the Romans and their expanding federation. Up to this point, when enemies had been defeated, they were brought into the Roman federal system and tied by treaty to Rome itself, bound to provide manpower for Roman wars, but otherwise left to rule themselves. This was usually accompanied by an annexation of a portion of land to Rome and the planting of Roman citizen colonies to secure the region. Interestingly, there is no mention of any of this happening. Rome's federal system seems to have remained strictly for Italians only.

In fact, we have no clear idea of what Rome's relationship was with Sicily between 241–228 BC. What is clear is that we have no record of any magistrates serving in Sicily during this period, nor any records of further military campaigns. This is in sharp contrast to Sardinia and Corsica, which saw a number of Roman campaigns during this period (see below). Therefore we have to conclude that the Roman occupation met with little overt opposition following Lutatius' pacification campaign. In terms of governance, Rome's control of Sicily does, in many ways, resemble her relationship with the territories in Illyria from 229 BC (see Chapter Four), which was based on Roman dominance of an enclave of territories, without formal annexation or the apparatus of provincial rule. However, this all changed in 228 BC.

Rome's First Overseas Provinces – Sicily 227–219 BC

It was in 228 BC that Rome took the first step towards turning her military domination into an overseas empire, through the creation of two new

Praetorships; one for Sicily and one for Sardinia (and Corsica) for the following year.[5] Frustratingly, this move comes during a period when we have virtually no sources for Roman domestic history, denying us the opportunity to have a clear understanding of what lay behind this decision.[6] What we do know about this period, however, is two other major events that occurred; the human sacrifice (by live burial) of two Greeks and two Gauls, and the negotiation of the Ebro Treaty with Carthage, both of which were brought about in great part due to Roman preparations for a major Gallic invasion (see Chapter Six). It may well be that the impending Gallic threat caused the Senate to worry about the safety of their overseas possessions and move to exert a tighter control over them, through a permanent governor. Breannan, however, argues that Rome's commitment to the Illyrian War and potential revolts in Sardinia had shown the Romans that they were potentially exposed in terms of sufficient military commanders.[7]

The Praetorship had been created (or re-founded)[8] in 367 BC to make additional capacity to support the two Consuls in their military and domestic duties. There remained only one Praetor until the 240s BC when a second Praetorship was created, again in response to the need for additional magisterial capacity.[9] Now this number was doubled to four, with the two newest Praetorships specifically assigned each year to rule Rome's new provinces of Sicily and Sardinia (and Corsica). We don't know if the Senate was alarmed by the prospect of native rebellions against their rule, stirred by the impending war with the Gauls or whether they feared a Carthaginian revival in their former territories, or even both. What we do know is that what was previously an ad-hoc arrangement had been converted into permanent rule.

We know the identity of the first Praetor for Sicily; it was C. Flaminius himself, who just five years earlier had gained notoriety for his year as a Tribune of the Plebs, during which he had pushed through a land distribution schemes, in the face of Senatorial opposition (see Chapter Three and Appendix Three). He would go on to be Consul in 223 BC and fight the Gauls (see Chapter Seven), and in 217 BC met his death at the Battle of Lake Trasimene, fighting against Hannibal. It is interesting to speculate what degree of involvement Flaminius had in the creation of these new prestigious offices, given his record in domestic politics, but as mentioned earlier, we are met with silence from our few surviving sources. Again we are left with no record of how he used his year of office governing Sicily.[10]

We have a similar problem from 227 to 219 BC, as our surviving sources do not record the identities of any of the Sicilian Praetors. Polybius does mention that in 225 BC the Romans sent a reserve legion of 4,200 infantry and 200 cavalry to Sicily, in response to the general mobilisation caused by the Gallic invasion of that year.[11] We are not told it was in response to a specific threat, be it Sicilian or Carthaginian, and there is no record of any campaigning. A similar legion was also sent to Tarentum, to provide military cover for the Illyrian protectorate if it was needed.

Thus it seems that the earliest years of the Roman occupation of Sicily were marked by a lack of military campaigning on the Roman part (after Lutatius' campaign of 241 BC) and an acquiescence on the part of the locals that was not to be matched elsewhere. It must be borne in mind that the island would have suffered heavily during the two decades of fighting during the First Punic War and did have a history of the towns and cities submitting to foreign rule, be it Carthaginian or even Epirote.

In the Shadow of Rome – Rome and Syracuse 241–218 BC

This acquiescence can best be seen in the case of Syracuse, which was the anomaly in Sicily during this period, remaining an independent kingdom. Syracuse represents an interesting case study, being the first client kingdom of Rome outside of Italy. Again no details of the exact relationship between Syracuse and Rome survive for this period. We know that their independence was guaranteed in the peace treaty between Rome and Carthage that ended the First Punic War, which gave them protection from Carthaginian attack.

In 241 BC it was Rome which presented the greater threat, not Carthage. Syracuse had fought throughout the preceding centuries to maintain their independence from outside powers, notably Carthage, whilst trying to expand her own control of the island.[12] However, this old balance of power had been shattered by the victory of the Romans, who soon made it clear that their presence on the island was not to be a temporary one.

At the time, Syracuse was ruled by a tyrant (in the ancient sense of the word), named Hiero.[13] He had ruled Syracuse since 275/274 BC, seizing power in the aftermath of the withdrawal of Pyrrhus, and ruled until his death nearly sixty years later in c. 216 BC. He proved to be an able general, leading the post-Pyrrhic Sicilian forces against the Mamertines, a group of former mercenaries who had carved out an empire for themselves in north-eastern Sicily. His victory at the Battle of Longanus River (c. 269–264 BC) crushed Mamertine power.[14] Unfortunately for Hiero, his victory was so comprehensive that the remaining Mamertines, who occupied the city of Messina sought out fresh allies, firstly in Carthage and then in Rome; these events led to the Roman intervention in Sicily, the First Punic War and ultimately Roman occupation of the island.

At the start of the Punic War, Hiero initially allied with his old foes the Carthaginians against Rome, but in a pragmatic move soon switched his allegiance to Rome and aided their war effort. It was this switch which preserved Syracuse's status as an independent kingdom, albeit one surrounded by the Roman Empire. Nevertheless, it seems that Hiero played the role of client king well, visiting Rome in 237 BC and lavishly distributing gifts of grain to the Roman people, though only Eutropius records the visit.[15]

With expansion in Sicily denied him, Hiero went on to cement his rule at home and by all accounts ruled moderately and was well-regarded. He famously patronised the inventor Archimedes, who interestingly designed and built a number of machines with which to defend both the city of Syracuse itself and its approaches. This last point perhaps provides us with an insight into Heiro's relationship with Rome in this period. He played the role of client king well, providing Rome with free grain and public protestations of loyalty, yet maintained and upgraded his city's defences, aware of Syracuse's precarious position as the last 'independent' city of Sicily.[16]

Hiero maintained this loyalty to Rome even with the outbreak of the Second Punic War in 218 BC, providing naval and logistical support to Rome in the early years of the war. It was only his death in c. 216 BC which saw Syracusan loyalty to Rome falter. Hiero was succeeded by his teenage grandson, Hieronymus, whose accession coincided with the crushing defeats that Rome suffered in the early years of the war. This convinced the young tyrant to abandon Rome and ally with Carthage, a decision which ultimately saw the siege and sack of Syracuse by the Roman commander M. Claudius Marcellus in 211 BC, extinguishing Syracuse's independence and completing Rome's conquest of the island.

The Annexation of Sardinia and Corsica 238–231 BC

The example of Sicily stands in stark contrast to that of the western Mediterranean islands of Sardinia and Corsica. Unlike Sicily, when the First Punic War ended these islands remained under Carthaginian control. In reality, this control was tenuous at best as the islands were garrisoned by mercenary forces whose control was unlikely to have spread much beyond the coastal regions. Nevertheless, officially Carthage remained in control of the two islands off the coast of Italy. Whilst on the face of it, it does seem odd that the Roman Senate allowed their enemy to maintain two strategic bases off their coast, there were good reasons for the Romans not to become entangled with controlling these islands. Unlike Sicily, the islands held little in the way of natural resources, and beyond the coastal areas were mountainous territories populated by native tribes who had proved adept at resisting outside forces. Pacifying the islands was beyond the resources of the Carthaginians and would not be as easy a task as securing Sicily was. Furthermore, of the two regions, Sicily presented the perfect staging ground to attack Italy, whereas Sardinia and Corsica had fewer resources to host an invading army and was further away from Africa, requiring control of the seas for any invading force to reach it.

Despite these factors, within just a few years the Senate reversed its earlier decision and in 238 BC Rome annexed the islands of Sardinia and Corsica from Carthage, in an apparent breach of the original peace treaty. This incident originated during the Mercenary War in 240 BC (as seen in Chapter One), when the mercenary garrison on Sardinia turned on their Carthaginian paymasters and seized control of the island. Reinforcements sent by Carthage to restore control of the island promptly deserted to the mercenary side, leaving the mercenaries in control of the island. They in turn, however, clashed with the natives, who took this opportunity to rise up and drive all the foreign occupiers from the island. Polybius reports that the surviving mercenaries fled to Italy.[17]

We do not know how much time elapsed between the expulsion of the rebellious mercenaries from Sardinia and the Senate's decision to invade. Even more importantly, we do not know what prompted the Senate to change their original decision and become involved. If anything, the native revolt had rendered Sardinia neutral territory, with the Carthaginian presence expelled. The Roman expedition of 238 BC was led by one of the Consuls,

Ti. Sempronius Gracchus, ancestor of the infamous Tribune of the same name. Gracchus' activities in 238 BC may shed some light on possible Roman intentions, as he began by leading an invasion of Sardinia but then moved on to campaign in Liguria in north-western Italy (as seen in Chapter Three). Thus we must question whether the move to invade Sardinia formed part of an overall grand strategy for Roman expansion into northern Italy and whether the strategic value of Sardinia lay not in stopping it being used by the Carthaginians to invade Italy, but in allowing the Romans to invade northern Italy themselves, opening up a fresh point of attack.

Naturally, the Romans faced two major obstacles in invading Sardinia. The first, and easiest to deal with, were the Carthaginians, whose empire Sardinia formally remained part of. Polybius says the following:

> When the Carthaginians objected on the ground that the sovereignty of Sardinia was rather their own than Rome's, and began preparations for punishing those who were the cause of its revolt, the Romans made this the pretext of declaring war on them, alleging that the preparations were not against Sardinia, but against themselves.[18]

Thus when Carthage raised a formal objection to the Roman breaking of the peace treaty, the Romans responded by an actual declaration of war against them, which technically meant that the Second Punic War started in 238 BC, not 218 BC. Even though Carthage was winning the war against their rebellious mercenaries, they were clearly in no condition to face Rome once again, and so it seems that the Carthaginians backed down and agreed to Roman demands, amending the original peace treaty, as noted again by Polybius:

> Later, at the end of the Libyan War, after the Romans had actually passed a decree declaring war on Carthage, they added the following clauses, as I stated above: "The Carthaginians are to evacuate Sardinia and pay a further sum of twelve hundred talents."[19]

Interestingly, later sources such as Appian and Eutropius have Sardinia ceded to Rome at the end of the First Punic War, thus reflecting an evolved tradition that exonerates Rome for their actions.[20] Another variant tradition has the Romans taking Sardinia in compensation for Carthaginian attacks on Roman shipping during the Mercenary War.[21] Clearly the lack of a detailed contemporary source, such as Fabius Pictor, denies us the opportunity to fully understand the circumstances behind this phoney Second Punic War. However, what is clear is that faced with no other practical option, Carthage backed down and Sardinia (and Corsica) fell into the Roman sphere of influence.

However, whilst removing Carthage's claims to Sardinia was one thing, actually securing the territory was another. Neither Carthage nor their mercenaries had been able to secure the islands beyond the coastal regions and this proved to be the case with Rome. Carthage may have stepped aside without a fight, the Sicilians may have capitulated without much struggle, but the same cannot be said of the native inhabitants of Sardinia and Corsica, who were determined to resist any outside rule. Strabo provides us with a description of the natives of Sardinia and Corsica, though we do not know how anachronistic it is:

> There are four tribes of the mountaineers, the Parati, the Sossinati, the Balari, and the Aconites, and they live in caverns; but if they do hold a bit of land that is fit for sowing, they do not sow even this diligently; instead, they pillage the lands of the farmers – not only of the farmers on the island, but they actually sail against the people on the opposite coast, the Pisatae in particular.
>
> But Cyrnus is by the Romans called Corsica. It affords such a poor livelihood – being not only rough but in most of its parts absolutely impracticable for travel – that those who occupy the mountains and live from brigandage are more savage than wild animals. [22]

It is unclear exactly what campaigning Gracchus undertook in Sardinia in 238 BC, but as his campaign seemed to be primarily focussed on the war in Liguria, we can only assume that he did little more than secure a coastal region as a secure base of operations from which to stage his attack on Liguria. In all probability, he most likely re-occupied the regions recently vacated by the Carthaginian garrison. There is no mention of Corsica in this campaign and we must assume that it was left alone this year. Therefore, the end of 238 BC saw Sardinia (and Corsica) Roman in name only; Carthage had been forced to cede their claim to the islands, but Rome had not yet been able to secure them.

This situation continued throughout 237 BC, with both Consuls too busy fighting against the Ligurians and the Boii to bother with the islands (see Chapter Three). It was only in the latter stages of 236 BC that the Consuls were able to turn their attention to the islands once more. Again both Consuls began the year campaigning in northern Italy against the Boii and Ligurians. It was only when these campaigns drew to a conclusion that the Consuls were free to return to the islands. In fact, 236 BC seems to mark the start of the Roman conquest of the islands proper. Given that the vast majority of the campaigning season had been taken with the Gallic Wars, it seems that the Romans decided to limit their conquest to the smaller of the two islands; Corsica, with a full blown campaign in Sardinia only following in 235 BC.

The Corsican campaign of 236 BC was led by the Consul C. Licinius Varus, for which he won a Triumph. The campaign was not without incident, however, as the surviving sources preserve the story of one of Varus' legates making a peace treaty with the Corsican tribes which the Senate refused to honour, leading to the legate's disgrace and perhaps execution, though the details of the story vary from source to source:

> Varus set out for Corsica, but inasmuch as he lacked the necessary ships to carry him over, he sent a certain Claudius Clineas ahead with a force. The latter terrified the Corsicans, held a conference with them, and made peace as though he had full authority to do so. Varus, however, ignored this agreement and fought the Corsicans until he had subjugated them. The Romans, to divert from themselves the blame for breaking the compact, sent Claudius to them, offering to surrender him; and when he was not received, they drove him into exile.[23]
>
> After Claudius had made terms with the Corsicans, and the Romans had then waged war upon them and subdued them, they first sent Claudius to them, offering to surrender him, on the ground that the fault in breaking the compact lay with him and not with themselves; and when the Corsicans refused to receive him, they drove him into exile.[24]
>
> The Senate surrendered M. Claudius [Clineas] to the Corsi because he had made a dishonourable peace with them. When the enemy would not take him, it ordered that he be put to death in the public jail.[25]

Thus, despite Varus winning a Triumph for the campaign, it did not get off to a successful start. Given that he had been fighting in northern Italy, it does seem that the early conclusion to the campaign offered the Consul a window of opportunity to campaign in Corsica, but that he had not adequately prepared for this, due to the lack of ships. Varus' legate Claudius was seemingly sent over with a smaller force to harry the native tribes, possibly until Varus himself could bring across his full forces. However, it seems that the tribes quickly offered terms, whether false or genuine, and Claudius, eager to secure a token victory, agreed. However, this token victory did not seem to be what the Consul had in mind, so he ignored the treaty and secured the tribes' submission by military might, rather than diplomacy. Claudius himself does seem to have been made the scapegoat for this Roman volte-face, though we will never know whether he did exceed his orders in this matter.

However, despite Varus gaining a Triumph and nominally securing the submission of the Corsican tribes, we must question how secure Rome's control was, especially when the army was withdrawn at the end of the campaigning season. Firstly, we do not know the scale of Varus' campaigns or victories, or just how many of the island's tribes he had defeated, or how severely. Another complete unknown is what, if any, measures had been taken to secure the defeated tribes' allegiance to Rome and whether they were bound by treaty, as in Italy, or left in limbo, as with Sicily.

Nevertheless, in the eyes of the Senate, the island of Corsica had been secured for the Roman people and the following year their attention turned to Sardinia. The Sardinian campaign of 235 BC was led by one of the Consuls, T. Manlius Torquatus. Manlius is widely credited throughout Roman history as being the commander who conquered Sardinia, but details of the campaign have not survived:

...the Romans made an expedition against the Sardinians, who would not yield obedience, and conquered them.[26]

Sardinia finally became subject to the yoke in the interval between the First and Second Punic War, through the agency of Titus Manlius the consul.[27]

It is interesting that Zonaras (based on Dio) emphasised that the Sardinians had not submitted to Roman control, backing up our hypothesis that the events of 238 BC had brought Sardinia under Roman control in name only. Nevertheless, by the end of 235 BC Manlius was awarded his Triumph and the Senate considered that both islands had been brought under their control.

This, combined with the peaceful conclusion to the renewed war with Carthage and the ending of the Gallic War, saw the Senate take the extraordinary step of declaring the Republic at peace by ceremonially closing the gates of the Temple of Janus.[28] This symbolic act of declaring the Republic at peace was the first time it had been undertaken in the whole Republican period, and had only supposedly happened on one prior occasion, during the reign of King Numa Pompilus (c.715–673 BC). It was not until 29 BC and the time of Augustus that the event happened again, making this occurrence in 235 BC unique in over 650 years of Roman history.

Unsurprisingly, however, the Gates of Janus had to be opened the following year (234 BC), and both Sardinia and Corsica were once again theatres of operation. As is common for this period, we do not know what caused the Senate to dispatch a Consul and a Praetor to Corsica and Sardinia respectively, and so soon after declaring peace, but we must assume that the tribes of the islands rose up against Roman rule once more. This again raises issues about how much control Rome actually had of both Sardinia and Corsica, and how comprehensive the victories in the preceding years actually had been.

Of the two theatres, it seems that Corsica represented the greatest challenge to Rome, as one of the Consuls, Sp. Carvilius Maximus, was dispatched there and one of the Praetors, P. Cornelius, was sent to Sardinia. We only have a brief note in Zonaras covering both campaigns:

> The following year the Romans divided their forces into three parts in order that the rebels, finding war waged upon all of them at once, might not render assistance to one another; so they sent Postumius Albinus into Liguria, Spurius Carvilius against the Corsicans, and Publius Cornelius, the praetor urbanus, to Sardinia. And the consuls accomplished their missions with some speed, though not without trouble. The Sardinians, who were animated by no little spirit, were vanquished in a fierce battle by Carvilius; for Cornelius and many of his soldiers had perished of disease. When the Romans left their country, the Sardinians and the Ligurians revolted again.[29]

Zonaras clearly ties all three campaigns (Corsica, Sardinia and Liguria) together, though whether this was the case in reality is unknown. Certainly it is possible that an uprising in one sparked off the others, even if they were uncoordinated. What is clear is that Carvilius was able to pacify Corsica, however temporarily, and was awarded a Triumph for his victory. As we can see, Sardinia proved to be a more difficult proposition, with the Roman Army and its commander succumbing to disease. This meant that Carvilius had to cross to Sardinia with his army, where he apparently won a battle.

The scale of his victory, however, must be judged by the fact the Sardinians rose up in revolt once the Roman Army had left the island, a common theme in these campaigns. The pattern continued in 233 BC, when again one of the Consuls, M. Pomponius Matho, was dispatched to Sardinia. Once again all we know is that Pomponius was awarded a Triumph for his campaigns, indicating a significant military victory over an element of the native tribes, but again the war continued into the following year.

In fact the situation in Sardinia seems to have deteriorated, as 232 BC saw both Consuls dispatched to the island, the fourth year in a row that a Consul had campaigned there. Once again we only have a brief note in Zonaras to cover these campaigns:

> When the Sardinians once more rose against the Romans, both the consuls, Marcus [Publicius] Malleolus and Marcus Aemilius [Lepidus], took the field. And they secured many spoils, which were taken away from them, however, by the Corsicans when they touched at their island.[30]

On this occasion, however, no Triumphs were awarded for the Consuls, mostly due to their blunder in losing the spoils they had won in Sardinia on Corsica. Thus it seems that the Consuls again met with some success in Sardinia and then decided to move their operations to Corsica, where they suffered some form of reverse.

It seems that this reverse and the knowledge that these supposedly straightforward campaigns of pacification were dragging on (now entering their sixth year across both islands) spurred the Senate into making a major push to end the wars. Once again, and for the second year running, both Consuls were dispatched to the islands; this time in a concerted effort. M. Pomponius Matho, kinsman of the Consul (of the same name) of 233 BC, was dispatched to Sardinia, whilst his colleague, C. Papirius Maso, was sent to Corsica.

As with all these campaigns, no record of the number of troops has survived for either side, but Zonaras does provide us with a more detailed account of the tactics involved:

> Hence the Romans now turned their attention to both these peoples. Marcus Pomponius proceeded to harry Sardinia, but could not find many of the inhabitants, who as he learned, had slipped into caves of the forest, difficult to locate; therefore he sent for keen-scented dogs from Italy, and with their aid discovered the trail of both men and cattle and cut off many such parties. Caius Papirius drove the Corsicans from the plains, but in attempting to force his way to the mountains he lost numerous men through ambush and would have suffered the loss of still more owing to the scarcity of water, had not water at length been found; then the Corsicans were induced to come to terms.[31]

In the scant descriptions we have of both campaigns, the problems facing Rome were laid bare. On both islands the Romans suffered from fighting a guerrilla war, with the native tribesmen retreating to the mountains, negating the superior tactical strength of the Roman military machine. Neither campaign seems to have been a resounding success, even though some measure of peace seems to have been brought to the islands. The nature of such a fragile peace meant that the Romans could never trust that either island would stay pacified for long, with the threat of a native rebellion ever present, especially in an era without a permanent Roman presence.

Again, and for the second year running, neither of the two Consuls celebrated a Triumph for their campaigns, though we do know that Papirius Matho requested one and was turned down, in retaliation for which he celebrated his own Triumph on the Alban Mount.[32] Nevertheless, it seems that these six years of continuous campaigning, the final two of which saw both Consuls involved, achieved some measure of temporary peace on the islands as there is no further record of Roman military involvement until 225 BC.

The Roman Provinces of Sardinia and Corsica (227–218 BC)

It was during this lull in military activity that Rome undertook its reform of provincial administration and introduced two new Praetors, one for Sicily (as detailed above) and one for Sardinia (and Corsica). Whilst the Praetor for Sicily would have been more of an administrative role, ensuring the regular exploitation of the island's natural resources, the Praetor for Sardinia and Corsica would have been far more focused on entrenching Rome rule in the islands and preventing native uprisings. Again we are not told what size force the regular Praetor for Sardinia took with him each year. We do know that the first Praetor for Sardinia was M. Valerius (Laevinus), though no details of his activities survive.

The natives of the islands appear to have been quiescent until 225 BC, when the Senate felt it necessary to dispatch a Consul to Sardinia, C. Atilius Regulus, despite the presence of a serving Praetor. This indicates a level of severity akin to the expected Gallic invasion. Again we have no detail as to Regulus' activities on Sardinia, and it is possible that he wanted to give his freshly assembled forces combat experience against a native enemy, but as will be detailed later, it was an unnecessary distraction that nearly cost Rome dear (see Chapter Six).

Aside from this one incident, which quite frankly we only know about thanks to its connection to the Gallic War, we are not told of any further military activity by Roman commanders on either Sardinia or Corsica for the rest of this period. Furthermore, we have no record of any further Triumphs being awarded for these theatres of operations (see Appendix Two). What we must assume is that after the large scale military operations of the Consuls of 232 and 231 BC, the natives of both islands avoided full-scale and open conflict with their new Roman overlords. This does not mean that the annual Praetors were not engaged in operations to ensure compliance, merely that full-scale warfare did not break out to the same extent as the 230s.

Thus we can see that the aftermath of the Fist Punic War saw Rome take her first strides towards overseas empire, with the islands of Sicily, Sardinia and Corsica. However, the two theatres of operations were quite different. On the one hand was the island of Sicily, with a significant degree of urbanization and a long history of undergoing foreign occupation. On the other were the islands of Sardinia and Corsica, composed of native tribes and mountainous terrain, which had only notionally been under foreign occupation.

It was not only these factors that accounted for the differing Roman experience in these islands. Sicily had fallen to Rome as a result of the First Punic War, and it made perfect strategic sense to hold onto the island. Sardinia and Corsica, however, represented something different; the Senate consciously decided to annex the islands, despite earlier leaving them in Carthaginian hands. They also invested heavily in pacifying the islands and bringing them under firm Roman control, despite offering limited material gain.

This move represented an evolution in Roman strategic thinking. From Rome's earliest days, the territories they conquered allowed Rome to develop a strategic buffer to protect the core Roman territories. At first this buffer was no more than the territories such as Alba and Veii that lay within a few days of Rome itself; however, as Roman territory expanded then so would the buffer zone needed to protect it. With all of Italy under their control, it was only logical that the buffer zone, which the Romans felt they needed, expanded too. Thus Sicily, Sardinia and Corsica all lay within Rome's outer zone of control, protecting Roman Italy itself, at least from the west and the south. Creating a 'buffer zone' of territories to the south and the west to protect Roman Italy raised obvious questions about the other regions; in particular the east and the north. However, it would not be long before the Senate sought to expand Roman control in these regions too.

Part II

Roman Expansion in Italy and the East
(238–228 BC)

Chapter Three

Roman Expansion in Italy – The Gallic and Ligurian Wars (238–230 BC)

In the decades following the First Punic War, Rome faced a far greater threat than the Carthaginians, one which was to threaten the very existence of the Republic itself. This threat came not from the south or the east, but from the north and from one of Rome's oldest and most dangerous enemies: the Gauls. At this point in time, no enemy posed a greater immediate threat, or a greater psychological one, than the tribes that had burnt the city of Rome to the ground in the early fourth century BC.[1]

Roman and Gallic Italy

When studying this period it is important to remember that not only was northern Italy (between the Alps and the Apennines) not under Roman control, but formed part of a wider Gallic rather than an Italian civilization. In fact the Roman name for this region was Cisalpine Gaul ('the Gaul on this side of the Alps', from the Roman perspective). The region, centred on the Po Valley, was home to a number of different Gallic tribes who had occupied the region for more than 300 years by this period.

Exactly when the Gallic tribes invaded Italy was a much discussed and argued over issue in Roman times. Williams presents a good in-depth modern analysis of the problems we face now.[2] At the heart of the debate is a much-repeated story throughout the ancient sources, that the Gallic tribes were invited across the Alps, c. 400 BC, by a certain Arruns of Clusium to use mercenaries in an internal conflict with his own ward (who had apparently seduced Arruns' own wife). However, when the Gallic troops saw how rich and fertile the region was, they attacked Clusium instead and settled in the region.

Despite the popularity of this myth, which had the traditional cocktail of sex and violence, there were many ancient writers who ridiculed it. Notable amongst these was Livy, who dismissed both the story of Arruns and the date. He instead dated the Gallic migration into Italy at c. 600 BC and as a consequence of over-population in Gaul, leading to pressure on land and thus forcing different tribes to find fresh lands to settle on.[3] One such tribe were the Insubres, who, led by Bellovesus, crossed the Alps, and encountered the Etruscan civilizations of the Po Valley, which naturally led to war:

> They themselves crossed the Alps through the Taurine passes and the pass of the Duria; routed the Etruscans in battle not far from the River Ticinus, and learning that they were encamped in what was called the country of the Insubres, who bore the same name as an Haeduan canton, they regarded it as a place of good omen, and founded a city there which they called Mediolanium.[4]

Over the next 200 years, wave after wave of Gallic tribes crossed the Alps to settle; the Cenomani, Libui, Salui, Boii, Ligones and Senones.[5] Thus, by 400 BC northern Italy, which had been Etruscan, was overrun and became a Gallic possession, centred on the Po Valley. The last tribe to migrate across the Alps seems to have been the Senones, who pushed deeper into Italy than any before and settled to the east of the Apennines, between the mountains and the coast (see Map 2).

The word 'Gaul' was applied to a vastly different array of Celtic tribes.[6] At first, Rome's knowledge of this new enemy must have been rudimentary, but as the contacts became more frequent, their knowledge will have become far greater.[7] These days we label the tribes as Celtic, after their ethnicity, but for the inhabitants of the ancient world they were Gauls, and many ancient writers refer to them with this title rather than their individual tribal name. [8]

The Gallic migrations were not confined to Italy, but also saw Greece and Asia Minor invaded. Most famously, in c. 279 BC, migrating Gallic tribes invaded Greece, defeating a defending force at the Battle of Thermopylae and attacking Delphi.[9] Gallic tribes even settled in Asia Minor, eventually becoming the Asiatic kingdom of Galatia. Thus, to most of the Mediterranean world, 'Gaul' conjured up the same image of rampaging tribesmen overrunning the more 'civilized' parts of the ancient world. The other major issue the Mediterranean civilizations faced when confronted by Gallic tribes was a completely different style of fighting than the ones they had been used to in their clashes with their neighbours. Ellis provides a good summary of the fighting techniques the various Celtic tribes used.[10]

Whilst the Gallic tribes were settling in northern Italy and expanding beyond the Po Valley, Rome had barely expanded beyond Latium, and was thus insulated from contact with them. However, given that Rome was slowly pushing northwards and the Gauls southwards, contact between the two civilizations was inevitable. When contact did occur, it ended disastrously for Rome. In the period 390–386 BC,[11] an army of Senones, headed by a chieftain named Brennus, crossed the Apennines and pushed deep into Etruria and down the Tiber Valley. There were many stories circulating in the ancient sources about why this occurred, usually connecting them to the Arruns of Clusium story and all naturally placing Rome at centre stage.

However, rather than having Rome as the intended destination of the Gauls, it would be more accurate to state that the Romans simply got in the way of the Gauls, who had another destination in mind. Exactly what the destination of Brennus and his forces was has long been debated. Cornell advocated a theory raised by Sordi, that this was connected to the campaigns of Dionysus of Syracuse (as seen in Chapter One).[12] From 390 BC onwards, Dionysus had launched a war of conquest aimed at annexing southern Italy and the Adriatic to his Syracusan empire. Although his land forces never ranged further than southern Italy, in 384 BC his navy sacked the Etruscan city of Pyrgi, which was ruled by the city of Caere, an old Roman ally. Thus, the argument goes that, lacking land forces in the region and determined to attack Caere, Dionysus hired Brennus and his forces as mercenaries to act in his name. Therefore, Brennus may have been moving on Caere itself or heading south to join up with the main Syracusan forces. That Dionysus used Gallic mercenaries is confirmed by a passage of Justin, who notes them being used in southern Italy.[13] Furthermore, as Cornell points out, there is a reference in Diodorus to a battle between a Caerean army and a Gallic army returning from the south:

Those Celts who had passed into Iapygia turned back through the territory of the Romans; but soon thereafter the Cerii made a crafty attack on them by night and cut all of them to pieces in the Trausian Plain.[14]

The Battle of the River Allia and the Sack of Rome (c. 390–386 BC)

Nevertheless, regardless of the intentions of the Senones marching through
Etruria, their path took them directly towards Rome. Whether they would
have attacked the city will forever remain unknown, but faced with an
advancing Gallic army, the Romans responded in the only way they could
and sent out their own army to intercept it. The two sides met at the River
Allia. The Roman forces were command by the Military Tribune (which had
replaced the Consulship in this period) Q. Sulpicius Longus. Livy preserves
an account of the battle:

> For Brennus, the Gallic chieftain, seeing the Romans to be so few, was
> especially apprehensive of a stratagem. He supposed that they had
> seized the higher ground for this purpose, that when the Gauls had
> made a frontal attack on the battle-line of the legions, the reserves
> might assail them in the flank and rear. He therefore directed his assault
> against the reserves, not doubting that, if he could dislodge them, it
> would be easy for his greatly superior numbers to obtain a victory in
> the plain. Thus not only luck but generalship as well were on the side of
> the barbarians. In the other army there was no resemblance to Romans,
> either amongst officers or private soldiers. Terror and dismay had got
> hold of their spirits, and such complete forgetfulness of everything that
> a much greater number fled to Veii, a hostile city, though the Tiber was
> across their way, than by the straight road to Rome, to their wives and
> children. For a little while the reserves were protected by their position.
> In the rest of the field, no sooner had those who were nearest heard
> the shouting on their flank, and those who were farthest the outcry in
> their rear, than – fresh and unhurt – they ran away from their strange
> enemies, almost before they had caught sight of them; and so far were
> they from risking a combat, that they did not even return their battle-
> cry. None were slain in fight; but they were cut down from behind as
> they blocked their escape by their own struggles in the disordered rout.
> On the bank of the Tiber, whither the whole left wing had fled, after
> throwing away their arms, there was great slaughter, and many who
> could not swim, or lacked the strength, weighed down by their corslets
> and other armour, sank beneath the flood. Nevertheless, the chief part
> got safely to Veii, whence they not only sent no succours to Rome, but

dispatched not even a messenger to tell of the defeat. From the right wing, which had stood at a distance from the river and closer to the foot of the mountain, the fugitives all made for Rome, and without stopping even to shut the city gates, sought refuge in the Citadel.[15]

Thus the first battle between the Romans and the Gauls ended with a comprehensive Roman defeat. As can be seen from Livy's narrative, Roman history has condemned the army that lost at Allia, which by the time of the late Republic, had not even put up a fight but fled at the sight of the Gauls and were driven into the Tiber. It seems, therefore, that the true story of the encounter has been lost to us and replaced with a 400-year-old version (by Livy's day) which emphasised the un-Roman conduct of the army and the incompetence and inauspicious actions of the Consular Tribunes.[16]

With the Roman Army defeated, Brennus then undertook one of the most notorious events in Roman history, the attack on and sack of the city of Rome itself.[17] It is generally considered that Rome in this time had little in the way of a defensive wall around the city. With no army to stop them, the Senones attacked and burnt the city itself, with the remaining defenders retreating to the Capitol, where they held out, eventually buying the Senones off with a ransom of gold.

Not only is the Sack of Rome one of the bitterest defeats in Roman history, it is also one of the most misrepresented. Later Roman historians sought to soften the blow to the Roman reputation with the story of M. Furius Camillus, who was able to rebuild the Roman Army after Allia, attacked the Senones as they were receiving the ransom of gold and thus ended the war with a victory. It has long been argued that this battle did not take place and that the Senones, having accepted the bribe, left the ruined city and continued their march south. There is even a variant tradition that has the Capitol falling to the Senones as well.[18]

The other major question that is asked is just how great the destruction of the city was? By the late Republic the historical tradition, as best seen in Livy, is that the city was burnt to the ground, with the exception of the Capitol; so much so, that the Senate debated relocating the city to the recently captured site of Veii. Livy further states that nearly all Roman records were lost in the blaze which destroyed the city.[19] Unfortunately, Livy's version of the city being burnt to the ground is not supported by the archaeological evidence. Nor does the scale of this disaster tally with the speed of the Roman recovery, and it is widely accepted that the Sack of Rome, although a major defeat, was not as destructive as the later ancient sources made out.[20]

The Gallic Wars (c. 390–334 BC)

The withdrawal of the Gallic army and their migration southwards allowed Rome to rebuild their military strength and re-establish their dominance in the Latium region. It was not long before another band of Gauls, probably also Senones, crossed into Latium and Roman territory, though the exact timing and location is disputed, as Livy himself acknowledges:

> Claudius [Quadrigarius] relates that the battle with the Gauls took place that year near the River Anio; and that this was the occasion of the famous duel on the bridge in which Titus Manlius slew a Gaul who had challenged him to combat, and despoiled him of his chain, while the two armies looked on. But I am more inclined to believe, with the majority of our authorities, that this exploit took place no less than ten years later, and that in the year of which I am now writing, the dictator, Marcus Furius, fought a battle against the Gauls on Alban soil. Notwithstanding the great terror occasioned by the invasion of the Gauls and the recollection of their old defeat, the Romans gained a victory that was neither difficult nor uncertain. Many thousands of barbarians fell in battle, and many after the camp was taken. The others roamed about, making mostly towards Apulia, and owed their escape from the Romans to their distant flight and the dispersion which resulted from their panic and their straggling.[21]

Whatever the exact year, this second clash appears to have resulted in a Roman victory. Despite the victory rhetoric in Livy, again it seems that this was little more than a Gallic incursion by another wandering warband.[22] A third conflict soon followed, in 361–360 BC, and was of a different nature. On this occasion the Gauls were allied to the Sabine city of Tibur (modern Tivoli) in their war against Rome. The first clash occurred at the River Anio and was famous for the victory of T. Manlius in single combat against a Gallic champion, which earned him the name Torquatus, after the Celtic torque he removed from the dead Gaul (a name which his family bore throughout the Republic), and earned the Romans a victory. The Gauls withdrew to Tibur and the war continued into 360 BC. On this occasion the Gallic army marched on Rome itself once more and a battle took place near the Colline Gate:

> The battle was fought not far from the Colline Gate. The Romans put forth all their strength in full sight of their parents and their wives and children. These are powerful incentives to courage even when unseen, but being then in full view, set the soldiers on fire with a sense of honour and compassion. The slaughter was great on both sides, but at last the Gallic army was driven off.[23]

Thus the second Gallic attack on Rome itself within a generation had been defeated. However, despite this victory the war with Tibur and their Gallic allies continued. A further attack on Rome occurred the following year, but Livy states that the force was only composed of solders from Tibur itself.[24] The Gauls reappeared the following year, in 358 BC, and another battle took place, this time at Praeneste. Once again this resulted in a Roman victory, which this time seems to have ended the Gallic participation in the war.

However, a familiar pattern emerges, when in 350 BC we have reports of a Gallic army reaching the Alban Hills, again most likely in the employ of Rome's local enemies. On this occasion the Consuls were dispatched and another battle was fought near the Alban Hills, which again resulted in a Roman victory. Once again this victory did not end the Gallic threat, with further clashes reported in 348 BC in the vicinity of the Alban Hills and again it seems in conjunction with Rome's enemies. The sources continue to report further encounters with the Gauls in both the 340s and 330s BC, though details are scant.[25] What is clear is that throughout this period the Gauls remained a pervasive threat for the Romans, with the threat of another Gallic Sack forever being brought to mind whenever a group of Gauls appeared in the vicinity of Latium, or were even rumoured to be in the vicinity. It must be pointed out though that in every subsequent encounter the Romans had emerged victorious in battle against the Gauls, and had successfully defended attacks on Rome on several occasions. What is also clear is that the Gauls were being used by Rome's regional opponents in their wars against Rome.

With this in mind, Polybius reports that in c. 334 BC the Romans and the Gauls (Senones?) negotiated a thirty-year peace. Interestingly, by Livy's day this treaty appears to have been omitted from the Roman historical consciousness. Polybius himself naturally presents this treaty in a typically pro-Roman light:

> After this panic, they kept quiet for thirteen years, and then, as they saw how rapidly the power of the Romans was growing, they made a formal peace with them, to the terms of which they adhered steadfastly for thirty years.[26]

Despite Polybius believing that the Gauls (Senones) sought peace due to their fear of Rome, the peace benefited the Romans greatly, perhaps more than the Senones themselves. Time and again over the previous fifty years, Rome's enemies had been able to hire Gallic mercenaries to bolster their armies and attack Rome, or threaten to do so. With Gallic reinforcements out of the picture, Rome would be free to consolidate their control of the region, especially following the dissolution of the Latin League and the subsequent political and manpower reforms (as seen in Chapter One). If anything, such a peace treaty built on these reforms and allowed Rome the time to expand their growing Italian empire without Gallic interference.

The Gallic Wars (334–283 BC)

We do not know if the treaty that Rome agreed with the Senones was originally meant to last for thirty years or whether that was simply how long an open-ended agreement lasted. In any event, for the next thirty-five years there were no further reported clashes between Rome and the Gallic tribes, allowing Rome to concentrate on fighting her nearest neighbours and expanding her territories. When the next clash did occur, in 298 BC, Rome was a far stronger power.

The year 298 BC saw the creation of a grand anti-Roman alliance, headed by the Etruscans, Samnites and Umbrians, but also including the Senones. The ancient sources offer a range of reasons for the ending of this Gallic truce, from being hired as mercenaries and pressure from fresh migrating Gallic tribes, to fear of encroaching Roman power. In truth, each of these elements may have been present in some form, but it was undeniable that Rome had benefited far more from the truce than the Senones. The creation of this grand anti-Roman alliance presented the gravest threat to date to Rome's expansion in Italy and led to what is now known (perhaps misleadingly) as the Third Samnite War. Whilst Rome started the war off well against the Etruscans and Samnites, it was the Senones who again struck the first blow for the alliance in 295 BC, ambushing two legions under the command of the former Consul of 298 BC, L. Cornelius Scipio.

Livy provides us with a brief account of the ensuing Battle of Clusium:

But before the consuls arrived in Etruria the Senonian Gauls came in immense numbers to Clusium with the intention of attacking the Roman camp and the legion stationed there. Scipio was in command, and thinking to assist the scantiness of his numbers by taking up a strong position, he marched his force on to a hill which lay between his camp and the city. The enemy had appeared so suddenly that he had had no time to reconnoitre the ground, and he went on towards the summit after the enemy had already seized it, having approached it from the other side. So the legion was attacked in front and rear and completely surrounded. Some authors say that the entire legion was wiped out there, not a man being left to carry the tidings, and that though the consuls were not far from Clusium at the time, no report of the disaster reached them until Gallic horsemen appeared with the heads of the slain hanging from their horses' chests and fixed on the points of their spears, whilst they chanted war-songs after their manner. [27]

Thus, once again, the Romans were defeated by a Senones force, though the loss was far from a critical one. Nonetheless, this did show that Rome could still be undone militarily by the Gallic tribes. The Gauls then joined up with the main Samnite army and faced the two Consuls at the Battle of Sentinum. Despite the death of one of the Consuls (P. Decius Mus), the Samnite–Gallic army was destroyed. Cornell describes the battle as the 'greatest military engagement that had ever taken place in Italy'.[28] Livy places the numbers killed as 25,000 Samnites and Gauls, with 8,700 Roman dead. Though the war continue until 290 BC, the Battle of Sentinum proved to be the turning point and ensured a Roman victory, and ultimately domination of central Italy. However, as Cornell points out, Livy's book ten ends in 293 BC, after which we have a large gap in our surviving sources for this period, including a gap in the list of Triumphs for 296 to 283 BC.[29]

Nevertheless, it seems with both the Samnites and Etruscans defeated, focus shifted back onto the Gauls. Although they had been defeated in battle, during the previous war, unlike their allies, they had not suffered a Roman invasion of their territory or been forced to submit. Thus the Gauls of northern Italy, and in particular the Senones of north-eastern Italy, became the next obvious rival for dominance of this region of Italy. Again the loss of Livy denies us a fuller narrative of events, but there can be doubt that a large-scale Gallic war broke out, initially focussed on the Senones. Polybius in his sketch on Roman–Gallic relations preserves a brief account of what followed:

> When Manius sent legates to Gaul to treat for the return of the prisoners, they were treacherously slain, and this made the Romans so indignant that they at once marched upon Gaul. They were met by the Gauls called Senones, whom they defeated in a pitched battle, killing most of them and driving the rest out of their country, the whole of which they occupied. This was the first part of Gaul in which they planted a colony, calling it Sena after the name of the Gauls who formerly inhabited it. This is the city I mentioned above as lying near the Adriatic at the extremity of the plain of the Po. Hereupon the Boii, seeing the Senones expelled from their territory, and fearing a like fate for themselves and their own land, implored the aid of the Etruscans and marched out in full force. The united armies gave battle to the Romans near Lake Vadimon, and in this battle most of the Etruscans were cut to pieces while only quite a few of the Boii escaped. But, notwithstanding, in the very next year these two peoples once more combined and arming their young men, even the mere striplings, again encountered the Romans in a pitched battle. They were utterly defeated and it was only now that their courage at length gave way and that they sent an embassy to sue for terms and made a treaty with the Romans. This took place three years before the crossing of Pyrrhus to Italy and five years before the destruction of the Gauls at Delphi. [30]

Thus Rome found themselves at war with not one, but two Gallic tribes; first the Senones and then the Boii. We find fragments of the conflict in the other surviving sources, which add crucial details. Appian has two notes revealing the origins of the war, which began with a revolt in Etruria to which the Senones supplied mercenaries. It is was this involvement which prompted the dispatch of Senatorial envoys, who were subsequently murdered, sparking off the first Roman invasion of Gallic territory:

> Once a great number of the Senones, a Celtic tribe, aided the Etruscans in war against the Romans. The latter sent ambassadors to the towns of the Senones and complained that, while they were under treaty stipulations, they were furnishing mercenaries to fight against the Romans. Although they bore the caduceus, and wore the garments of their office, Britomaris cut them in pieces and flung the parts away, alleging that his own father had been slain by the Romans while he was waging war in Etruria.[31]

The Periochae of Livy provides us with details of a Roman defeat:

> When Roman envoys were killed by Gallic Senones, war was declared against the Gauls. Praetor Lucius Caecilius [Metellus] and his legions were killed by them.[32]

Orosius actually provides the most details of this defeat:

> The praetor Caecilius was sent with an army to avenge their murder and to crush the uprising of the enemy. He was however overwhelmed by the Etruscans and Gauls and perished. Seven military tribunes were also slain in that battle, many nobles were killed and 30,000 soldier likewise met their deaths.[33]

Thus the Romans opened the war with another heavy defeat against the Senones. Given the poor quality of our sources, we do not have an exact chronology but the battle is likely to have taken place in 284 BC when Caecilius Metellus was Consul, and took place at Arretium.[34] Despite this initial disaster, however, it seems that the two Consuls of 283 BC, P. Cornelius Dolabella and Cn. Domitius Calvinus Maximus, both scored notable victories over the Senones and their Etruscan allies.[35]

It was during this war that Rome took two major steps. First came the invasion of Gallic territory for the first time, accompanied by the first Roman colony (Sena) planted on Gallic territory. Naturally this alarmed not only the Senones but the other Gallic tribes of the region, who for centuries had been used to being the aggressor and the expansionist power. This brought the Boii into the war (see Map 2), who allied with the Etruscan rebels and faced Rome at the Battle of Lake Vadimon (283 BC), which saw the combined Etruscan and Boian army destroyed. According to Polybius a further battle was fought, though his chronology of the conflict is uncertain.[36]

The victory at Lake Vadimon seems to have brought the war against the Gallic tribes to a successful conclusion, though Rome did continue to fight in Etruria and Umbria. The conclusion of these wars came just in time to allow Rome to focus on the invasion of southern Italy by the Epirote King Pyrrhus (see Chapter Four). Thus Rome had in one short war defeated both the Senones and the Boii. Furthermore, the defeat of the Senones was such that Rome was able to confiscate large portions of their land on the Adriatic coast and plant a fresh colony at Ariminum (Rimini).[37] Furthermore the Senones, Rome's most long-standing and bitter Gallic foe, were never to engage in a conflict with Rome again. Rome had taken a major step in its relations with Gallic Northern Italy. For the first time, and after a century of being on the defensive, Rome went on the offensive and invaded and annexed a portion of Gallic Northern Italy, reversing centuries of Gallic annexations. However, although the Senones had been defeated and bowed, the same could not be said of the Boii, whose defeat merely created a new leading Gallic foe for the Romans, replacing the Senones. The other Gallic tribes further north would have taken note that Rome was now expanding northwards towards them, setting the scene for further conflict.

Roman and Northern Italy during the First Punic War

Although the Gallic phase of Rome's northern expansion had ended in the 280s, fighting against other regional enemies such as the Volsinii continued sporadically until 264 BC. The final defeat of the Volsinii and M. Fulvius Flaccus' Triumph in 264 BC seem to have marked an end to this particular period of warfare in northern Italy. The reduction of these races came just in time for Rome, as Fulvius' colleague Ap. Claudius Caudex, was dispatched by the Senate to cross into Sicily and secure the city of Messina from the Carthaginians, an act which led to the outbreak of the First Punic War (see Chapter One). Given that northern Italy up to Cisalpine Gaul had finally been secured by Rome, the Senate must have felt more secure in the fact that they could involve themselves in a war to the south with a pacified northern border.

For the next twenty years the attentions of our surviving sources focus on the war with Carthage and ignore any events on Rome's northern border, the only one which adjoined hostile territory. In reality it may have been the case that the Senate directed the full military resources of the state to the war in Sicily and left the northern region to settle. We do have accounts of Roman–Gallic clashes from this period, but these are the result of the Carthaginians making use of Gallic mercenaries in their armies. This arrangement did not seem to be a happy one as there are a number of occasions recorded when the Gallic mercenaries deserted or threatened to desert to the Romans.[38] These occasions caused Polybius to comment on the untrustworthiness of the Gallic race.[39] Polybius also reports that upon the end of the war, Rome exiled a number of Gallic mercenaries, whom they had captured or had deserted to them, from Italy by ship.[40]

It is notable that there is not even a trace of military activity in our surviving sources against either the Gauls of northern Italy or the freshly conquered Italic peoples of Rome's northern border region, but perhaps this silence would not be the case if we had the books of Livy (see Appendix One). Nevertheless, given that the Punic War in the south had descended into one of attrition, requiring Rome's full military and fiscal resources (as seen in Chapter One), such inactivity is understandable, at least on Rome's part. What is more unusual is that Rome's recently defeated former enemies did not take this opportunity, offered by Rome's commitments in the south, to rise up once more. The only trace of discontent against Rome is recorded in 259 BC, when there was an aborted plot in Rome itself by 3,000 slaves and 4,000 Roman allies serving in her navies; whom Zonaras names as Samnites. Orosius states that as Rome was without a garrison such a plot could have taken the city.[41]

It is notable that the first recorded revolt of an Italian ally against Rome in this period did not occur in the region that had freshly been conquered by Rome, but came closer to home in 241 BC, following the end of the war.

As we have seen, it was the Falisci, a long-standing and often defeated enemy of Rome, who lived in Etruria, who revolted and were summarily crushed by both Consuls in just six days (as seen in Chapter One). This year also saw the founding of Spoletium (in the southern Apennines), which the Periochae of Livy places after the revolt and the creation of two new voting tribes in Picenum (the final two of the thirty-five).[42] Whilst these measures may have been planned for some time, it is possible to view them as pre-emptive responses to counter tensions within Rome's other restive allies.

Rome and Northern Italy in the 230s – The Gallic and Ligurian Wars

Forty-five years of peace between Rome and the Gallic tribes of northern Italy came to an end in 238 BC when a fresh conflict broke out. This saw Rome face an alliance of old and new enemies; principally in the form of a renewed conflict against the Boii and a new front opening up against the Ligurians. There are three principal accounts surviving for this period of conflict; a short section of Polybius, one in Florus and a lengthier description from Zonaras, along with short notes in Orosius and the Periochae of Livy.

The war seems to have originated with the Boii tribe, whose lands bordered those of Rome. Polybius ascribes this next outbreak of hostilities to a fresh generation of Gallic leaders who had not tasted defeat and that the collective Gallic memories of the previous wars had faded. Polybius' comments on the war are interesting for understanding the interplay between the various Gallic tribes and also the absence of any open warfare with Rome, in stark contrast to our other sources for this period. However, his account seems to be set in 236 BC and the conclusion is a garbled account of what we find in other sources (see below):

After these reverses, the Gauls remained quiet and at peace with Rome for forty-five years. But when, as time went on, those who had actually witnessed the terrible struggle were no more, and a younger generation had taken their place, full of unreflecting passion and absolutely without experience of suffering or peril, they began again, as was natural, to disturb the settlement, becoming exasperated against the Romans on the least pretext and inviting the Alpine Gauls to make common cause with them. At first these advances were made secretly by their chiefs without the knowledge of the multitude; so that when a force of Transalpine Gauls advanced as far as Ariminum, the Boian populace were suspicious of them, and quarrelling with their own leaders as well as with the strangers, killed their kings, Atis and Galatus, and had a pitched battle with the other Gauls in which many fell on either side. The Romans had been alarmed by the advance of the Gauls, and a legion was on its way; but, on hearing of the Gauls' self-inflicted losses, they returned home.[43]

Thus Polybius' account, written only a century later, details this as a Gallic alliance which collapsed into internal warfare between the tribes of northern Italy and those from across the Alps, and thus did not trouble Rome. This is in stark contrast to the details in the other three, much later, sources, which detail several years of warfare and the first belligerent contact between Rome and the Ligurian tribes. In Zonaras' account, we have little detail about the war's origins, only that it initially involved the Boii and some of their neighbouring tribes. The danger lies in combining these two campaigns, or these two enemies, into one, as analysis reveals that there were two separate peoples and the conflict had two distinct origins.

The Boian War (238–236 BC)

In many respects, the war between Rome and the Boii picked up where the previous generation of warfare had left off. The wars of the 280s had seen the Senones tribe destroyed and a Roman colony of Ariminum planted on both their and Boian lands. Such a defeat was bound to create lasting resentment, as would the deliberate planting of a Roman colony, and so a renewal of hostilities between the two sides did not come as a surprise. The only surprise was that it took as long as it did to break out again (nearly fifty years). It is possible that the Roman victory in the south paradoxically may have convinced the Gallic tribes that they could not rely on others to defeat Rome, and that a victorious Rome would soon turn their attentions back to the north. Dyson also postulates that there may well have been short-term reasons for the renewed conflict, through local disagreements between the tribesmen and the colonists on issues of trading and land disputes.[44] Therefore there should be no issue about accepting that the Boii amassed a fragile alliance of tribes behind them and attacked Roman territory. In terms of aims, it seems clear that the Boii at the very least wanted to reverse the obvious effects of the previous defeat and remove the Roman colony from their territory, as can be seen by their demands to the Senate in 235 BC (see below). In terms of their wider aims, all the tribes of the region would have welcomed pushing the Roman power back beyond the Apennines and restoring the old status quo.

Zonaras provides us with an overview of three years' worth of campaigning by Rome against the Boii and their allies. The opening of the conflict seems to confirm that the Boii and their allies had the strategic initiative. The Roman campaign was led by one of the Consuls, P. Valerius Falto, who fought two battles this year with mixed success.

In the first, and unnamed, battle of the conflict, for which we have no location or detail, merely a conclusion, Valerius was defeated by the Boii:

After this the Romans again waged war upon the Boii and upon the Gauls who were neighbours of the latter…in a conflict with the Gauls, however, Publius Valerius was at first defeated.[45]

In the first conflict, when Valerius was Consul, three thousand Romans fell.[46]

Despite reportedly losing 3,000 men, it seems that Valerius was able to retreat with the rest of his forces intact and await fresh reinforcements. We do not know what actions the Boii and their unnamed allies took following this victory, nor do we have any timescale for the period between this battle and the subsequent one.

Zonaras reports that Valerius, on receiving reinforcements, was determined to bring the Boii to battle again, primarily in order to erase the shame his earlier defeat had brought on him. It must also be pointed out that in this period of Roman warfare, commands tended not to be rolled over into the subsequent year, so for Valerius this campaigning season was his only opportunity. Again we are given no name, location, tactics or overall numbers, merely the outcome:

…But later, learning that troops had come from Rome to his assistance, he renewed the struggle with the enemy, determined either to conquer by his own exertions or to die – for he preferred death to living in disgrace – and by some good fortune or other he gained the victory.[47]

…In the second [battle], fourteen thousand Gauls were slain, and two thousand captured. [48]

It is again thanks to Orosius that we are able to see the scale of the victory Valerius won. Again we have no further detail as to the other events of the campaign. However, we can suppose that after such a defeat the Boii fell back into their own lands and Valerius retired his army for winter and returned to Rome, where he was refused a Triumph on account of his earlier defeat.[49] For the second year of the Boian War (237 BC) we only have a short account in Zonaras to rely on. His account does seem to suggest that the two Consuls acted in concert and invaded Boian territory:

The next year Lucius [Cornelius] Lentulus [Caudinus] and Quintus [Fulvius] Flaccus made a campaign against the Gauls; and as long as they remained together, they were invincible, but when they began to pillage districts separately, with the purpose of securing greater booty, the army of Flaccus became imperilled, being surrounded by night. For the time the barbarians were beaten back, but after gaining accessions of allies they proceeded anew with a huge force against the Romans.[50]

Thus it seems that Q. Fulvius Flaccus was lured into an ambush but was able to extricate himself from it. The year's campaign appears to have been one of mixed success, with the Roman armies punishing the Boii and their allies, but then nearly losing another army to an ambush. It seems that the year's campaigning ended with fresh allies arriving to aid the Boii, most likely from the tribes of Cisalpine Gaul, possibly the Insubres tribes and thus stalemate was achieved once more.

The third and decisive year of the war (236 BC) seems to have opened with a fresh Gallic thrust into Roman territory, seemingly towards the Roman colony of Ariminum. Once again both Consuls appear to have taken to the field to oppose them, showing the seriousness of the threat. It is also interesting to note that one of the Consuls was another Cornelius Lentulus Caudinus (Publius), a kinsman, possibly even brother, of the

Consul of the previous year. From the passage of Zonaras below it is clear that, despite the presence of both Consuls, the Roman were outnumbered by the reinforced Gallic armies. Battle between the two sides was averted on this occasion:

> When confronted by Publius [Cornelius] Lentulus and [Caius] Licinius Varus, they hoped to terrify them by their numbers and prevail without a battle. So they sent and demanded back the land surrounding Ariminum and commanded the Romans to vacate the city, since it belonged to them. The consuls, because of their small numbers, did not dare to risk a battle, nor would they undertake to abandon any territory; accordingly they arranged an armistice, to enable the Gauls to send envoys to Rome. These came before the Senate with the same demands, but obtained no satisfaction, and returned to camp. There they found their cause was lost. For some of their allies repented, and regarding the Romans with fear, turned upon the Boii, and many were killed on both sides. Thereupon the remainder went home and the Boii obtained peace at the price of a large portion of their land.[51]

Thus we can see the incident referred to by Polybius earlier (above). However, this description does portray the Romans in a different light; until the dissensions between the Gallic tribes, the Romans were facing a far larger army with no guarantee of success. The Romans emerged from the war victorious and with greater lands than before, but only on account of the collapse of the Gallic alliance and not from their own force of arms. As such, this was hardly a repeat of the victorious campaigns of the 280s and would not have discouraged further Gallic activity, or reduced the threat to their borders. Nevertheless, the Boii had been defeated and the gains of the 280s had been solidified and built upon.

The Ligurian War (238–233 BC)

The Ligurian War represented something different altogether. The Ligurians were not a Gallic people but a native Italic one, who had been pushed by the Gallic invasions into the mountainous region in north-west Italy that lay sandwiched between the coast, the Alps and the Apennines (see Map 2).[52]

Unlike the Boii and the other Gallic tribes of the Po Valley, the terrain was mountainous and favoured guerrilla warfare rather than set piece battles. Furthermore, it offered little in the way of arable land for expansion. Given its location and character there had been no hostile contact between Rome and the Ligurians in the previous period, except by proxy. Dyson provides the best background discussion of the region and its peoples.[53]

Whilst the region had a strategic significance, controlling the coastal routes between Italy and Gaul and overlooking the Po Valley, the Ligurians were not an obvious opponent for the Romans, based on their prior thrust of expansion. The few comments we have from our surviving sources present a picture of the Ligurians having a basic tribal existence, with a pastoral economy, little urban development and no overarching leadership structures. However, it is clear that these were a martial people, with banditry, piracy, raiding parties and mercenaries being key activities.

It is through this mercenary activity that the Ligurians would have first come into hostile contact with the Romans. The sources record that as early as 480 BC Ligurians were serving as mercenaries in Carthaginian armies, as detailed by Herodotus.[54] The proximity of Sardinia to Liguria would have brought them into contact with the Carthaginians and they found employment in their armies throughout the following centuries. It is this connection that links the campaigns against Liguria in 238 BC to those against the Carthaginian possessions of Sardinia and Corsica of the same year, and thus separates them from the Boian conflict (see Chapter Two). If Rome moved on Corsica then it created the problem of the Ligurian connection. Not only were Ligurians providing mercenaries to fight in Carthaginian armies, but the coastline was a hotbed of piracy and by moving on Corsica, Rome acquired the responsibility for the seas of the region. Thus in effect Liguria, with its Punic links, became a third area of potential Punic influence in western Italy, along with Sardinia and Corsica. The linkage is affirmed by the fact that it was the Consul of 238 BC Ti. Sempronius Gracchus who led the attack on Sardinia and then against the Ligurians. However, in terms of detail we have less for the Ligurian War than we do for the Boian one. All Zonaras provides is the following for the first year of the campaign (238 BC):

After this the Romans again waged war upon the Boii and upon the Gauls who were neighbours of the latter, and upon some of the

Ligurians. So the Ligurians were conquered in battle and harried by Sempronius Gracchus. [55]

Exactly what or whom Gracchus attacked is another challenge, given the mountainous and scattered nature of the Ligurian lands. There were no chief settlements or leaders to attack and bring under submission. Furthermore, the Ligurians could easily melt back into the mountains and conduct a guerrilla campaign, mirroring Rome's experience in Corsica (as seen in Chapter Two).

We have no details for any campaigns the following year either (237 BC), with both Consuls seemingly engaged in the Boian War. This seems to be borne out by the narrative of events we have for 236 BC, when the Consul P. Cornelius Lentulus Caudinus only campaigned in Liguria after the end of the Boian War:

> When the Gallic wars had now been ended, Lentulus conducted a campaign against the Ligurians; he repulsed those who attacked him and gained possession of several fortresses. [56]

As is common for this period we have no other details of Lentulus' campaigns, especially where these fortresses were. They may have controlled key valleys and passes, guarded the coastal route, or been in the south bordering Roman allied territory. In any event, Lentulus was awarded a Triumph for his campaigns when he returned to Rome. At best we must assume that these campaigns were to show the Ligurians that they now fell under Roman, rather than Punic influence, and secured some key strategic targets for Roman control. This was not a campaign of conquest.

Nevertheless by 234 BC Rome was campaigning in Liguria once more. This is most commonly ascribed by the ancient sources to the Carthaginians stirring up the native tribes, here and in Corsica, against Rome:

> Later the Carthaginians secretly persuaded the Sardinians to rise against the Romans. In addition to this the Corsicans also revolted and the Ligurians did not remain quiet... the following year the Romans divided their forces into three parts in order that the rebels, finding war waged upon all of them at once, might not render assistance to one another; so they sent [Lucius] Postumius Albinus into Liguria.[57]

Whether or not the Carthaginians needed to spur the Ligurians to taking up arms against Rome, fresh hostilities broke out once more and once again a Consul (L. Postumius Albinus) was dispatched to campaign in Liguria, yet once again we have no details as to his actions. What we do know is that Albinus was not able to bring the war to a conclusion and he was succeeded by a Consul of 233, Q. Fabius Maximus (who was to find fame during the Second Punic War). Fabius clearly had greater success against the Ligurians, as he is recorded as celebrating a Triumph against them the following year; and whilst the wars in Sardinia and Corsica continued, there is no record of the Ligurian War continuing beyond this year. Whilst Zonaras simply records that Fabius was dispatched to Liguria, Plutarch's Life of Fabius preserves a slightly fuller account of an unnamed battle:

> The first of the five consulships in which he served brought him the honour of a Triumph over the Ligurians. These were defeated by him in battle, with heavy loss, and retired into the Alps, where they ceased plundering and harrying the parts of Italy next to them.[58]

Again we have no details of the battle's location, or each side's strengths and tactics. Nevertheless, this extract does provide us with some insight into the conflict. The Ligurians had clearly been raiding regions of Roman-controlled Italy which bordered their territory. Fabius appears to have brought them into battle in a coastal region, and after inflicting a heavy defeat forced them to scatter once more into the mountains. Despite this victory in battle, the limitations of Rome's policy in Liguria are clear to see. Even on the occasions that the Ligurians gave battle, they could retreat back into the safety of the mountains, regroup and harry any Roman military presence. Therefore at best the Romans could launch punitive campaigns against the Ligurian tribes and exercise some measure of control of the coastal regions, but had little in the way of permanent control over the region or its peoples. Fabius' victory seemed to bring a halt to the fighting in Liguria during this first war. However, Zonaras records that the Consuls of 230 BC, M. Aemilius Barbula and M. Iunius Pera, were travelling to campaign in Liguria when they were diverted to face the Boii once more (see below). We are given no other details, not even if the Consuls returned to fight in Liguria, but this again shows that even a major Roman victory, such as that of Fabius', proved to be, at best, a temporary setback for the Ligurians, who were soon able to harry Roman interests in the region.

This again shows the limitations of the Roman's half-hearted approach to Liguria in terms of their temporary forays into the region and punitive campaigns. Nothing short of a complete conquest of the region would quell the Ligurian tribesmen, and this does not seem to have been part of the Roman strategy. At best, these campaigns had brought Liguria from the Carthaginian sphere of influence to the Roman one, but not under their control. It was clear from the continued outbreaks of fighting that Roman warfare in Liguria was to be of a different sort to that on the plains of Northern Italy, much more akin to the long drawn-out conflict in Sardinia and Corsica and that of Spain in the centuries which followed. Thus, after five years of warfare and several Roman Triumphs, the Ligurian tribes were still as unbowed as they had been at the start of the war and Rome had gained a long-running issue on its north-western borders which was to be a concern for the next fifty years.

Land Distribution and the Tribunate of Flaminius

Fabius' Triumph in 232 BC coincided with another important event in Rome; a controversial land distribution law, proposed by the Tribune C. Flaminius.[59] Flaminius' Tribunate and his proposals have long garnered attention for their parallels to the later Tribunates of the Gracchi, which may have actually influenced much of the later historiographical treatment of the earlier Tribunate of Flaminius (see Appendix Three). Fortunately, we have Polybius' testimony which predates the Gracchi.[60]

Flaminius' proposal seems to have been to distribute lands captured from the Senones in the *ager gallicus* around Ariminum and Picenum amongst the Roman populace. We have little detail of the law itself, only that it was promulgated in the face of Senatorial opposition, though this detail comes from later sources and not from Polybius himself. If we are to believe the sources for the early Republic, which itself is a vexed issue, then land distribution schemes for conquered territories had been a staple of Tribunician activities in the fifth century using lands around Rome.[61] As Roman control expanded through Italy, however, this had been supplanted by a colonisation policy controlled by the Senate. Flaminius' proposal seems to have challenged the Senate's policy here, but in what manner we are not told (see Appendix Three).[62] However, it does seem that additional colonisation took place on Gallic lands in this period, possibly under the supervision of L. Caecilius Metellus.[63]

Whilst many commentators have since focussed on the domestic repercussions of Flaminius' actions, especially in light of the similarities to those of Ti. Sempronius Gracchus a century later, Polybius instead looks at the effect on the Gauls of this policy. Widespread Roman settlement meant the displacement and dispossession of the local population, which in turn would create widespread anger and resentment in the region. The timing of this proposal is interesting, given that it came so long after the lands of the Senones had been annexed but so soon after the Boian War. The recent war may have acted as a spur, by showing the Romans how vulnerable their northern border was, and thus Flaminius' proposal could have been a move to strengthen it by creating additional Roman colonies whose manpower could be mobilised to block any Gallic advance and strengthen the ring of defensive Roman colonies in the border region.[64]

However, it is equally true that such a move, far from strengthening Rome's northern borders, could actually have undermined it. From the Gallic perspective, this move could have been seen as a provocation in what was a region that had only just seen a massive Gallic incursion defeated, not by Roman force of arms but by inter-Gallic dissensions. Whether the Senate and people may or may not have thought of it in this way, or even cared how it looked to the Gauls, is a matter we will never resolve, though Develin does argue that this may have accounted for the Senate's opposition to Flaminius' proposal.[65]

In any event, whether the colonisation programme that took place was Flaminius' or not, and regardless of the tactics used in Rome, a widespread programme of dispossession and Roman settlement seems to have been enacted on the border regions between Roman and Gallic Italy. To Rome, this would have been a move to secure her northern frontier and draw the lands firmly into Roman Italy. For the Gallic tribes, it was Roman encroachment and settlement, evidence of a Roman policy of a permanent land expansion programme that would only have one logical conclusion. Coming on the heels of the poor military showing during the Boian War and the aggressive expansion into the islands and Liguria. Thus the stage was set for a further and more intensive period of warfare between the two great and contrasting civilisations of Italy.

The Aborted Campaigns of 230 BC

The year 230 BC forms a postscript to both the Boian and Ligurian Wars of this period. For these events we only have the direct testimony of Zonaras, who records three interesting events this year, all of which shed further light on the instability on Rome's northern frontier. The first involved the activities of the Boii:

> In view of the fact that the Boii and rest of the Gauls were offering for sale various articles and an especially large number of captives, the Romans became afraid that they might someday use the money against them, and accordingly forbade anybody to give to a Gaul either silver or gold.[66]

Although this is a brief note, there are a number of interesting aspects here. Whilst it is not clearly stated, the danger the Romans perceived was most likely the use of the monies to hire further Gallic tribesmen as mercenaries for the Boian cause. Another key aspect is just whom the Boii had enslaved. This clearly indicates that they had been at war with other Gallic tribes, perhaps a continuation of the conflict between them and their erstwhile allies from the previous war with Rome. Not only does this indicate continued instability in the region, but also that the Boii had emerged victorious and were now back in a position, or were perceived to be in a position, to challenge Rome once more.

The second point Zonaras notes is that both Consuls were sent to Liguria (see below), though for what purpose is not stated. Interestingly, this comes in the narrative after the earlier point about the Boii using their wealth against Rome. Given that the Ligurians were famous for their exploits as mercenaries, was this a case of the Senate backing up its economic move with a military one: to ensure that the Ligurians did not send men to fight with the Boii? This would explain the presence of both Consuls, and so soon after Fabius' seemingly major triumph in Liguria.

The third point Zonaras makes is that an unidentified foe was preparing to attack Roman territory this year:

Soon afterward the Carthaginians, learning that the Consuls, Marcus Aemilius and Marcus Iunius, had started for Liguria, made preparations to march upon Rome. But when the Consuls became aware of this and proceeded suddenly against them, they became frightened and went to meet them as if they were friends. The Consuls likewise feigned that they had not set out against these people, but were going through their country into the Ligurian territory.[67]

Unhelpfully, Zonaras, or one of his transmitters, has inserted the name of the Carthaginians as the enemy, well ahead of the Second Punic War, rather than the true foe. However, given that they occupied the north of Italy we must assume a Gallic tribe, and the Boii are the most likely. We must as always exercise caution; there may have been no overt move by the Gallic tribes to attack Rome, merely the fear, or rumour, on the Roman side rather than the reality, but it nevertheless shows the fragile state of affairs in this region. Thus we can see that Rome again faced a threat from her northern borders, one which was again only prevented by a show of force, which would be nothing more than a temporary solution. It also shows that the Gallic tribes were preparing for another attack on Roman Italy, but on this occasion wanted to be sure of their superior strength before attacking, rather than risk another failure, as had occurred in the previous war; where they were defeated not by Rome, but their own disunity.

Interestingly, Polybius has none of this detail for the period, and moves quickly on to the events of the 220s. Nevertheless, an undated section does talk about the Boii and Insubres making a fresh alliance against Rome and details Roman insecurity about the region:

All this time, the Romans, either hearing what was happening or divining what was coming, were in such a state of constant alarm and unrest, that at times we find them busy enrolling legions and making provision of corn and other stores, at times marching to the frontier, as if the enemy had already invaded their territory, while as a fact the Celts had not yet budged from their own country.[68]

Summary

We can see that the Gallic and Ligurian Wars of the 230s, although technically victories for Rome, did little to secure Rome's northern frontiers and in many ways added to the instability. In the north-east, a major attack by the Boii had only failed due to a collapse of a Gallic tribal alliance and infighting, and showed how vulnerable Rome's northern frontiers were to a combined attack from the Gallic tribes. If anything, the events of 230 showed that, in this region, Rome seemed to be shying away from open confrontation with the tribes and made efforts to try to undermine them economically and deny them mercenary reinforcements from Liguria. No doubt they also made efforts to foster disunity amongst the tribes, which seems to have been Rome's most effective tactic.

Events in the north-west had hardly fared better for Rome. Following a string of Consuls campaigning in Liguria, with many being awarded Triumphs, the region had been brought into the Roman sphere of influence, but their control of it was limited at best, perhaps, to the coastal regions, which soon melted away when Roman armies returned home. If anything, the Ligurian War reflected a half-hearted, or disjointed, approach to strategic military action. The Senate was seemingly aware that these regions needed to be brought under Roman influence, but without the commitment to bring them into Roman control and into the Roman system. This would lead to endless years of campaigning in these territories and against enemies who the Romans were unsuited to fighting, echoing Roman military policy for the next century: military dominance without full annexation.

These two theatres of conflict reflect the state of affairs in the conquest of Sardinia and Corsica. On the face of it, Rome had aggressively taken steps to secure her borders by annexing Carthaginian territory off her coastline. In reality, both wars had become drawn-out guerrilla campaigns in terrain which was seemingly unsuited to Roman tactics. Piecemeal campaigns and nominal victories had only a limited effect on a mountainous people who desired to remain outside of anything more than nominal Roman control. Furthermore, unlike the peoples of central Italy, they could not be easily integrated into the Roman system.

Overall, we can see that the wars of the 230s were something of a mixed bag for Rome. Despite a string of Triumphs celebrated in Rome, the strategic situation was still far from secure. Rome had taken action to secure both the north-west and north-east of Italy, but had become bogged down in Liguria and had shown her vulnerability against the tribes of the Po Valley. The actions of the Consuls of the 230s BC seemed to quieten the tensions in the region for the time being but further warfare was inevitable. As it happens, events transpired which shifted Rome's focus further eastwards still, across the Adriatic.

Chapter Four

Roman Expansion in the East – The First Illyrian War (230–228 BC)

Having campaigned in the north against the Gauls and in the west against the natives of Sardinia and Corsica, 230 BC saw Rome take a momentous, but logical step; namely, conducting military operations across the Adriatic on the Greek mainland. Yet this event did not occur in isolation and to fully understand the war, its origins and wider implications we must first have an understanding of the interactions between Rome and the Greek world prior to 230 BC.

Rome's Evolving Relationship with the Wider Greek World

It is important to understand that during the period prior to the one under review here, Italy, and Rome, occupied the periphery of the 'civilized' world. The earliest civilizations had sprung up in the Middle East, Egypt and Anatolia. By the foundation of the Roman Republic, the largest empire of the ancient world had been created, spanning from India to Macedonia, in the form of the First Persian Empire. It was from the Middle East that the first wave of colonization across the western Mediterranean came, in the form of the seafaring Phoenician city states. They planted colonies as far as Gades (Cadiz) in Spain and, most famously, Carthage on the North African coast.

The flourishing of the Greek city states brought about the second great wave of colonization of the western Mediterranean through the plantation of colony cities on various coastlines, from Emporion (Ampurias) in Spain to Massilia (Marseilles) in southern Gaul and Syracuse in Sicily. These colonies allowed the Greek city states to alleviate population growth at home, gain access to a wider range of natural resources and ultimately create a Mediterranean-wide trading network. Given the proximity of southern

Italy to the Greek mainland, it is no surprise that a number of Greek colonies were founded there, beginning in c. 750 BC when Cumae was founded by colonists from Euboea.[1] There followed several centuries of Greek expansion, from the eighth century down to the fifth; including Tarentum, Rhegium, Thurri and Heraclea. The whole region of these southern Italian Greek cities became known in Latin as Magna Graecia, or Greater Greece.[2] Thus southern Italy was firmly in the orbit of the Greek world from the seventh century BC onwards, albeit on the periphery.

Therefore, throughout its history, Rome developed in an Italy which had a distinctly Greek flavour to it. It is impossible to say how much Greek influence penetrated 'Dark Age' Rome, but by the late Republic a number of key events in Roman history had taken on a Greek tinge. At some point in its history, Rome acquired a foundation myth involving Aeneas and the Trojan War. The chronology of the overthrow of the monarchy and the foundation of the Republic became suspiciously close to the overthrow of the Peisistratid Tyranny of Athens and the creation of the Athenian Democracy. In c. 454 BC, a Senatorial delegation apparently travelled to the Greek city states, including Athens, to study their low codes, leading to the creation of the Twelve Tables, the very cornerstone of the Roman constitution.

The most obvious impact of Greek culture upon Rome, however, can be seen in the Roman style of fighting. At the core of Greek armies, until the fourth century, sat the hoplite phalanx; heavy infantry fighting as a closed unit with long spears. As this military innovation swept the Greek world in the eighth and seventh centuries, it soon spread to the periphery of this world. Given the lack of contemporary sources there is no firm evidence of when Rome adopted the hoplite and phalanx military tactics, but it is most commonly ascribed to the period of King Servius Tullius (c. 578–535 BC): the so-called Servian reforms.[3]

The Wars for Southern Italy (395–275 BC)

More tangible military links came in the late fifth and early fourth centuries BC, when two major military campaigns linked the Greek and Italian worlds. It began in 415 BC, when the Athenians, taking advantage of a break in the Peloponnesian War, launched an audacious and ultimately disastrous attempt to conquer Syracuse and add Sicily to their maritime empire, now known as the Sicilian Expedition.[4] Although we do not wish to indulge in counter factual history, had they succeeded, and by all rights they should have, Rome would have entered one of its most critical periods with the Athenian Empire as their neighbour.

However, just as the Sicilian Expedition proved to be Athens' downfall, it proved to be the foundation upon which Syracuse then launched an attempt to carve out a Greco-Italic Empire of their own. In c. 390 BC The Tyrant of Syracuse, Dionysius I, launched an ambitious war of conquest with an invasion of Italy and was able, albeit temporarily, to conquer the Greek cities of southern Italy and add them to his empire.[5] With southern Italy secure, he was then able to launch an attack on Epirus itself, defeating both the Epirotes and the Illyrian tribes of the region and installing a puppet on the throne of Epirus. Although Dionysius' land forces did not penetrate into central Italy, his navy ranged up the entire length of the western Italian coast, sacking the Caerean city of Pyrgi (as seen in Chapter Three). Although our sources for these campaigns are poor, it does seem that southern Italy remained part of the Syracusan Empire until after the death of Dionysius in 367 BC.

It is not known when the Syracusan control of southern Italy collapsed, but Dionysius' successor, Dionysius II, appears to still have control of much of southern Italy throughout his initial reign (367–357 BC and then later in 346–344 BC). However, Champion points out, even when the southern Italian cities were able to escape Syracusan domination, they had been weakened so much by the constant warfare in southern Italy that they proved to be easy pickings for the native peoples of the region: the Lucanians and Apulians.[6] This in turn led to them seeking military assistance from Greece itself and a period of sixty years in which five major interventions were made in southern Italy by Greek commanders, culminating in the famous campaigns of the King of Epirus, Pyrrhus.

The first of these interventions came in 343 BC, when Archidamus III, King of Sparta (360–338 BC), travelled to southern Italy to take command of the forces of the city of Tarentum. He spent the next five years fighting against the Lucanians, but was killed at the Battle of Manduria in 338 BC:

> For at about the same time the people of Tarentum were engaged in prosecuting a war against the Lucanians and had sent to the Lacedaemonians, who were the stock of their ancestors, envoys soliciting help, whereupon the Spartans, who were willing to join them

because of their relationship, quickly assembled an army and navy and as general in command of it appointed King Archidamus. But as they were about to set sail for Italy, a request came from the Lyctians to help them first. Consenting to this, the Lacedaemonians sailed to Crete, defeated the mercenaries and restored to the Lyctians their native land. After this Archidamus sailed to Italy and joined forces with the Tarentines but lost his life fighting gallantly in battle.[7]

During his years of fighting in southern Italy, he apparently had no contact with Rome. The same cannot be said of his replacement and the next Hellenic ruler to intervene in southern Italy. In c. 334 BC, the Tarentines invited the King of Epirus, Alexander I (342–331 BC), brother-in-law of Philip II of Macedon, to take command, this time against both the Lucanians and Samnites:

> Samnium likewise had now for two years been suspected of hatching revolutionary schemes, for which reason the Roman Army was not withdrawn from the Sidicine country, but an invasion by Alexander of Epirus drew the Samnites off into Lucania, and these two peoples engaged in a pitched battle with the King, as he was marching up from Paestum. The victory remained with Alexander, who then made a treaty of peace with the Romans; with what faith he intended to keep it, had the rest of his campaign been equally successful, is a question.[8]

Alexander proved to be more successful in battle against the natives of Italy and even made a treaty with Rome, which was itself at war with the Samnites in this period (as seen in Chapter One). Thus Rome had its first treaty of alliance with a Greek ruler (agreed in 332 BC). We do not know its terms, but there is no record of direct Roman military intervention. Unfortunately for Alexander his triumph was short lived as he was assassinated in c. 331 BC by a Lucanian exile.[9]

The next thirty years passed without any further Greek intervention in southern Italy, no doubt greatly due to the upheavals caused in Greece and the wider ancient world by the rise and fall of Alexander III of Macedon (the Great). His death in 323 BC saw his new empire torn apart by civil wars between his various generals, a conflict known as the War of the Diadochi.[10] Despite the eastern Mediterranean suffering fifty years of warfare between Alexander's successors, Italy remained untouched by the fighting. Interestingly, Livy breaks off his narrative of Roman history to engage in one of the earliest and most famous discussions of counter factual history in ancient history: namely, what would have happened if Alexander the Great had invaded Italy?[11]

Though unconnected, it was in this period that the Romans rapidly expanded their empire in Italy (as seen in Chapter One) and pushed further southwards. Again the city of Tarentum turned to Greece for a commander to lead their forces, and again they turned to their ancestral home city of Sparta. On this occasion it was a Spartan pretender to the throne, Cleonymus, who answered their call, arriving with a force of 5,000 mercenaries.

Cleonymus' involvement highlights the evolution in Rome's relationship with these Greek adventurers. When Archidamus arrived, there was no apparent contact between him and Rome, showing that they as yet had no conflicting interests in southern Italy. When Alexander arrived, the two sides concluded a treaty, as they had common enemies, the Samnites. By 302 BC, however, and the arrival of Cleonymus, Rome's southward expansion meant that the foreign intervention was now a threat to Roman interests, as seen from Livy:

> During the year a fleet of Greek ships under the command of the Lacedaemonian Cleonymus sailed to the shores of Italy and captured the city of Thuriae in the Sallentine country. The Consul, Aemilius, was sent to meet this enemy, and in one battle he routed him and drove him to his ships. Thuriae was restored to its former inhabitants, and peace was established in the Sallentine territory. In some annalists I find it stated that the Dictator, Iunius Bubulcus, was sent into that country, and that Cleonymus left Italy to avoid a conflict with the Romans.[12]

There were clearly two versions of this period of history circulating in Rome by the late Republic. In one, Rome went to war with Cleonymus, which would be their first with an overseas foe, and the Consul M. Aemilius Paullus defeated him in an unnamed battle. It is probably no coincidence that there was a version of history circulating which had an Aemilius Paullus being the first man to defeat a Greek foe, given that it was L. Aemilius Paullus who defeated the Macedonians at the Battle of Pydna in 168 BC. The other version has a Roman Dictator (specially appointed sole military commander), C.

Iunius Bubulcus Brutus, sent to defeat Cleonymus, but the latter withdrew rather than fight Rome.[13]

Cleonymus did not return to face Rome in battle, but withdrew to the island of Corcyra (Corfu), from where he launched an incursion northwards, landing in Gallic northern Italy, where he was defeated in the territory of the Veneti. In any event, it was now clear that Rome would oppose any foreign intervention in southern Italy.

Another result of the defeat (or retreat) of Cleonymus was that Rome and Tarentum entered into a treaty of alliance which guaranteed Tarentine independence for the time being and set a limit on where Roman ships could sail: not beyond the Cape of Lacinium. Beyond this, no other details are known. This treaty, however, provided only short-term respite. Rome's attentions turned away from Magna Graecia towards a war against an alliance of Samnites, Etruscans, Umbrians and Gauls (the Third Samnite War, 298–290 BC). It was this period that saw the arrival of the fourth of the overseas rulers, in the form of Agathocles, the then Tyrant of Syracuse.

Agathocles seems to have been intent on reviving the Dionysian project of an empire which spanned from Sicily to Greece, and in c.299 BC sent his fleet to Corcyra to defend it from a Macedonian attack, destroying the Macedonian navy in the process. Diodorus records that he had Ligurians and Etruscans as mercenaries in his armies,[14] which he then sent to intervene in southern Italy, but was defeated by the Bruttians in c. 298 BC. In 295 BC he allied himself to King Pyrrhus of Epirus and King Ptolemy I of Egypt and launched an attack on southern Italy, conquering and garrisoning the coastal city of Croton, after which he returned to Syracuse. He was again drawn back into southern Italy by an appeal by Tarentum, this time threatened by the Bruttians. On this occasion (c. 294 BC) he launched a full-scale invasion of southern Italy:

> Agathocles assembled an army and crossed over into Italy with thirty thousand infantry and three thousand cavalry. The navy he entrusted to Stilpo with orders to ravage the territory of the Bruttians; but while Stilpo was plundering the estates along the shore, he encountered a storm and lost most of his ships. Agathocles laid siege to Hipponium… and by means of stone-throwers they overpowered the city and captured it. This terrified the Bruttians, who sent an embassy to treat for terms. Agathocles, having obtained six hundred hostages from

them and having left an occupying force, returned to Syracuse. The Bruttians, however, instead of abiding by their oath, marched out in full force against the soldiers who had been left behind, crushed them, recovered the hostages, and so freed themselves from the domination of Agathocles.[15]

Further involvement in southern Italy was curtailed by Agathocles, failing health and he died in c.289 BC. As is often the case, the death of a tyrant led to a collapse in the power and empire of Syracuse, both within Sicily and further afield, and Syracuse collapsed into internal dissension, freeing the Greek cities of southern Italy from the danger of Syracusan intervention, but also leaving them vulnerable to the native Italian peoples once more.[16] By 285 BC the city of Thurii was so threatened by the Lucanians that they made a fateful, and some would say inevitable step, and appealed to Rome for military assistance. Having emerged victorious form the Third Samnite War as unquestioned masters of central Italy, the Romans were only too willing to extend their influence into southern Italy, and soon had a string of Greek cities under their protection; notably Locri, Rhegium and Croton. This led Tarentum to once again appeal to Greece for aid and this time another Epirote king answered; Pyrrhus.

Unlike the events detailed above, the Pyrrhic Wars have been well documented and analysed elsewhere.[17] However, in this context the war between Rome and Pyrrhus can be seen as the natural evolution of the prior interventions. Whilst it may not have been the first clash between Rome and a Greek king (see Cleonymus, above), it was certainly the first full-blown war between the two, Pyrrhus invading Italy in 280 BC with a battle-hardened army of 25,000 men (along with twenty elephants). Rome's first encounter with a full Hellenistic army ended in defeats at the Battles of Heraclea (280 BC) and Ausculum (279 BC). However, their manpower reserves meant that they did not need to sue for terms and were able to fight on. Paradoxically, Pyrrhus did not have the manpower to fight a protracted war in Italy and left to take up command of the Greek cities of Sicily (which were in chaos following the death of Agathocles), and fight the Carthaginians. His return in 275 BC saw the third battle between him and Rome (Beneventum), which finally saw a Roman victory and his retreat back to Greece. Inevitably, the Romans then moved on Tarentum, which fell in 272 BC, completing the Roman conquest of southern Italy.

We can see that from 395–272 BC the history of southern Italy was fundamentally linked to the Hellenic and then Hellenistic worlds, and their ever-changing wars. Throughout this period, parts of southern Italy fell under an Adriatic-spanning Syracusan Empire (twice), saw two Epirote kings try to extend their empires in the opposite direction, and even witnessed two royal Spartan commanders take up arms in Italy. The further south the Romans moved their empire in Italy, the more they were drawn into this world and its ever-changing series of wars. Furthermore, it was apparent to anyone who reviewed this history that southern Italy was prone to invasion from both Greece in the east and Syracuse in the west; not even mentioning Carthage, with had a significant presence in Sicily as well.

Rome and the Hellenistic World 273–230 BC

The following forty years did not see any further military engagements with the states of the Greek mainland or wider Hellenistic world. Naturally, Rome's full military attention was soon focussed on the war in the south against the Carthaginians. Yet the meagre sources that survive for this period (and which are not focused on the Punic War) do preserve a number of interesting references to Rome's widening participation in Greek affairs. The first occurred as early as 273 BC and is perhaps the most well-known; an agreement of friendship between the Senate and People of Rome and King Ptolemy II of Egypt, one of the three premier Hellenistic powers.[18] Victory over Pyrrhus, widely regarded at the time as one of the Hellenistic world's foremost generals (if not statesmen), seems to have brought Rome to wider attention:

> Ptolemy, nicknamed Philadelphus, King of Egypt, when he learned that Pyrrhus had fared badly and that the Romans were growing powerful, sent gifts to them and made a compact. The Romans, accordingly, pleased that a monarch living so very far away should have come to regard them highly, despatched ambassadors to him in turn. From him the envoys received magnificent gifts; but when they offered these to the treasury, they were not accepted.[19]

Aside from the exchange of envoys, the agreement seems to have had little of substance but it did mark an important step in Rome's gradual advancement from Italian power to regional power. The 260s BC saw the arrival of another embassy, this time from the Illyrian city of Apollonia, though there are scant details:

> Q. Fabius and Cn. Apronius, former Aediles, struck some envoys sent to Rome from the city of Apollonia in a quarrel. When the Senate learnt of this they immediately serenaded them through Fetials to the envoys.[20]

Unfortunately, the sources choose to focus on the incident and not the reason for that embassy, but it is interesting that an Illyrian city was sending embassies to Rome in the 260s BC. Whatever the reason, the outcome was clear. Rome did not intervene, if that was the request, across the Adriatic, into a region which fell under the sphere of influence of Epirus at that time (see below). The 240s BC saw two other vague references to Roman involvement in the wider Hellenistic world. There is a curious reference in Suetonius' *Life of Claudius* to an agreement of friendship between Rome and a King Seleucus of the Seleucid Empire:

> ...reciting upon the occasion a letter in Greek, from the Senate and People of Rome to King Seleucus, on which they promised him their friendship and alliance, provided that he would grant their kinsmen the Iliensians immunity from all burdens.[21]

The reference is undated and it is not clear to which Seleucus it refers, but it has been argued that it may well date from the 240s BC and thus refer to Seleucus II (246–225 BC).[22] If it does then it shows Rome's continued progress on the international stage, albeit as a small participant. The final reference comes from c. 238 BC with Rome, having emerged as victorious in the Punic War and master of Sicily, making their first intervention across the Adriatic, albeit a diplomatic one. The only source to reference this is Justin (which, if it can be trusted, represents an interesting omission from Polybius):

> The Acarnanians also, fearing to trust for support to the Epirotes, requested of the Romans assistance against the Aetolians, and prevailed on the Senate to send ambassadors to order the Aetolians 'to withdraw

their garrisons from the cities of Acarnania, and allow those to be free, who alone, of all the people of Greece, had not contributed aid to the Greeks against the Trojans, the authors of the Roman race.[23]

Justin goes onto recount, in some, detail, that the Aetolians rejected the Roman embassy, pouring scorn on their character, with a suspiciously impressive account of Roman history from the Gallic sack onwards. The content of this speech and the omission of this embassy from every other surviving ancient source does raise serious questions about its authenticity. Justin also record the outcome of the embassy:

> They thus dismissed the Roman embassy, and, that they might not seem to speak more boldly than they acted, laid waste the borders of Epirus and Acarnania.[24]

Despite the very real issue about the authenticity of this episode, the event does have some interesting implications. If we are to believe that this episode was based on a real event, then Rome's first intervention overseas was to support Acarnania, a region which bordered the Ionian Sea, just south of the Adriatic, and which had been recently partitioned between Epirus and the Aetolian League. The collapse of Epirote power (see below) does give this incident resonance with Rome's first military intervention on the Greek mainland (see below).

The First Illyrian War (230–228 BC)

Before we can examine the First Illyrian War itself in detail, it is important to understand the nature of the enemy Rome fought. Illyrians was the name given to the communities which inhabited the region of the eastern shores of the Adriatic (see Map 4). However, unlike the kingdoms that bordered Illyria, namely Macedon and Epirus, Illyria itself was not a homogenous kingdom or even an area with a clear racial identity.[25] The region boasted a number of different communities, city states and quasi-kingdoms in what seems to have been an ever shifting pattern.[26]

In the 280s BC, southern Illyria appears to have fallen under the domination of its neighbour, the Kingdom of Epirus, ruled by King Pyrrhus, whose fourth wife came from one of the ruling families of Illyria. Following Pyrrhus' death (in 272 BC), his son Alexander II and grandson Pyrrhus II continued the policy of dominating southern Illyria. However, this Epirote dominance collapsed with the deaths of Pyrrhus II (c. 237 BC) and his brother Ptolemy (c. 234 BC). By c. 232 BC Epirus had collapsed into civil war, which saw the monarchy overthrown by a noble coup. This sudden collapse of Epirus naturally led to a power vacuum in Illyria. It was against this background of a collapse in Epirote power in the region that Rome chose to intervene. It is interesting that the alleged Roman embassy to the Aetolians in 238 BC also came in this period of Epirote weakness and concerned coastal territories.

The Rise of the Ardiaei and the Outbreak of the War

Whilst the Aetolians may have benefited from the Epirote collapse to the south, in Illyria it was the Ardiaei, a native Illyrian race, under a leader named Agron, who capitalised on this power vacuum. Little is known about the Ardiaean tribe prior to their appearance in the sources at this time, and their early development has either been lost to the historical record or never bothered it at all.[27] Dzino presents the most recent summary of the arguments to date, though Badian's account must never be overlooked.[28] By this period the Ardiaei occupied the coastal regions of the Adriatic to the north of Epirus, though where they may have originated from has long been debated.[29] We do not know their internal structures, apart from the fact that by this period the Ardiaei had unified under the leadership of one king and a ruling dynasty. We must assume that prior to this period that the Ardiaei fell under the hegemony (to whatever degree) of Epirus. However the collapse of Epirus in the 230s presented Agron with an opportunity, which he grasped enthusiastically. Again we have no exact chronology for this, but by 231 BC Agron had expanded southwards and carved out a nascent Ardiaean Empire. Polybius describes him thus:

> Agron, king of Illyria, was the son of Pleuratus, and was master of stronger land and sea forces than any king of Illyria before him.[30]

By 231 BC, Agron had come to the attention of the Macedonian King Demetrius II, who bribed him to intervene against the Aetolian League, which was laying siege to the city of Medion in Acarnania (as seen above, in the 238 BC incident). Agron led his forces to relieve the siege with a combined land and naval assault, and defeated the Aetolian forces, further establishing his growing regional dominance.

Soon afterwards, however, Agron died (c. 231 BC), but his widow Teuta took command of the Ardiaei as regent for his son Pinnes. She seems to have continued the Ardiaean expansionist campaign in the region and soon attacked and defeated the Epirotes, and captured and ransomed the regional capital of Phoenice.[31] The sources are confused as to the exact chronology of the conquests of the Ardiaei, but they also seem to have attacked the island of Issa (see Map 4). Naturally, given the confusion about these events amongst our surviving ancient sources, there are a number of differing causes given for what triggered Roman involvement in this region:

> To return to the Illyrians. For a long time previously they had been in the habit of maltreating vessels sailing from Italy, and now while they were at Phoenice, a number of them detached themselves from the fleet and robbed or killed many Italian traders, capturing and carrying off no small number of prisoners. The Romans had hitherto turned a deaf ear to the complaints made against the Illyrians, but now when a number of persons approached the Senate on the subject, they appointed two envoys, Caius and Lucius Coruncanius, to proceed to Illyria, and investigate the matter.[32]

> Agron captured a part of Epirus and also Corcyra, Epidamnus, and Pharus in succession, where he established garrisons. When he threatened the rest of the Adriatic with his fleet, the isle of Issa implored the aid of the Romans. The latter sent ambassadors to accompany the Issii and to ascertain what offences Agron imputed to them.[33]

> When the Issaeans had attached themselves to the Romans, the latter, desiring to show them some prompt and ready favour in return, so as to get the reputation of aiding such as joined their cause, and also to punish the Ardiaeans, who were annoying those who sailed from Brundisium, sent envoys to Agron, to ask for clemency for the Issaeans and at the same time to censure the king for wronging them without cause.[34]

> Issa is an island situated in the Ionian Gulf. Its inhabitants, known as Issaeans, had of their own free will surrendered themselves to the

Romans because they were angry with their ruler Agron, who was king of the Ardiaeans and of Illyrian stock. To him the consuls sent envoys.[35]

As can be seen, there is an interesting division amongst our surviving ancient sources as to the event that actually sparked off Rome's interest in the shifting balances of power in Illyria. Our earliest source, Polybius, links this to the Ardiaean piracy and the capture of the city of Phoenice, and a massacre of Italian traders there.[36] The later sources, Appian, Dio and Zonaras, tie the intervention into a Roman alliance with the island of Issa (modern Vis), which was seeking protection from the advance of Ardiaeans and leading to a Roman intervention on its behalf. Polybius does mention Issa, but only in connection with the Ardiaeans already besieging the city at the time the Roman envoys arrived.

Thus, on the one hand we have the Senate intervening over the massacre of Italian traders, who seem to have gone to their allies in the Senate to protect their trade routes. On the other hand we have Rome intervening on behalf of one of her very small allies in the Adriatic, which if accurate is interesting in itself. It is entirely possible that our later sources, or one of their annalistic predecessors, had mistaken the besieging of Issa when the envoys arrived as the cause of their dispatch, rather than a coincidence of timing.

Nevertheless, the unifying factor in both explanations – trade and Adriatic allies – lies in the collapse of Epirote power, with Rome willingly stepping into the breach and acting as the regional power broker. Previously, the protection of the Adriatic shipping routes, overseas trade and the island communities of the Adriatic would have fallen to Epirus and its monarchs. It is clear that there were many in the Senate with a pecuniary interest in trade and the Adriatic trading routes, which had only fallen to Roman control a generation earlier with the conquest of southern Italy.[37] Neither the trade protection nor the defence of a tiny ally adequately explain Roman intervention, nor does an argument that Agron and his expansion threatened Rome, as he hardly commanded the resources of a great Hellenistic king such as Pyrrhus.

What does tie all these elements together is the Roman Senate viewing itself, not only as hegemon of Italian affairs, but now stepping into the recently vacated role as hegemon of the Adriatic, mirroring a similar expansion of the Roman sphere of influence to the western isles of Sardinia and Corsica, and

Sicily in the south. The only key difference being that this position was not the result of a successful war, but Rome stepping into a vacuum created by the collapse of a regional rival (Epirus) and possibly a desire to curtail the expansion of the Aetolian League. Thus we can see Rome acting as protector of trade in the Adriatic (especially when it was being conducted by Italian traders) and possibly acting as protector of the smaller city states.

The Senate dispatched two envoys, Caius and Lucius Coruncanius, to the Ardiaean leadership to emphasise the will of the Senate. The choice of these two men is an interesting one; the only other known Coruncanius was a Consul of 280 BC who had fought Pyrrhus.[38] In any event, the audience between the Senate's envoys and Teuta went badly, with Polybius providing an embellished account of the crossed words that were spoken, followed by a somewhat misogynistic analysis of the temper of female rulers.[39] On the voyage back to Rome, the envoys were attacked and one of the brothers or kinsmen was murdered, the other possibly captured and imprisoned.[40]

Though Rome clearly had one eye on the Gallic situation (as seen in Chapter Three), such a clear challenge to Rome's authority could not go unpunished and it gave the Senate the excuse that they may have been looking for to intervene across the Adriatic and project their power more directly on the Greek mainland; thus cementing their place in the post-Epirote world.[41] Thus, war was declared against Teuta and the Ardiaei; a momentous event, being the first time Roman forces had fought on the Greek mainland, though it would hardly be the last.

The Ardiaean Campaign of 229 BC

Undeterred by the impending clash with Rome, according to the Polybian narrative the Ardiaeans continued and, if anything, actually increased their offensive in Illyria. Polybius relates that Teuta deployed a larger navy than before and attacked a number of targets, such as the city of Epidamnus and the island of Corcyra.[42] Whilst the attack on Epidamnus failed, that on Corcyra brought an appeal for help to both the Achaean and Aetolian Leagues (the two largest federations of Greek city states), who both moved to aid the Corcyrans. The result was a naval battle off Corcyra in which the Aetolian and Achaeans were defeated and driven off.[43] With the loss of their allies, the Corcyrans capitulated to the Ardiaeans and agreed terms of surrender. An Ardiaean garrison was installed on Corcyra under the command of a man known as Demetrius of Pharos. Although Corcyra had fallen, the Ardiaeans continued with their siege of Issa and resumed that of Epidamnus.

Teuta had taken the offensive, added a key strategic island to her bourgeoning empire and defeated a naval contingent from the two key Greek leagues. Clearly she hoped to secure a number of key assets in the Adriatic before the Romans had a chance to mobilise and intervene. If anything, her actions would have merely confirmed the Roman fear of a bourgeoning aggressive power rising in the Adriatic, which, whilst no material threat to the Roman federation itself, clearly threatened its interests and challenged their newly assumed hegemony.

The Roman Campaign of 229 BC

In Rome, the Consuls for 229 BC were L. Postumius Albinus and Cn. Fulvius Centumalus. Interestingly, Postumius had been Consul just five years earlier (234 BC) and had campaigned in Liguria (as seen in Chapter Three). For Fulvius we have no details on his background prior to this Consulship. Of the two, Fulvius was placed in command of the Roman fleet, whilst Postumius had command of the land forces, in what clearly needed to be a combined land and naval campaign against the Ardiaei.

There are a number of surviving sources which provide some details of this war, but again the most detailed account is that of Polybius. Whilst their land forces were assembling for transport across the Adriatic, via Brundisium, the Romans began their campaign with a naval expedition to Corcyra. Polybius ascribes two different, and possibly mutually exclusive, motivations for this. Firstly, he states that the Consul Fulvius was unclear on the outcome of the Ardiaean siege of Corcyra and was therefore hoping to relieve the city. Secondly, he adds that, upon hearing of the city having fallen, Fulvius was in communication with its new Ardiaean governor, Demetrius of Pharos. The obvious point here is that if Demetrius had written to the Romans then he would have mentioned that he was in charge of Corcyra and that, ergo, the siege was over. [44]

In truth, we have no way of determining which of the above reasons drew Fulvius to Corcyra, but the impact of the Roman arrival did set the tone for the war which followed; namely that the Corcyrans rose up and Demetrius, the Ardiaean governor, surrendered his garrison to Fulvius without a fight. This does make it likely that Demetrius had been in contact with the Romans prior to their arrival and had arranged for the surrender of the island to Rome. Polybius ascribes this act to a falling out between him and Teuta, but in any event it was the logical move in the face of war with the Romans, and one which he personally benefited from (see below). Thus the Romans' first potential engagement of the Illyrian War had ended with an Ardiaean surrender without a fight. Interestingly, Dio and Zonaras present a variation on this Corcyran campaign:

> Then she [Teuta] again grew fearful and sent a certain Demetrius to the Consuls, assuring them of her readiness to heed them in everything. And a truce was made with this emissary, upon his agreeing to give them Corcyra.[45]

The key differences here centre on a more active role for Teuta, who is absent for the early Polybian narrative of the campaign. Here it was her idea to send Demetrius to the Romans, not his own treachery. This potential peace treaty, which seems to have included the handing over of the murderers of the Roman envoys and the freeing of Corcyra, was then apparently broken by her dispatch of armies to attack other cities (see below), which Zonaras (based on Dio) ascribes to 'yet woman-like, such was her vain and fickle disposition'.[46] It is interesting that Dio and Zonaras chose to focus more on Teuta herself, and her flaws as a female leader, whereas she is wholly absent from Polybius' narrative for this year's campaigning, which is a somewhat glaring omission, given her leadership and role in the instigation of the war. As always, the truth may be somewhere between these two extremes.

With Corcyra secure, Fulvius moved the Roman naval force to rendezvous with his fellow Consul (Postumius) and the Roman Army at Apollonia (see Map 4). Polybius states that Rome had mobilised a force of 20,000 infantry and 2,000 cavalry.[47] Upon the arrival of this combined land and naval force, it seems that Apollonia too threw open its gates, welcomed the Romans and placed themselves under their protection. The role of Apollonia is interesting given its earlier embassy of the 260s BC (as seen above). Having secured a bridgehead, the Romans then moved north towards the coastal city of Epidamnus, apparently still under Ardiaean siege. Once again, battle was avoided when the Ardiaean forces laying siege to the city broke off and withdrew in the face of the Roman advance. Thus the Romans had now taken three major strategic coastal or island cities without a single blow in combat.

This continued submission of the Illyrian cities can be seen to be the culmination of three key factors. Firstly, the Romans had overwhelming military superiority in comparison to the Ardiaeans, who had been taking advantage of the collapse of Epirote power to carve out a new empire. Secondly, the Romans offered a return to peace and stability, which these cities had seen under Epirus, rather than the bloodshed seen under the rise of the Ardiaeans. Thirdly, the Romans seemed to offer a more attractive form of rule. As we have seen, the Ardiaeans ruled via garrisons and governors, whereas the Roman Federation was known for its light touch in terms of overt signs of domination. There would be no garrisons or governors, local elites would be left to rule as before and local laws and customs left alone. Again this was something that they would not find under the Aetolian League. Thus the Romans, through both a combination of overwhelming military force and local pragmatism, were able to portray themselves as the liberators and defenders of these communities on the Adriatic. Again, Zonaras (and Dio) present a slightly different view of these events, centred on the character of Teuta herself:

> When the Consuls had crossed over to the island, she became emboldened again, and sent out an army to Epidamnus and Apollonia.[48]

Thus, for Dio and Zonaras, Teuta dispatched an Ardiaean army to attack Epidamnus and Apollonia, which undermined any prospective peace treaty with Rome. In Polybius' narrative, Epidamnus is already being besieged from the year before, whilst Apollonia seems to be as yet untouched by the Ardiaeans. For these two sources, the failure of this attack on Epidamnus and Apollonia (though we are not told whether this involved an actual military clash) is the last major offensive Teuta launched this year. Whilst we have the greater detail of Polybius, there are no reports of any positive moves being made by Teuta. There is logic to an Ardiaean push towards Epidamnus and Apollonia, however, in terms of denying the Romans a bridgehead in Illyria, yet the execution of these moves in the Dio/Zonaran narrative seems hopelessly disjointed and ill-timed.

Returning to Polybius, it seems that the Ardiaeans did intend to make a stand to defend their newly-won empire and retreated from Epidamnus back into the Illyrian interior. Unfortunately, Polybius chooses to gloss over this conflict with the following statement:

> The Romans, taking Epidamnus also under their protection, advanced into the interior of Illyria, subduing the Ardiaeans on their way.[49]

Given that the Ardiaean homeland lay further north, we are unclear as to exactly who the Romans subdued. The most likely explanation is that it was the Ardiaean army that had been laying siege to Epidamnus, who retreated and then either chose to turn and attack the pursuing Roman forces or were forced into battle. In any event, we have no further details for this first military clash between Rome and the Ardiaeans, merely the inevitable outcome: a Roman victory.

A clear victory over an Ardiaean force seems to have merely emphasised the disparity in power between the two sides of this war and led to a number of local tribes sending embassies to the Consuls and pledging their support for Rome. Polybius names the Parthini and Atintanes (see Map 4), both of whom became allies of Rome.[50] Thus, Rome's sphere of influence now extended beyond the coastal cities and into the Illyrian hinterland, further securing Rome's bridgehead.

With this bridgehead secure, the Consuls continued their policy of relieving the cities that the Ardiaeans had been besieging. Having relieved Corcyra and Apollonia, the next target was the siege of Issa. It is unclear from Polybius' account whether the siege of Issa was relieved by force, or whether the besieging Ardiaean force fled without a fight.[51] Later in his account, however, he does refer to the Ardiaei who had been laying siege to Issa:

> Of the besiegers of Issa those now in Pharos were allowed, through Demetrius' influence, to remain there unhurt, while the others dispersed and took refuge at Arbo. [52]

Given this, it is more likely that the Ardiaei who had been besieging Issa gave up without a fight. Many, it seems, fell under the protection of Demetrius himself, who was coordinating efforts with the Consuls in a liaison capacity.

Others fled to the unknown location of Arbo. Walbank compiled several suggestions for its location, either being the town of Albanopolis (modern Arbunc) or even Narona, on the Adriatic coast opposite Pharos.[53] The latter would fit in with a possible Roman attack on the city later in the campaign (see below).

The relief of Issa seems to have brought a successful conclusion to the first stage of Roman operations, to relieve the cities and islands being besieged by the Ardiaei and thus stop their advance in its tracks. This seems to have been completed with remarkably little bloodshed, with the advancing Ardiaean forces seemingly no match in terms of numbers or quality for the Roman Army. On this occasion it does seem that the Romans were welcomed as genuine liberators by the locals, though many must have been wary whether they were swapping one overlord for another. Certainly, given the overwhelming Roman military superiority, it is hardly a surprise that the local cities and tribes were willing to throw their support behind Rome. For the Romans, this success had the added bonus of stripping away support for the Ardiaean Empire, leaving behind only the core supporters of Teuta. This made the Consuls' campaign far more manageable, as they would be able to more effectively target their resources on key objectives, rather than having to subdue entire regions.

In Polybius' narrative the fall of Issa heralded the next stage of the Roman campaign, namely the reduction of the remaining key Ardiaean Adriatic strongholds. To accomplish this, the Romans would have needed control of the Adriatic, but we hear of no naval engagements with the Ardiaean fleet in our surviving sources. This may be masking the fact that the Ardiaean fleet had no more enthusiasm to engage the Romans than their land forces did, or our surviving narrative may well be missing a number of naval engagements. In either event, the campaign by the Roman navy, commanded by the Consul Fulvius Centumalus, targeted the Ardiaean Adriatic strongholds which possibly still housed the Ardiaean fleet. With these ports under Roman control, the Ardiaean challenge to Roman mastery of the Adriatic would be ended. Unfortunately, Polybius provides us with few details of the Roman assaults, merely covering them with one sentence:

The fleet too took several Illyrian cities by assault as they sailed along the coast.[54]

We can surmise that the Romans moved northwards up the Adriatic coast, further into territory that had been Ardiaean for longer and thus was more loyal to Teuta.[55] We have no way of telling whether the majority of the towns and cities fell without a fight, or how many resisted the Roman advance and were subdued by force.

What we do know is that these Adriatic strongholds put up the stiffest resistance that the Romans had faced to date during the war. One detail Polybius does provide us with is that the Romans were defeated when attacking the city of Nutria in 229 BC. Unfortunately, there is no clear identification of where Nutria was. Bagnall surmised that it may have been the town of Narona, on the Adriatic coast opposite the island of Pharos (see Map 4).[56] Polybius only provides us with a passing reference to the defeat:

…losing, however, at Nutria not only many soldiers, but some of their military tribunes and their quaestor.[57]

That the Romans face stiffer resistance the further north they campaigned, and thus the deeper into Ardiaean territory they pushed, is not surprising. We have no idea of the total numbers lost, but we must speculate that this reversal was a temporary one and that a renewed attack by the Roman forces eventually took the town. However, we hear no more about the incident.

One additional consequence to the Roman control of the Adriatic came with the capture of Teuta's treasure fleet of twenty ships, as reported by a number of sources.[58] There is some difference of opinion where this fleet came from and its destination. Zonaras states that they were travelling from the Peloponnese, whilst Polybius writes that it was fleeing the Adriatic with the plunder from the Ardiaean advance. Whatever the truth, the important aspect for the Romans was that they had seized a considerable part of Teuta's economic resources and thus reduced her ability to continue fighting this war, as well as paid for the Roman campaign itself.

The brief narrative that Polybius provides us with has little in the way of a chronology for the campaign, but it seems that the coastal campaign continued until late into the year. Prior to the end of the campaigning season, Polybius does not provide us with any further details of military action. However, a fragment of Dio, which is difficult to place in a chronological context, does seem to refer to a further battle between the Romans and the Ardiaei, possibly with Teuta herself:

Meanwhile they mounted to a high place above the sea, and were defeated near the Atyrian hill; and she now waited, hoping for their withdrawal, in view of the fact that it was already winter.[59]

This fragment seems to the referring to a battle between Teuta's forces and the Romans towards the end of the campaigning season of 229 BC. We have no other details about this clash, and all we know is that the Ardiaei, under the command of Teuta, took up a position on the high ground near the Atyrian Hill (whose location is unknown) and were defeated. Strangely, we find no reference to the battle in Polybius, nor in the account of Zonaras. This naturally means that we must treat this possible clash with a degree of scepticism. Nevertheless, Polybius does refer to Teuta retreating at the end of the year:

Teuta, with only a few followers, escaped to Rhizon, a place strongly fortified at a distance from the sea and situated on the River Rhizon.[60]

Polybius' account may be referring to the aftermath of the battle we find in the Dio fragment. It seems that the majority of the Ardiaean forces that took part in the battle were destroyed or captured, leaving Teuta with just a small remnant, who retreated with her. The location of her stronghold of Rhizon has been much debated. Evans identified it with the later Roman colony of that name on the Rhizonic Gulf (modern day Risano in Montenegro). [61]

Roman Military and Imperial Evolution 229–228 BC

The Battle of Atyrian Hill seems to have brought a close to the campaign for the year. In just one season Rome had broken all the Ardiaean sieges, secured the loyalty of the Epirote towns and the native tribes of the region, gained mastery of the Adriatic and reduced the Ardiaean coastal strongholds. It also seems likely that they had defeated Teuta herself in battle and driven her into exile in the Illyrian interior.

The two Consuls, who are largely absent from Polybius' narrative, seem to have commanded the campaign well, blunting the Ardiaean advance, liberating the Epirote cities, gaining the allegiance of the local cities and tribes, and defeating and capturing those towns and cities which remained loyal to Teuta. Again, we have few details as to their personal actions during the campaign, but the outcomes speak for themselves. It is also interesting to note the coordination of the naval and land campaigns during this war, with Fulvius in command of the Roman fleet and the naval assaults on the Ardiaean strongholds, whilst Postumius commanded the army and the campaigns to relieve the Epirote cities and subdue the Illyrian interior.

With the onset of winter, the Dio fragment refers to Teuta waiting for the Romans to withdraw back to Italy following the end of the campaigning season, as was their custom, allowing her time to regroup after a disastrous year's campaigning. However, it seems that Teuta was to be gravely disappointed as, in an innovation to usual practice, the Romans kept a strong presence in Illyria over the winter of 229/228 BC:

> After accomplishing so much and placing the greater part of Illyria under the rule of Demetrius, thus making him an important potentate, the Consuls returned to Epidamnus with the fleet and army. Cnaeus Fulvius now sailed for Rome with the greater part of both forces, and Postumius, with whom forty ships were left, enrolled a legion from the cities in the neighbourhood and wintered at Epidamnus to guard the Ardiaeans and the other tribes who had placed themselves under the protection of Rome.[62]

These few sentences from Polybius reveal three innovations to the Roman way of warfare. Firstly, we have the use of Demetrius of Pharos, the first major Ardiaean commander to defect to the Romans. Throughout the war he seems to have occupied a position as official liaison to the Consuls, advising them on local conditions and seemingly negotiating the surrender of a number of Ardiaean forces. Arguments have long raged over just how much influence Demetrius retained over Illyria (see below), but it is clear the Romans were happy to use him as a figurehead, or client ruler, to govern various areas of Illyria in their interests. The use of client rulers was to become a feature of Roman Republican policy for a number of centuries, but it is interesting to see it being used here, in a small way, in Rome's first excursion onto the Greek mainland.

The second notable feature is that whilst the Consul Fulvius Centumalus, who had commanded the naval campaign, returned to Rome at the end of the campaigning season, as was custom, Postumius Albinus remained in the city of Epidamnus to maintain a Roman presence in Illyria and prevent Teuta from exploiting the absence of Roman forces whilst a change of Consuls was underway.[63] Whilst proconsular commands were a standard feature of later Republican warfare, this was not the case at this time. They had certainly been used during the First Punic War, but that revealed more about the prolonged nature of the war. Fulvius' proconsulship is the only one recorded between the First and Second Punic Wars. [64]

It is, therefore, an interesting innovation to find a Consul staying overseas against a foe who had been heavily defeated during the year. Clearly the Romans were thinking ahead and did not want to have their good work undone by creating a power vacuum in Illyria, which Teuta could exploit to rebuild her strength. The fear must have been that their new allies could desert Rome or some other potentate could step into the vacuum (perhaps including Demetrius himself). According to the Dio fragment, Teuta was hoping to exploit such a weakness to rebuild her position.[65] Therefore a permanent Roman presence in Illyria, under the Consul who had commanded the land forces that year, merely emphasised to all the hopelessness of her position. However, on the other hand, emphasising a permanent Roman presence in Illyria would have done little to re-assure the local cities and tribes that this was to be a temporary Roman excursion across the Adriatic.

The third innovation came with the levying of a legion of Illyrian axillary troops to bolster the forces that had remained behind with Postumius. This again is an important step in the evolution of Roman imperial power, the use of non-Italian native forces. The Consuls had arrived in Illyria with a standard army composed of Roman citizens and Italian allies; all of whom would have been expecting to return home after a short victorious campaign. Yet the situation clearly called for a garrison to remain in Illyria for at least the winter months, until a fresh consular army arrived in 228 BC. Native troops were thus levied to make up the shortfall, again pre-empting what was to become a regular feature of Roman imperial military practice. The basis of serving in the Roman Army up to this point was either citizenship or treaty obligation. Neither of these existed in this situation between the Romans and the native Illyrians and Epirotes; it was merely a short-term alliance, driven by expediency. This would also have the bonus of introducing elements of Roman military culture into the region, even if the auxiliary force disbanded shortly thereafter. It is unlikely that this garrison legion was ever meant to be anything other than an immediate solution to see the Romans through the winter. However, it nevertheless shows the evolution of Roman military thinking, whereby practical innovations were being introduced to solve issues thrown up by the ever-changing nature of Roman imperial endeavours.

The End of the War and the Peace Treaty of 228 BC

Back in Rome, the new Consuls for 228 BC were Sp. Carvilius Maximus and Q. Fabius Maximus Verrucosus. Interestingly, both men had been Consuls once before, in 234 and 233 BC respectively. Both had proven military records and had celebrated Triumphs; Carvilius over the Sardinians, and Fabius over the Ligurians (as seen in Chapter Three). Fabius Maximus would go on to find fame during the Second Punic War, and ever since, for his delaying tactics against Hannibal. Carvilius had served his first Consulship with L. Postumius Albinus, the Consul of the previous year, who was still the commander of the Illyrian land forces quartered in Epidamnus.

Unfortunately for the new Consuls, however, the war ended before they could cross over to Illyria. Having suffered heavy defeats during the previous year, bereft of allies and with a permanent Roman presence in Illyria throughout the winter, Teuta sent ambassadors to Rome to offer terms. With the fighting all but concluded, and perhaps with one eye on the situation in Gallic northern Italy (as seen in Chapter Three), the Senate accepted the offer and imposed harsh terms on Teuta and the Ardiaei; details of which are preserved by Polybius and Appian:

> In the early spring Teuta sent an embassy to the Romans and made a treaty, by which she consented to pay any tribute they imposed, to relinquish all Illyria except a few places, and, what mostly concerned the Greeks, undertook not to sail beyond Lissus with more than two unarmed vessels.[66]

> After these events the widow of Agron sent ambassadors to Rome to surrender the prisoners and deserters into their hands. She begged pardon also for what had been done, not by herself, but by Agron. They received for answer that Corcyra, Pharus, Issa, Epidamnus, and the Illyrian Atintani were already Roman subjects, that Pinnes might have the remainder of Agron's kingdom and be a friend of the Roman people

if he would keep hands off the aforesaid territory, and agree not to sail beyond Lissus nor to keep more than two Illyrian pinnaces, both to be unarmed. The woman accepted all these conditions.[67]

There seem to have been four key elements to the terms the Romans demanded; the standard payment of a war indemnity, the return of prisoners and deserters, the future shape of the Ardiaean kingdom and a permanent Roman influence in Illyria, and the wider issue of control of the Adriatic and the shipping lanes. In terms of the Ardiaei, it seems that Teuta was to abdicate the regency, leaving Agron's son (Pinnes) to rule a much-reduced Ardiaean kingdom. Teuta herself seems to have gone into internal exile but it is unclear who exactly took over the regency; whether it was Pinnes' natural mother (Triteuta), or possibly even Demetrius himself.[68] The wider Ardiaean federation was dismantled, with all conquered territories being freed, and practical limits set to its ability to expand southwards, either by land or sea. Thus the Ardiaei were returned to being a small tribal kingdom, as they were before the rise of Agron; being kept in check by a regional superpower, in this case Rome, instead of Epirus.

What form this check took on land has long been a source of much debate. If we are to believe Appian, who was writing at the time of the Roman Empire, Corcyra, Pharus, Issa, Epidamnus and the Atintani all became Roman subjects and thus Rome added the province of Illyria.[69] However, it has long been argued that Appian is being anachronistic here and that Rome did not formally annex any fresh territory. It seems that, in what was the start of a new eastern policy, the Romans declared the freedom of the Illyrian cities that had been dominated or threatened by the Ardiaei, guaranteed by Roman military might. We are unclear if this process was even supported by formal treaties between Rome and the Illyrian cities and tribes.[70]

In truth, the Romans did not need to annex the region and probably had little desire to do so. Annexation meant government, and Rome had enough to deal with in terms of Sicily, Sardinia and Corsica, which had been taken to secure Rome's strategic position *vis a vis* Carthage. In Illyria there was no such imperative; Epirus had collapsed and the Ardiaei had been crushed. Rome had secured control of the Adriatic for both strategic and trade reasons and now had a clearly established zone of influence on its eastern shore, which they took pains to advertise.

It is also clear that Rome did have a clear proxy or client ruler in terms of Demetrius of Pharus, who was the first leader of the region to turn to Rome and who had apparently advised them throughout their campaign. Again, the size of the region he directly ruled is much disputed and frequently inflated. What is clear is that he ruled the strategic island of Pharus and the region around it. Appian says the following:

> To Demetrius they gave certain castles as a reward for his treason to his own people, adding the express condition that they gave them only conditionally, for they suspected the man's bad faith; and before long he began to show it.[71]

It is unclear at this point if Demetrius was given some form of role involving the regency of the underage Ardiaean King Pinnes (see Chapter Eight). What is clear is that Demetrius had the favour of Rome, a position which would enable him to keep a close eye on the cities and tribes of the region and act as Rome's proxy if need be.

The final provision of the peace treaty was a limit to the distance which Ardiaean (pirate) ships could sail; not beyond the point of Lissus (modern Lezhë) with more than two unarmed boats. This served several purposes. Not only did it limit the activities of the Ardiaei, but it would in theory stop the piratical activities of any ships that sailed under their banner. This in turn freed the Adriatic and the trade routes from Italy to Greece from piracy. With Rome as the guarantor, it meant the Adriatic was theirs to police and thus fell under their control. It also meant that the trade of the region fell under nominal Roman control. After just one year's campaign, the Adriatic fell under Roman control and Rome established a strategic and economic prominence in the region and secured a zone of influence on the Greek mainland. Just fifty years after Pyrrhus attempted to incorporate southern Italy into his empire, Rome had effectively done the same to the eastern seaboard of the Adriatic.

Building on the Peace (228 BC)

As well as securing these advantages through the peace the Senate imposed on the Ardiaei, they extended this victory one stage further by sending embassies to the regional powers of Greece to advertise the peace (and victory) and thus cement Rome's newly acquired position. A number of sources record these symbolic embassies:

When this treaty had been concluded Postumius sent legates to the Aetolian and Achaean leagues. On their arrival they first explained the causes of the war and their reason for crossing the Adriatic, and next gave an account of what they had accomplished, reading the treaty they had made with the Illyrians. After meeting with all due courtesy from both the leagues, they returned by sea to Corcyra, having by the communication of this treaty, delivered the Greeks from no inconsiderable dread; for the Illyrians were not then the enemies of this people or that, but the common enemies of all.[72]

...and of their first coming into relations through an embassy with Greece. But having thus begun, the Romans immediately afterwards sent other envoys to Athens and Corinth, on which occasion the Corinthians first admitted them to participation in the Isthmian Games.[73]

The Romans were thanked by the Corinthians for their action, and took part in the Isthmian Games, in which Plautus won the stadium race. Moreover they formed a friendship with the Athenians and were admitted by them to citizenship and to the Mysteries.[74]

These embassies were highly symbolic. The Romans had no need to explain themselves to the regional Greek powers, but they emphasized a clear point; namely that Rome had done what they could not in defeating the Ardiaei and freeing the shipping lanes of pirates. If the Romans promoted the view that the Ardiaei were enemies of all Greece, then by implication, Rome had saved them as well. It is interesting that Polybius gives the initiative for these embassies again to Postumius Albinus. Not only had he stayed in Illyria over the winter and organized native Illyrians into Roman military units, but he seems to have taken a leading role in the peace negotiations with Teuta and then commissioned these embassies to the regional Greek powers to cement Rome's position. Thus, although it was the Consul Fulvius Centumalus who won the Triumph, the greatest credit for the conduct of the whole war and its aftermath seems to belong to Postumius Albinus.

These embassies were also a highly public declaration that Rome had arrived on the Greek (civilized world) stage and was now a force to be reckoned with. This arrival was not just a military one, but a cultural one as well thanks to Rome's admission to the Isthmian Games, which officially brought them within the cultural Greek world, if not as equals then as least not *barbaroi* (barbarian, or non-Greeks).[75]

To fully understand this act, we need to understand the context of the Greek world in this period. For over a century mainland Greece had been dominated by one of the three Hellenistic superpowers: Macedon, whose garrisons controlled a number of key strategic sites on the Greek mainland known as the 'Fetters of Greece' (Acrocorinth, Chalcis and Demetrias). They also had a garrison controlling the Piraeus at Athens. Aside from Macedon the other key regional power blocks were the two alliances of city states known as the Aetolian and Achaean Leagues. The former powers of Athens and Sparta remained separate from these Leagues, but were shadows of their former selves. Ironically, shortly after the Romans had left the region, Sparta, under King Cleomenes III, made their final bid to recover their former status, when war broke out between them and the Achaean League.[76]

Not only had Rome benefited from the collapse of Epirote power, but in 229 BC the Macedonian King Demetrius II, who had himself made use of Agron and the Ardiaei as allies, was killed in battle by an invading force of Dardani (a Thracian tribe). Macedon soon collapsed into chaos, with the established king dead and his successor being his son (Philip V), who was too young to rule in his own right, thus requiring a regency. Thus the one regional superpower that had the most to fear from Roman influence extending across the Adriatic was in no position to do anything about it. Neither of the two Greek city leagues were on a par with Rome and many would have welcomed a fresh power to counter-balance that of Macedon.[77] As it turned out, Rome's influence in the region extended for the next 500 years until the division of the Roman Empire in the fourth century AD.

The First Illyrian War was a turning point in the history of Roman imperial expansion. Taking advantage of the collapse of Epirus and with a clear economic, as well as strategic imperative, Rome fought her first war on the Greek mainland. In reality Rome's opponents, the Ardiaei, were hardly of the calibre of the Gauls or the Carthaginians, but that must have suited the Senate very well. It allowed them to conduct a short, sharp campaign; securing control of the Adriatic and its shipping routes and securing their eastern flank with a zone of influence on the Adriatic seaboard, giving them an opportunity to place itself as a participant on the main stage of the ancient world.

Chapter Five

Carthaginian Expansion in Spain and the Roman Response (237–226 BC)

There is one important aspect which we must not lose sight of, namely that Rome was the not the only power expanding in the western Mediterranean. There was one power which was pursuing a far more ambitious policy of expansion than Rome itself. We are of course referring to Rome's recent foe, Carthage. If victory in the First Punic War acted as spur for Rome to expand both the areas they directly governed and those under their sphere of influence, then in Carthage's case the opposite was true. For them, defeat in the First Punic War and the loss of their Mediterranean empire (Sardinia and Sicily) was swiftly followed by near destruction at the hands of their former mercenary army and their Numidian allies (as seen in Chapter One). Yet their response to both military setbacks was to go on the offensive, in a campaign aimed to replace their Mediterranean losses with a large land empire in the previously untouched European mainland of Spain.

In terms of our surviving sources we must sound a further note of caution as the majority of the reporting comes third-hand, from only Roman era sources. There are no surviving native or even Punic sources for the period, merely Roman or Greco-Roman reports based on their understanding of events taking place at this time or using, or on lost Punic sources (see Appendix One). Nevertheless we must persist, as Spain not only plays an increasing role in the geopolitics of the period, in terms of the rise of a Carthaginian Empire, but perfectly showcases the development of Roman tactical thinking as the period progressed and their strategic horizons expanded.

Spain in 237 BC

Whilst the history of the Iberian Peninsula prior to this period falls outside the remit of this work, a brief sketch of the background is useful in setting the scene. Like much of the western Mediterranean, Spain at this time was a mixture of native tribes in the interior with a collection of Greek and Phoenician trading colonies on the coast. From the eighth century onwards, the Mediterranean coastline saw a number of Phoenicians and Greek colonies established which created an international network of trading ports across the Mediterranean. Carthage was one such foundation, an eastern Mediterranean city planted on the coastline of a tribal interior.

Although on the far side of the so called 'civilized' ancient world, Spain had numerous economic resources which would attract international trade; notably its abundant mineral and natural resources, from silver mines to timber. These coastal colonies acted as conduits funnelling trade from the interior, mostly utilising Spain's river and valley network to the coast and then the Mediterranean trade routes. Spain had one other notable trade, that of mercenaries, who served in a number of Mediterranean theatres of conflict. Justin provides us with an explanation of its economic importance:

> From hence, indeed, comes not only great plenty of corn, but of wine, honey, and oil. Its iron is excellent, and its breed of horses swift. Not only is the produce of the surface to be admired, but the abundant riches of the metals hidden beneath it. There is great plenty, too, of flax and hemp, and certainly no country is more productive of vermilion. The courses of the rivers are not violent and rapid, so as to be hurtful, but gentle, watering the vineyards and the plains; they are also well stocked with fish from the estuaries of the sea, and most of them are rich in gold, which they carry down with their water.[1]

One aspect that is unclear is how great the Carthaginian presence was in Spain, prior to the First Punic War. Certainly Carthage was the nearest major trading power to Spain and would have had a sizeable share of any trade that emanated from the coastal cities. However, what is not known is whether this Carthaginian presence had taken on any more tangible form, in terms of the physical possession of some of these coastal cities, and if so whether this control was lost as a result of the First Punic War.

Unsurprisingly, historical opinion is divided on the subject, ranging from the Carthaginians having destroyed the native Tartessian kingdom and carving out a land empire to the Carthaginians having nothing more than a mercantile relationship with the former Phoenician colonies on the coast. Miles argues against a large land empire, and the archaeological evidence does seem to favour the minimalist approach.[2] On balance the evidence points to the Carthaginians having control of no more than some Phoenician coastal colonies and certainly not having expanded inland into the native Spanish territories.

Hamilcar Barca and the Spanish Proposal

Central to this new wave of post-war Carthaginian expansion in Spain was the figure of Hamilcar Barca. As we have already seen (in Chapter One), Barca was perhaps Carthage's most experienced general, having fought against the Romans in Sicily and the mercenaries and Numidians in Africa. However, it seems that following the conclusion of the Mercenary War, Hamilcar entered, or re-entered, Carthaginian politics at the head of a populist faction and through some unrecorded method got himself appointed for an indefinite command in Spain, with a remit to carve out a new empire.[3]

The obvious question was why, having suffered twenty years of warfare across the Mediterranean, followed by four more gruelling years in Africa, the Carthaginians opted for an attempt to carve out a land empire in a vast European territory? This was not just a case of personal aggrandisement for Hamilcar or a matter of restoring lost martial pride. Both the Punic and Mercenary Wars had not only exacted a heavy military and economic toll on Carthage, but had highlighted a serious flaw in their military system, especially when compared to Rome, in terms of military and economic resources.

Rome had fought the First Punic War based on a foundation of having the resources of Italy to draw upon, both in economic support and manpower. On the other hand, Carthage only had control of the Numidian hinterland around the city itself and the coastal region of North Africa, along with the overseas islands of Sardinia and Sicily. Her economic power was not agricultural but trade, which was easily disrupted by warfare, and whilst Sicily was always considered a breadbasket in the ancient world, it lay as close to Italy as it did to Carthage. Carthaginian military force was based on the use of mercenaries, who were both costly and, as the recent war showed, unreliable.

If Carthage was to recover from the losses of the Punic War, both militarily and economically, they clearly needed to build a fresh powerbase, one which eliminated the flaws of relying on Mediterranean trade and mercenaries. To Carthage's east lay desert and beyond that the Hellenistic superpower of the Ptolemaic Empire, whilst to the north lay the Mediterranean islands which were now part of Rome's sphere of influence. This left two potential directions; to the south and south-west lay the African hinterland and the Numidian tribes, and to the north-west lay Spain and the European tribes. Carthage had already established some measure of dominance over the Numidian tribes, the largest being the Massylii and Masaesyli, which they had recently cemented, having crushed a Numidian rebellion. The Numidian lands were not purely desert and were capable of agriculture, as the strength of the Second Century unified Numidian kingdom attested. Yet the Numidian tribes were fiercely independent and whilst they accepted nominal Carthaginian suzerainty, would not easily be converted into loyal Carthaginian subjects.

An empire in Spain, however, offered a number of advantages, as detailed above. If the native Celt-Iberian tribes could be tamed and made loyal subjects, then Carthage would have access to as big a potential pool of manpower as Rome had. Furthermore, there was significant mineral and material wealth to be gained, most notably in the form of gold and silver mines. With these resources, Carthage could not only rebuild her strength, but eliminate the structural weaknesses that had been highlighted in the recent war with Rome.

However, despite the possibilities such an empire would bring Carthage if successful, it must be acknowledged that such an adventure at this time was highly risky, coming so soon after two decades of warfare and the devastation of the war in Africa. Hamilcar was taking a calculated risk in committing the remnants of the Carthaginian military machine in an effort to subdue a vast region populated by numerous tribes, none of whom would be easily beaten by an overseas power. To his enemies in Carthage, Hamilcar's death overseas would probably have been welcomed, but the defeat of his enterprise would have had serious consequences for Carthage itself.

Carthaginian Expansion under Hamilcar Barca 237–231 BC

Despite the lack of native Punic sources, there are a number of later accounts which preserve some details of Hamilcar's campaigns, notably Polybius and

Diodorus.[4] Unfortunately, the surviving sources that do preserve accounts of the campaign are short of detail and all conflate nine years' worth of campaigning into one section, denying us an accurate chronology of the war. We are not told how large a force Hamilcar took with him to Spain, though Polybius does label it an 'adequate force'.[5] Hoyos estimates it to have been no more than 20,000 strong, 2–3,000 of which would have been cavalry, along with a force of elephants.[6] Diodorus also refers to the use of elephants in Spain by the Carthaginians. Hoyos has the best modern account of the campaigns.[7]

In the history of this period and that of the ancient world, this was an important war, being the first concerted effort to conquer an area of 'barbarian' Western Europe. Diodorus preserves the best description of Hamilcar's campaigns, which provides us with a flavour of the overall progress of the war and an insight into the tactics used and outcomes achieved. Diodorus' narrative is in three parts, of which the below is the first and only indication we have of the timescales involved:

> When Hamilcar was placed in command at Carthage he soon enlarged the empire of his country and ranged by sea as far as the Pillars of Heracles, Gadeira, and the ocean. Now the city of Gadeira is a colony of the Phoenicians, and is situated at the farthest extremity of the inhabited world, on the very ocean, and it possesses a roadstead. Hamilcar made war on the Iberians and Tartessians, together with the Celts, led by Istolatius and his brother, and cut to pieces their whole force, including the two brothers and other outstanding leaders; he took over and enrolled in his own army three thousand survivors. Indortes then raised an army of fifty thousand men, but before the fighting even began he was put to flight and took refuge on a certain hill; there he was besieged by Hamilcar, and although, under cover of night, he again fled, most of his force was cut to pieces and Indortes himself was captured alive. After putting out his eyes and maltreating his person Hamilcar had him crucified; but the rest of the prisoners, numbering more than ten thousand, he released. He won over many cities by diplomacy and many others by force of arms.[8]

Crucially, Diodorus, supported by Appian, provides us with a description of how Hamilcar opened his campaign.[9] His starting point was the city of

Gadir (modern Cadiz) on the south-western cost of Spain, beyond what is now the Straits of Gibraltar. Gadir was a long-established trading city of Phoenician origin, sharing a common background with Carthage in that respect. What is not clear from Diodorus' account is whether Gadir was already in Carthaginian hands or was the initial point of attack. However, the account of Appian has Hamilcar launching an expedition against Gadir, which would support the notion that his Spanish campaign began with an attack on and the capture of Gadir. No details have been preserved as to how difficult Hamilcar found it to take the city or if a siege was involved.

The city would have been part of a trading network which Carthage was part of, but it is unknown whether this attack was the first attempt by Carthage at controlling the city or merely a re-assertion of a position lost in the aftermath of the First Punic War. In any event, the capture of Gadir provided Hamilcar with a base of operations on the Spanish coast, to act as a bridgehead for a conquest of the interior. The Diodorus excerpt implies that the first major campaign was against an alliance of three major ethnic groupings, Iberians, Celts and Tartessians, the latter of which are an identifiable group who lived in the vicinity of Gadir by the Guadalquivir River. Despite this alliance, Hamilcar was able to emerge victorious and thus secure a portion of the interior of Spain around Gadir.

A subsequent campaign was fought against a Spanish leader named Indortes, though it is unclear whether he hailed from one of the three ethnic groupings that formed the previous triple alliance or the leader of a different native people. Despite apparently raising an army of 50,000, which must have dwarfed the Carthaginian army, Hamilcar was seemingly able to ambush and rout the force before battle commenced. He then trapped them on top of a hill and destroyed them when they tried to flee, apparently killing more than 40,000 of them.

As well as campaign details, Diodorus' account also purports to provide an insight into Hamilcar's thinking about winning the peace. After his first campaign, he integrated the surviving tribesmen into his own army, and on the second occasion freed the prisoners, possibly again recruiting them to the Carthaginian cause. Not only would this solve his immediate need for manpower, given the limited nature of Carthaginian resources (especially so far from home), but this provides us with an insight into the longer term solution to Carthage's manpower deficiently: the enrolment of native levies.

Thus Spain could become for Carthage what Italy was for Rome, a source of potentially limitless manpower.

As well as providing details of the fighting, both Diodorus and Polybius make reference to Hamilcar's twin strategies of subduing the native tribes by a mixture of force and diplomacy. Given the overwhelming victories on the battlefield and the mixture of clemency for the soldiers and brutality towards their commanders, it is not surprising that many tribes and towns chose to voluntarily submit to Carthaginian overlordship rather than fight. Pursuing these twin policies of conquest and diplomacy, it is clear that Hamilcar carved out an embryonic Carthaginian Empire in southern Spain.

Diodorus' account goes on to show that Hamilcar was laying the foundations for a permanent Carthaginian presence in Spain, with the foundation of a new Carthaginian city: Acra Leuce, on the eastern coast, which is described as a large city.[10] Diodorus refers to it as being the winter quarters for the Carthaginian Army, so it was clearly a military foundation, acting as a base for his expanding campaigns. We have no date for its foundation, but its location in Diodorus' narrative, after the Numidian War (see below), would seem to place it later in the period, c.230 BC[11] Thus Hamilcar was laying the foundations for a permanent European empire for Carthage.

The Numidian War of the late 230s BC

Diodorus preserves a passage which details an important interruption in Hamilcar's campaign; namely the outbreak of another war with the Numidian tribes:

> Hasdrubal, the son-in-law of Hamilcar, having been sent by his father-in-law to Carthage to take part in the war with the Numidians who had revolted against the Carthaginians, cut down eight thousand men and captured two thousand alive; the rest of the Numidians were reduced to slavery, having formerly paid tribute.[12]

Again, we have no other details, and do not know what led to the war, nor are we aware of any other campaigns. We do not even have a secure chronology for the campaign, but logically it must be placed c.235–230 BC It is interesting to note that a portion of the Numidians rebelled against Carthage within a decade of the previous one, and demonstrates how precarious a grip on North Africa Carthage had at this time.

Hamilcar sent back a portion of his Spanish forces to fight against the Numidians. However, we do not know whether this was the only fighting or whether Hasdrubal was reinforcing Carthaginian forces already in Africa. What it does show is the key role that Hamilcar was playing in the Carthaginian military machine, as well as the fact that Carthage now possessed a permanent and battle-hardened army, ready to be deployed across the Mediterranean if necessary.

The Benefits of Empire

Though his accounts are short of campaign detail, it is Appian who on more than one occasion makes reference to the benefits that Hamilcar's conquests brought to both Carthage and himself:

> For whatever property he took he divided, giving one part to the soldiers, to stimulate their zeal for future plundering with him. Another part he sent to the treasury of Carthage, and a third he distributed to the chiefs of his own faction there.[13]

Nepos also makes reference to the goods shipped back to Africa:

> He (Hamilcar) subdued some very powerful and warlike nations, and supplied all Africa with horses, arms, men, and money.[14]

Thus we can see the benefits that Carthage's fledgling European empire was bringing. Hamilcar's soldiers were motivated to fight for their commander in the ongoing wars of conquest, giving them a stake in what they were fighting for; mirroring the Roman military system, rather than relying on mercenaries to fight for them. The Senate and people of Carthage could see the tangible benefits that this empire brought, which would have entrenched support for Hamilcar's campaigns and his position as commander. This was aided by his policy of ensuring that his own domestic supporters benefited directly. Finally, the Carthaginian state as whole can be seen to be have benefited, both economically and militarily.

The economic benefits came in the form of the flow of monies from Spain into the state coffers, helping them to recover from the effects of the First Punic War and the loss of their island possessions. The military benefits included not only the possession of a permanent battle-hardened army fighting on the European mainland, with an ability to be redeployed across the Mediterranean if necessary (see above), but also the ability to recruit soldiers from the subdued Spanish tribes and thus reduce their reliance on mercenary forces. This manpower reserve would go a long way to making up for the military imbalance Carthage suffered *vis a vis* Rome. Thus, after its first few years, Hamilcar's expedition was seemingly paying handsome dividends for Carthage, and helping them to recover from the damage inflicted by the First Punic War far more quickly than they would have been able to under normal circumstances.

The Roman Intervention of 231 BC

Given this expansion of the Carthaginian Empire and its associated benefits to Carthage as a whole, it is not surprising that the Roman Senate began to take an interest in Spanish matters. It is more surprising that they took so long to do so. As detailed earlier, Rome's focus throughout the 230s had been on securing Sardinia and Corsica and fighting a Gallic War in Italy, yet by 231 BC the Senate's attention turned to Carthaginian activities in Spain. Here we must exercise caution, however, as we only have the one reference to this Roman involvement in Spain, coming from a fragment of Dio Cassius:

> On one occasion they sent envoys to investigate the movements of Hamilcar, in the consulship of Marcus Pomponius and Caius Papirius [231 BC], in spite of the fact that they had no interests in Spain as yet. Hamilcar showed them all due honour and offered them plausible explanations, declaring, among other things, that he was obliged to fight against the Spaniards in order that the money which was still owing to the Romans might be paid; for it was impossible to obtain it from any other source. The envoys were consequently embarrassed to know how to censure him.[15]

Dio, presumably based on an earlier source, certainly has the correct consular pairing, adding validity to this being an accurate record of events. If this is the case then it is clear that the Senate had become aware of Hamilcar's activities in Spain and was sufficiently concerned to send a Senatorial enquiry. Again, this highlights a wider tactical thinking developing in the Senate. It is of course tempting to link this visit to the aforementioned Numidian revolt, which roughly dates to this period, and the dispatch of military forces from Spain to crush the Numidian tribes, perhaps highlighting the growing Carthaginian military strength. We do not know the size or scale of the Numidian rebellion, but it does seem that Carthage defeated it with far more ease than the one which immediately followed the First Punic War.

In any event, whilst Dio is correct in saying that Rome had no formal interest in Spain, in terms of either territory or allies, something sparked off a concern in the Senate that Hamilcar's activities in Spain may have construed as a threat to Roman power. The sentiment behind Dio's words imply that the Senatorial delegation was sent there specifically to censure Hamilcar, with the Romans having already made up their minds that these activities constituted a danger to them which needed to be curtailed.

It seems, however, that Hamilcar showed off his diplomatic skills and was able to allay Roman concerns about his campaigning in Spain, and that no further action was undertaken at this time. However, it is clear that this commission was a turning point in both Carthage's campaigning in Spain and Rome's relationship with that region; the Senate of Rome was now keeping the Carthaginian expansion in Spain in their sights. This commission would have been the first time that Romans officials had visited Spain; although merchants may well have travelled to the west before. It is also interesting that this expansion of Rome's sphere of interest to the west occurred just the year before such an expansion occurred in the east with the First Illyrian War (as seen in Chapter Four). Apparently the Roman Senate, or factions within it, were expanding their tactical horizons further than Italy and the Mediterranean islands that they directly controlled.

Carthaginian Expansion in the Shadow of Rome 231–226 BC

The effects of the Roman commission of 231 BC seem to have been far more symbolic than practical, and Hamilcar was left free to pursue his policy of expansion and carving out an empire in Spain. Nevertheless, it must have been at the back of his mind that the Romans were now paying more attention to his activities and that a further Roman commission may well reach a different conclusion.

As before, we have no detailed chronology for events in Spain following 231 BC, so we must assume that Hamilcar continued his polices of expansion by both diplomacy and force. It is not until the winter of 229 BC that we have a securely datable campaign of Hamilcar's, this time against the city of Helice.[16] Diodorus preserves the fullest account, but Zonaras also preserves some additional details:

> While Hamilcar was encamped before the city of Helice and had it under siege, he sent off the greater part of his army and the elephants into winter quarters at Acra Leuce, a city of his own foundation, and remained behind with the rest. The king of the Orissi, however, came to the aid of the beleaguered city, and by a feigned offer of friendship and alliance succeeded in routing Hamilcar. In the course of his flight Hamilcar contrived to save the lives of his sons and his friends by turning aside on another road; overtaken by the king, he plunged on horseback into a large river and perished in the flood under his steed, but his sons Hannibal and Hasdrubal made their way safely to Acra Leuce.[17]
>
> About this time also Hamilcar, the Carthaginian general, was defeated by the Spaniards and lost his life. For, as he was arrayed in battle against them, they led out in front of the Carthaginian army waggons full of pine wood and pitch and when they drew near they set fire to these vehicles, then hurried on the animals drawing them by goading them to madness. Forthwith their opponents were thrown into confusion, became disorganized, and turned to flight, and the Spaniards, pursuing, killed Hamilcar and a great many besides.[18]
>
> The Spaniards, when fighting against Hamilcar, hitched steers to carts and placed them in the front line. These carts they filled with pitch, tallow, and sulphur, and when the signal for battle was given, set them afire. Then, driving the steers against the enemy, they threw the line into panic and broke through.[19]

Thus Hamilcar was defeated and killed in an ambush by the tribe of the Orissi. Aside from the death of Hamilcar himself, we are not given any other casualty figures. However, Diodorus does state that the greater part of the army had been sent to winter quarters whilst he maintained the siege of Helice, so they cannot have been that substantial. Nevertheless, the figurehead and driving force behind the Carthaginian expansion into Spain had been killed.

Fortunately for the Carthaginians, it seems that Hamilcar had already, if not formally nominated a successor, had at least made his preferred candidate clear, and thus his son-in-law, Hasdrubal, commander of the Carthaginian navy in Spain and victor in the recent Numidian War, was confirmed as the new commander in Spain. Hasdrubal was clearly Hamilcar's second in command and seems to have no issue with securing the army's support in Spain and having this appointment confirmed by the Senate and people of Carthage. Thus we can see that command remained within the wider Barcid family, ensuring a continuity of purpose, vision and authority.

In terms of wider issues, the ambush at Helice shows that at least one of the tribes that remained outside of Carthaginian control, the Orissi, had decided to take a proactive stance to meeting the Carthaginian challenge and target the figure of Hamilcar himself, obviously hoping that doing so would cause the Carthaginian campaign to collapse. In this respect the killing of Hamilcar not only failed to achieve its objective, but backfired spectacularly as it brought down the immediate wrath of the Carthaginian forces upon the Orissi themselves. Diodorus preserves details of Hasdrubal's campaigns:

Hasdrubal, the son in law of Hamilcar, immediately upon learning of the disaster to his kinsman broke camp and made for Acra Leuce; he had with him more than a hundred elephants. Acclaimed as general by the army and by the Carthaginians alike, he collected an army of fifty thousand seasoned infantry and six thousand cavalry, together with two hundred elephants. He made war first on the king of the Orissi and killed all who had been responsible for Hamilcar's rout. Their twelve cities, and all the cities of Iberia, fell into his hands. After his marriage to the daughter of an Iberian prince he was proclaimed general with unlimited power by the whole Iberian people. He thereupon founded a city on the sea coast, and called it New Carthage; later, desiring to outdo Hamilcar, he founded yet another city. He put into the field an army of sixty thousand infantry, eight thousand cavalry, and two hundred elephants.[20]

For the first time, we have details of the numbers that the Carthaginians were able to put into the field. Hasdrubal was apparently able to field 50,000 infantry, (which must have contained a sizeable Spanish contingent), 6,000 cavalry and 200 elephants. Armed with such a force Hasdrubal attacked and overran the Orissi, and then continued with Hamilcar's policy of expansion, overrunning all of the Iberian territories (see Map 3). We have no timescale for this expansion, but Diodorus' account implies that it was a fairly swift conquest, taking place in 228 BC and perhaps the following year.

As well as military victories, Hasdrubal continued his father-in-law's policy of securing diplomatic ties though his own marriage to a ruling Iberian family (though we are not told whether this was a polygamous union or not). He also continued the policy of building up the infrastructure of the new Spanish province with the founding of cities, and even provided a new capital for the Carthaginian Empire in Spain; New Carthage (modern Cartagena).

Strabo maintains a passage on New Carthage, showing not only its strategic importance but its economic role as a conduit for trade between the interior of Spain and overseas markets:

> New Carthage is by far the most powerful of all the cities in this country, for it is adorned by secure fortifications, by walls handsomely built, by harbours, by a lake, and by the silver mines of which I have spoken. And here, as well as at the places nearby, the fish–salting industry is large. Furthermore, New Carthage is a rather important emporium, not only of the imports from the sea for the inhabitants of the interior, but also of the exports from the interior for all the outside world.[21]

Diodorus' excerpt also provides us with a figure for the total strength of the Carthaginian Army in Spain at this time; some 60,000 soldiers (though we are not told the balance between Carthaginian and native Spanish), 8,000 cavalry and 200 elephants. Thus the Carthaginians were able to field a significant sized army including battle elephants, a first for European warfare. Aside from military strength, the death of Hamilcar showed the strength and continuity of the Carthaginian presence in Spain. The whole concept of the Spanish campaign seems to have been a highly personal one, centred on the figure of Hamilcar himself. Yet upon his death his son-in-law and number two was able to effortlessly step into his place and continue his policies, representing a strength of continuity.

Hasdrubal was able to build upon the achievements of Hamilcar and even utilise the anger surrounding his death to inject a fresh impetus to Carthaginian expansion in Spain, adding a number of new territories. The permanence of the Carthaginian presence was confirmed with the building, and even naming, of a new capital city for the province, New Carthage.

Roman Expansion in Spain – the Ebro Treaty and Saguntum (227–226 BC)

None of this can have been lost on the Senate of Rome and it must have been clear now that this was no mere series of temporary campaigns to secure booty, but the creation of an empire to rival their own. This process had a clear momentum that could not be stopped by the death of its originator and had seen a second Carthage being founded on the European mainland. Furthermore, it has been argued that Rome's old ally of Massilia (Marseilles) had become alarmed by the growth of the Carthaginian Empire in western Europe and had been briefing against Carthage in the Senate. [22] However, Roman intervention, when it came, did not take the form of a military commitment but a diplomatic one, complicated by the involvement of at least one third party.

It is interesting to note the evolution in the power dynamic between Rome and Carthage which becomes evident in Spain at this time. Whereas, just a decade before, Rome had acted unilaterally against a weakened Carthage, now Rome chose to negotiate, showing a more equal relationship. There are two clear factors at play here. Firstly, Carthage was now no longer in a weakened state, but had carved out a substantial land empire in Spain, backed by significant military resources, including a battle-hardened army of 60,000 men.

Secondly, for Rome at this time, Carthage was not the main foreign policy issue or the primary threat.[23] Here we must move away from the mind-set of the two Punic Wars and the whole narrative that has built up surrounding the period in-between being nothing more than a lull between wars. In 226 BC, Rome did face a clear and impending threat to their empire and very existence, but it came from north Italy and the Gallic tribes, rather than

Spain or North Africa. As is detailed elsewhere (see Chapters Three, Six and Seven), the Gallic tribes both sides of the Alps posed a far greater threat to Rome, and although the Romans had emerged victorious from the previous Gallic Wars of the 230s, this was more a matter of Gallic weaknesses than Roman strength. As previously detailed (in Chapter Three), the Romans had been able to merely set back the Gallic tribes without establishing a permanent dominance over them, and seem to have been expecting a fresh outbreak of warfare.

Thus Rome was not in a position to throw their weight around against Carthage over the matter of Spain and their main imperative must have been to secure their western (and southern) flanks to enable them to focus on the threat from the north. The Senate, despite any concerns they may have had about the growth of Carthaginian power, had to negotiate and avoid any military entanglement, at least in the short-term. To that end, envoys were sent to Hasdrubal in Spain to negotiate a treaty between the two powers.[24]

As is common, it is Polybius who provides the best surviving summary of the Roman position:

> The Romans, seeing that Hasdrubal was in a fair way to create a larger and more formidable empire than Carthage formerly possessed, resolved to begin to occupy themselves with Spanish affairs. Finding that they had hitherto been asleep and had allowed Carthage to build up a powerful dominion, they tried, as far as possible, to make up for lost time. For the present they did not venture to impose orders on Carthage, or to go to war with her, because the threat of a Celtic invasion was hanging over them, the attack being indeed expected from day to day. They decided, then, to smooth down and conciliate Hasdrubal in the first place, and then to attack the Celts and decide the issue by arms, for they thought that as long as they had these Celts threatening their frontier, not only would they never be masters of Italy, but they would not even be safe in Rome itself. Accordingly, after having sent envoys to Hasdrubal and made a treaty, in which no mention was made of the rest of Spain, but the Carthaginians engaged not to cross the Ebro in arms, they at once entered on the struggle against the Italian Celts.[25]

It is interesting to note that the changing balance of power between the two states is seemingly reflected in the treaty that came out of these negotiations, which is commonly described as the Ebro Treaty. Once again the Senate sent a delegation to Spain, but unlike the one of just five years earlier, this delegation was not there to inspect Carthaginian actions but to seek a treaty between the two powers. It is clear that Hasdrubal took it upon himself to negotiate the Carthaginian terms, presumably sending them to the Carthaginian Senate for rubber stamp approval afterwards.

Despite the fact that a number of our surviving sources refer to the so-called Ebro Treaty, frustratingly there is little detail as to its terms and actually no firm chronology for its negotiation or enactment. [26]

For had it been a matter for argument, what ground was there for comparing Hasdrubal's treaty with the earlier one of Lutatius.[27] In the latter it was expressly stated that it would only be of force if the people approved it, whereas in Hasdrubal's treaty there was no such saving clause. Besides, his treaty had been silently observed for many years during his lifetime, and was so generally approved that, even after its author's death, none of its articles were altered. But even if they took their stand upon the earlier treaty – that of Lutatius – the Saguntines were sufficiently safeguarded by the allies of both parties being exempted from hostile treatment, for nothing was said about "the allies for the time being" or anything to exclude "any who should be hereafter taken into alliance."[28]

Under its terms, the River Ebro was to form the boundary between the two empires, and Saguntum, occupying an intermediate position between them, was to be a free city.[29]

It was agreed between them that the limit of the Carthaginian power in Spain should be the River Iberus (Ebro); that beyond that river the Romans should not carry war against the subjects of Carthage, nor should the Carthaginians cross it for a similar purpose; and that the Saguntines and the other Greeks in Spain should remain free and autonomous.[30]

The details we do have are all filtered through a pro-Roman prism, reflecting on the obligations placed upon the Carthaginians and not any on the Romans. As noted by Polybius the clearest detail that emerges from the treaty is that Hasdrubal apparently agreed not to cross the River Ebro under arms. How this clause is interpreted depends entirely upon the reader's point of view. At first glance this could seem to be a Roman-imposed restriction on Carthaginian expansion. Yet the Ebro lay far north of current Carthaginian possessions and the great unanswered question has always been whether this meant that everything south of the Ebro had been agreed by the Roman Senate to be in the Carthaginian sphere of influence (with the exception of Saguntum – see below). Polybius states that the rest of Spain was not mentioned, but then it was hardly in the later Roman interest to admit that they acquiesced to the Carthaginian annexation of the majority of Spain. In Appian's account, however, which was written some 300 years after the event, the Ebro clause is taken to its logical conclusion and the Romans too would not cross it in arms either, thus placing a formal limit on where Roman armies could operate. Naturally, modern opinion on the treaty varies widely as well.[31]

Even if the rest of Spain was not explicitly mentioned, the underlying theme of choosing the Ebro is that it marked the demarcation between the Romans and Carthaginian spheres of influence, as noted by Livy, who labels it, somewhat anachronistically, the 'boundary between the two empires'.[32] As noted above, it must be remembered that this treaty was negotiated by the Romans from a position of relative weakness; the Carthaginian Empire in Spain was now a reality and Rome feared, correctly as it turned out, that a fresh Gallic War was imminent in Italy.

It is interesting that this treaty represented something of a victory for both sides, emphasizing their equal nature, but one that was only ever likely to be temporary. On the Carthaginian side, this was a massive turnaround from the position of 231 BC, when Rome sent a delegation of 'inspectors' to judge Carthaginian actions. Now, just five years later, there was an acknowledgement not only of the Carthaginian Empire in Spain, but that everything south of the Ebro fell into their sphere of influence. For the Romans, although they now had to acknowledge the growth and permanence of a Carthaginian Empire in Spain, they had negotiated a northern limit to their expansion and had secured a pro-Roman outpost in Spain itself, which could monitor Carthaginian growth and represent their interests.

Aside from the details of the so-called Ebro Treaty not being clear, there is a further major complication in the form of Rome's relationship with the Spanish city of Saguntum. Whilst Rome certainly must have harboured concerns about the growth of the Carthaginian Empire in Spain itself, the danger the Carthaginians posed was much more immediate. In those parts of Spain which had not yet fallen under Carthaginian sway, the fall of the Orissi had provided a clear foretaste of things to come. Hamilcar may have been killed and the Carthaginians defeated in one battle, but the war of conquest continued, and with added impetus. When facing the difficult question of what to do to preserve their independence, the city state of Saguntum (see Map 3) took an alternate strategy to the stark choice of fight or capitulate; they looked for the protection of another power; in this case Rome. This is a clear example of the old adage that the 'enemy of my enemy is my friend' and thus Saguntum sent ambassadors to Rome to seek an alliance with the one power strong enough to challenge the Carthaginians. Furthermore, given the physical distance between Saguntum and Rome, they were unlikely to be swapping one potential superpower domination or another.

For the Roman Senate, this offer from Saguntum must have represented an opportunity and a major expansion of their sphere of influence; an alliance with a city in Spain, which could act as Rome's eyes and ears monitoring Carthaginian expansion in Spain. Once again this was a logical expansion of Rome's influence. Rome had recently allied with a number of cities in Illyria, although they had no direct territorial possessions in the region. This fitted into a wider policy of developing a series of buffer zones to the east, west and south (Illyria, Sardinia and Corsica, and Sicily and Syracuse respectively), which protected Roman interests. Further afield, Rome also had a long-standing alliance with the Greek city of Massilia (Marseilles).[33] This ally was useful as an early warning post against tribal migration in the region and to keep an eye on Carthaginian expansion in Spain.

Saguntum seems to have fallen into the same category as Massilia, a Roman ally in the region. However, there are two fundamental problems with the relationship between Rome and Saguntum which cloud all events that were to follow. Firstly, when was this alliance agreed; prior or post the Ebro Treaty? Secondly, what type of agreement was it and more importantly was Rome pledged to defend Saguntum from Carthage? Both have a critical impact on our understanding of the nature of the Ebro Treaty itself.[34]

Critically, our surviving sources do not provide us with a firm date for Rome's agreement with Saguntum, nor even an indication of whether this predated the Ebro Treaty. Either way we are left with a problem; given that Saguntum lay 100 miles south of the Ebro, despite what some of the ancient sources believe.[35] Thus, if the agreement predated the Ebro Treaty, did the treaty make provision for the continued relationship between Rome and Saguntum and thus not prevent Rome from having allies south of the Ebro, even if they perhaps were not able to cross the Ebro in arms? If so, then was the Ebro the defining boundary between the two empires, which we are led to believe? Furthermore, if the alliance dated to after the signing of the Ebro Treaty, then this too leads us to the conclusion that the treaty did not prohibit the Romans from making alliances south of the Ebro. If this did not break the letter of the agreement, it most likely broke the spirit of it.

Commentators have argued for centuries over whether the alliance predated or post-dated the Ebro Treaty and still have not come to a firm conclusion either way, given the lack of evidence, and will probably never do so.[36] Nevertheless, given the critical impact this alliance between Rome and Saguntum was to have (see Chapter Eleven), it is worth stating a position on this matter. An important consideration is whether the Senate had the desire to form such an alliance pre-226 BC, given that their attention was primarily focused on matters in Italy (see Chapters Six to Nine). The Ebro Treaty itself seems to have been all Rome had the desire for; to secure their western flank. There is also the issue that there was a clear Roman intervention in Saguntum's internal politics (see Chapter Eleven), which is most commonly placed in the late 220s, and that this may well have been the catalyst of Saguntum, or a portion of its elites, to contact Rome. Furthermore, Heichelheim argued that due to the coinage Saguntum issued, the alliance must have been towards the end of the 220s.[37] For these reasons this author believes that the Saguntum alliance came after the Ebro Treaty and that it confirms that the treaty provided a far less rigid boundary than is commonly assumed.

Even if we argue that this alliance dated from after the Ebro Treaty, there is nothing to provide us with a firmer date for the alliance itself. However, given that Rome was occupied with the north of Italy from 225 BC, a later date seems the more reasonable, perhaps even caused by Hannibal's succession to the leadership of Carthaginian forces in Spain. It is possible to argue that whilst the Ebro Treaty represented a defensive measure for Rome, agreed at a time their attention needed to be elsewhere, the Saguntum alliance indicated a fresh confidence in Roman foreign affairs, with the Gallic threat dealt with (see Chapters Six to Nine). Thus the Senate agreed to the Saguntine request despite the Ebro Treaty being in place, perhaps to test Carthaginian resolve and in an effort to subvert the spirit if not the letter of the agreement.

The next issue is perhaps even more contentious; namely, what type of alliance Rome and Saguntum agreed? Once again, the surviving ancient sources are frustratingly vague about this and most commentators are split. Opinion ranges from it being a formal alliance which bound Rome to defend Saguntum in the face of third party attack, to a far looser expression of friendship. Again, whilst there will never be a definitive answer, a statement of which version this work most identifies with is necessary. Given the restrictions of the Ebro Treaty, a looser form of friendship seems the more likely, on a par with the Massilian model, especially given that when Saguntum was attacked Rome did nothing for nine months (see Chapter Eleven) and seemingly was not expected to rush to their defence.

Thus the Ebro Treaty does not seems to have barred Rome from making alliances with non-aligned states south of the Ebro, especially if this alliance was nothing stronger than an expression of friendship between the two states. Nevertheless, it must be acknowledged that whilst both sides emerged from the Ebro Treaty with some short-terms gains, neither was likely to hold to it in the longer-term. For the Carthaginians, Spain was now securely in their orbit and the continuing growth of the empire would soon chafe at any restrictions placed on it and at the presence of a Roman outpost in the region. For the Romans, the treaty brought them time to deal with the threat from the north. If that threat could be resolved on a more permanent basis, then the Senate could turn its attention back to the resurrection of Carthaginian power in the west as the factions in the Senate would never be comfortable with a Carthaginian Empire which stretched from the Ebro to North Africa (see Map 8).

Overall, it is clear that this period represented a triumph for Carthage and a setback for Rome. The gamble Hamilcar took in 237 BC had paid off handsomely. Carthage had carved out a substantial land empire on mainland Europe, giving it access to a range of natural resources and manpower, with which it could not only recover from the losses of the First Punic War but grow stronger. Thus it is clear that this period not only saw an expansion of the Roman state, but also the Carthaginian one, sparking off a 'cold war' between the two greatest powers in the western Mediterranean.

Part III

Roman Expansion in Italy and the Gallic War
(228–218 BC)

Chapter Six

The Gallic War I – The Road to Telamon

I n the years that followed the defeat of the Boii and their allies in the
230s BC (as seen in Chapter Three), Rome's northern frontier (where the
Apennines met the Po Valley) had seemingly remained quiet for a five-
year period between 230 and 225 BC, and our few surviving sources have no
mention of any direct activities in this region. However, this does not mean
that the region did not pose a threat and it seems that it underwent a 'cold
war', with both Rome and the Gallic tribes consolidating their positions for
a renewal of the conflict.

The Cold War in Northern Italy 230–225 BC

Naturally our view of this period is severely affected by the limited
number of ancient sources which survive for this period (see Appendix
One). Nevertheless, both Polybius and Zonaras do shed some light on
the manoeuvring which both Rome and the Gallic tribes seem to have
undertaken in this period.

The Alliance of Gallic Tribes

Despite their previous alliance having collapsed into disarray and inter-
tribal warfare, it is clear from Polybius that the largest tribes of Cisalpine
Gaul, the Boii and Insubres, once again reached out to their cousins from
across the Alps to create a grand alliance of Gallic tribes with which to face
the Romans. Reconstructing an accurate chronology in regard to the length
of time these negotiations would have taken between the tribes is impossible
given the paucity of evidence, especially when it involved overcoming the
mistrust caused by the collapse of the previous alliance. Nevertheless, there

is perhaps some indication as to timescale in the actions of the Romans. In 229 BC, the Romans felt secure enough to launch their first war across the Adriatic on the Greek mainland, in Illyria (as seen in Chapter Four). Yet by 226 BC two key events in Rome indicate that they believed that a Gallic attack was imminent. Thus we could hypothesise that it was between these years (228–226 BC) that the Gallic tribes created a fresh 'grand alliance', and that news of this filtered to Rome.

As before, the leading tribes in this anti-Roman alliance in Cisalpine Gaul were the Boii and Insubres. According to Polybius, their chief allies from north of the Alps were a group known as the Gaesatae, which literally means spear carriers, a name given to a group who hired themselves out as mercenaries: [1]

> The two largest tribes, therefore, the Insubres and Boii, made a league and sent messengers to the Gauls dwelling among the Alps and near the Rhone, who are called Gaesatae because they serve for hire, this being the proper meaning of the word. They urged and incited their kings Concolitanus and Aneroëstus to make war on Rome, offering them at present a large sum in gold, and as to the future, pointing out to them the great prosperity of the Romans, and the vast wealth that would be theirs if they were victorious. They had no difficulty in persuading them, as, in addition to all this, they pledged themselves to be loyal allies and reminded them of the achievement of their own ancestors, who had not only overcome the Romans in combat, but, after the battle, had assaulted and taken Rome itself, possessing themselves of all it contained, and, after remaining masters of the city for seven months, had finally given it up of their own free will and as an act of grace, and had returned home with their spoil, unbroken and unscathed.[2]

Interestingly, both Zonaras and Plutarch, later authors, mention only the Insubres as the driving force behind the Gallic War, with no mention of the Boii.[3] Polybius, however, introduces a fourth major tribal grouping; the Taurisci. His accounts of the Battle of Telamon describe the Gallic army as having four distinct components; the Boii, Insubres, Gaesatae and Taurisci, though we are not given any numbers for each tribal element. However, we can speculate that the Boii committed more forces to this venture than the

Insubres, based on the fact that the Insubres had to leave forces behind to defend their territory from the Cenomani and from the relative strengths of both tribes, post Telamon (see Chapters Seven and Eight).

The Taurisci are an interesting addition to this alliance, as the other of the tribes had fought the Romans as part of the previous Gallic alliance in the 230s BC (as described in Chapter Three). Polybius is the only source for their involvement and even then they appear suddenly in his account of Telamon, without any explanation of how they became involved. Early in his work, Polybius does mention the Taurisci as dwelling 'on the slopes of the Alps'.[4] As they had no direct contact with Rome before, we must assume that they were recruited as mercenaries alongside the Gaesatae.

Thus we have an alliance of four distinct tribal groups invading Roman Italy. We are given no details as to how this alliance worked in practice or what made this alliance stronger than the one a decade earlier. Polybius names two kings or chieftains of the Gaesatae, but does not state who had overall command of the alliance.

The Roman Federation

From Polybius' statements it is clear that the Romans were monitoring the situation in Cisalpine Gaul, which given the close nature of the conflict a few years previously is not a surprise. What is unclear is the mechanism the Romans used to monitor the Gallic tribes; whether they employed spies, used allies amongst the other tribes of Gaul or a combination of the two. As noted above, the Romans certainly felt confident enough to launch their first expedition on mainland Greece in 229 BC, so they cannot have been that concerned about Cisalpine Gaul in this year.

Nevertheless, from 228 BC Rome undertook a number of preparations for a further Gallic War; some were diplomatic, some military and others religious. This process seems to have begun in 228 BC when we have reports of an extraordinary human sacrifice made in Rome, with the live burial of two Gauls and two Greeks, a man and a woman of each race, in the Forum Boarium. Both Zonaras and Plutarch provide us with details behind this unusual practice, though there is no mention in Polybius:[5]

Inasmuch as an oracle had once come to the Romans that Greeks and Gauls should occupy the city, two Gauls and likewise two Greeks, male and female, were buried alive in the Forum, in order that in this way destiny might seem to have fulfilled itself, and these foreigners, thus buried there, might be regarded as possessing a part of the city.[6]

...at the time when this war burst upon them they were constrained to obey certain oracular commands from the Sibylline books, and to bury alive two Greeks, a man and a woman, and likewise two Gauls, in the place called the "forum boarium", or cattle-market; and in memory of these victims, they still to this day, in the month of November, perform mysterious and secret ceremonies.[7]

Thus the Romans made a human sacrifice in accordance with an oracle found in the Sibylline Books, to prevent the Gauls and Greeks from occupying the city. It would have been interesting to find out exactly what race each of the Gauls and Greek were from, especially given that Roman emissaries were touring Greece promoting their victory over the Ardiaei, at the same time as burying Greeks alive in Rome itself. It is no surprise that we do not find this event in Polybius, as the Romans would have hardly wanted to advertise such an act to the civilized Greek world. This is the first recorded human sacrifice of this nature in Rome and does show the depth of worry the Romans had about the impending threat.[8] Dio also records another version of the Sibylline oracle concerning the Gauls:

The Romans were alarmed over an oracle of the Sibyl which told them that they must beware of the Gauls when a thunderbolt should fall upon the Capitol near the temple of Apollo.[9]

Having made an attempt to assuage the Gods and cheat destiny, the Senate seems to have taken a more practical step this year and doubled the number of Praetors. We only have two brief references to this event in our surviving sources, and no detail as to the cause.[10] Certainly, Sardinia and Sicily were to be governed by Praetors (as seen in Chapter Two), but what were the wider reasons behind the timing of this decision? Brennan argues that it was the revolt of Sardinian tribes at the same time as the Consuls were fighting in Illyria the year previously that brought home to the Senate that Rome needed more commanders with imperium, given the increasing number of theatres of operation the Romans were now fighting in (as seen in Chapters Two and Four respectively). Furthermore the Senate had needed to grant one of the Consuls, Cn. Fulvius Centumalus, a Proconsulship, which was the first since the Punic War.[11] Nevertheless, given that the Romans were seemingly making preparation for an impending Gallic War, it does seem logical that this too had a major bearing on the decision to increase the number of Praetors and thus more commanders were available when the war came.

Eckstein provides a further argument based on the unusual inactivity of the Consuls of 228–226 BC, who are not recorded as engaging in any major military conflicts.[12] He argues that these Consuls were held in reserve by the Senate to respond to a supposedly imminent Gallic invasion. Polybius says the following:

> ...that at time we find them [the Romans] busy enrolling legions and making provision of grain and stores, at bother times marching to the frontier, as if the enemy had already invaded their territory, while in fact the Gauls had not yet moved from their own territory.[13]

Thus the Consuls of these years seem to have been charged with preparing Roman defences; raising and training troops, stockpiling supplies and marching to the northern border in response to false alarms. Having undertaken religious and military measures in the previous years, 226 BC saw two major diplomatic measures come to fruition which helped to underpin the Roman position. The first and most well-known came in the form of the so called Ebro Treaty between Rome and Carthage, concerning their respective spheres of influence in Spain (as seen in Chapter Five). Polybius clearly states that it was the danger of the Gauls in Italy that forced Rome to make peace with Carthage over Spain, allowing them to focus on the main danger; the Gauls, not the Carthaginians:

> They therefore secured themselves against the Carthaginians by the treaty with Hasdrubal, the terms of which I stated above, and threw their whole effort into the struggle with their enemies in Italy, considering it their main interest to bring this to a decisive conclusion.[14]

Thus the Romans were able to focus their attentions on the impending war in Italy, with the added security that they need not worry about

the Carthaginians. Given the subsequent history between Rome and
Carthage, this treaty has also been over-emphasised in its importance.
The Carthaginians at this point were an unnecessary distraction and this
agreement allowed Rome to deal with a potential distraction and focus on
the far more important and dangerous enemy, the Gauls. To these ends, the
Romans' second diplomatic triumph of this period is far more important;
an alliance with a number of Gallic tribes in northern Italy itself. Polybius
reports the following:

> The Insubres and Boii held stoutly to their original purpose; but the
> Veneti and Cenomani, on the Romans sending an embassy to them,
> decided to give them their support; so that the Celtic chiefs were
> obliged to leave part of their forces behind to protect their territory
> from invasion by these tribes.[15]

Thus the Romans secured the first victory of the impending war, a diplomatic
one, and secured allies from amongst the Gallic tribes of northern Italy. As the
previous Gallic War had shown, one of the Gallic tribes' greatest weaknesses
was the divisions between them. Each tribe may have had a common origin,
having migrated from over the Alps, but would have been competing with
the others for access to resources in northern Italy and maintained a fierce
independent identity to the others. Whilst tribes like the Boii were directly
affected by the northern advance of the Roman Federation, to tribes like
the Cenomani and Veneti, Rome was further away and not a direct threat.
Furthermore, there were distinct advantages to having Rome as an ally in
their struggles with their fellow tribes, as subsequent events showed.

Thus, through these two pieces of diplomacy, Rome gained three major
advantages. Firstly, it stopped the grand alliance which the Boii and Insubres
were building from adding any more northern Italian tribes, thus increasing
their manpower further. Secondly, as Polybius points out this Roman alliance
forced the hostile tribes, and the Insubres in particular, to leave behind forces
to defend their territory from the pro-Roman tribes, and the Cenomani in
particular (see Map 2). Therefore, the army which invaded Roman Italy was
reduced. The unexpected bonus for the Insubres, however, was that post-
Telamon they had more forces to resist the Romans with (see Chapters
Seven and Eight). The third advantage was that the Romans seemed to gain
additional forces from this alliance, and Polybius speaks of Cenomani and

Veneti forces being placed at Rome's disposal. Polybius' narrative dates these alliances to 225 BC and the year of the invasion; however, the Roman emissaries must have been negotiating for longer than his narrative allows and must come incredibly early in the year to allow for the events that were to follow. Therefore, we can argue that these diplomatic missions must have started earlier than 225 BC.

Thus, we can see that the Romans took a number of steps to prepare for what they correctly assumed would be an impending Gallic invasion, through religious, military and diplomatic preparations, albeit with some of more practical value than others. Furthermore, in 225 BC, when the invasion was confirmed, and following the Roman mobilization, the Romans took steps to secure their eastern and western flanks, again showing a high level of tactical thinking. Polybius reports that two reserve legions were raised, one in Sicily and one in Tarentum.[16] In Sicily a legion was deployed to ensure both the Roman subjects and Syracusans did not use this invasion to stage a revolt. A reserve legion would not have stopped a Carthaginian invasion, but then again, in this period, such a notion must have been discounted.[17] The legion in Tarentum, must have served two purposes; firstly to secure the most direct route into Italy from the Greek mainland and secondly to be ready, if need be, to cross the Adriatic and defend the Roman position in Illyria, whether from rebelling local cities or tribes or ultimately Macedonian interference.

The Senate can be seen to be thinking about the whole of Rome's growing empire, which shows how far it had developed in just over a decade. Even though the threat was from the north, consideration had to be given to their position on the islands of Sardinia and Corsica in the west, Sicily in the south and Illyria in the east. All this came on top of a diplomatic settlement with Carthage to further secure the far west and south. However, in detailing all of these steps Rome took to face the impending Gallic threat, we have yet to touch on the most important one: the mobilization of Rome's armies from her vast manpower reserves.

Polybius and the Roman Army of 225 BC

Polybius states that the Romans, who were apparently prepared for an imminent invasion, were alerted to the Gaesatae crossing the Alps; whether by friendly tribes, spies or a combination of both is never stated.[18] Having expected a Gallic invasion for some time, as Polybius states, the Romans had had plenty of time to make preparations and had thus mobilized one of the largest Roman armies ever:

> Each of the Consuls was in command of four legions of Roman citizens, each consisting of five thousand two hundred foot and three hundred horse. The allied forces in each Consular army numbered thirty thousand foot and two thousand horse. The cavalry of the Sabines and Etruscans, who had come to the temporary assistance of Rome, were four thousand strong, their infantry above fifty thousand. The Romans massed these forces and posted them on the frontier of Etruria under the command of a Praetor. The levy of the Umbrians and Sarsinates inhabiting the Apennines amounted to about twenty thousand, and with these were twenty thousand Veneti and Cenomani. These they stationed on the frontier of Gaul, to invade the territory of the Boii and divert them back from their expedition. These were the armies protecting the Roman territory. In Rome itself there was a reserve force, ready for any war-contingency, consisting of twenty thousand foot and fifteen hundred horse, all Roman citizens, and thirty thousand foot and two thousand horse furnished by the allies.[19]

Thus, according to Polybius, the Romans had five separate armies drawn up and awaiting the Gallic invasion, and two legions in reserve: [20]

First Consular Army (L. Aemilius Papus)	25,400 Infantry, 1,600 Cavalry
Two Legions of Roman Citizens	(10,400 Infantry, 600 Cavalry)
Italian Allied Forces	(15,000 infantry, 1,000 Cavalry)
Second Consular Army (C. Atilius Regulus)	25,400 Infantry, 1,600 Cavalry
Two Legions of Roman Citizens	(10,400 Infantry, 600 Cavalry)
Italian Allied Forces	(15,000 infantry, 1,000 Cavalry)
Italian Allied Army (Unnamed Praetor)	50,000 Infantry, 4,000 Cavalry
Sabines and Etruscans	
Mixed Italian Allied and Gallic Allied Army	40,000 (Mixed)
Umbrians, Sarsinates	(20,000 Mixed)
Veneti, Cenomani	(20,000 Mixed)

Reserve Army (Citizen and Allies)	50,000 Infantry, 3,500 Cavalry
Four Legions of Roman Citizens	(20,000 Infantry, 1,500 Cavalry)
Italian Allied Forces	(30,000 Infantry, 2,000 Cavalry)
Sicilian Legion (One Legion)	4,200 Infantry, 200 Cavalry
Tarentine Legion (One Legion)	4,200 Infantry, 200 Cavalry

If we believe Polybius' figures, the Romans had three armies, totalling over 150,000 infantry and 10,000 cavalry, ready to face the Gallic invasion. It is interesting to note that over 70 per cent of the total infantry and cavalry came from Rome's Italian allies, showing the fundamental strength of the Roman manpower system (just over 100 years old at this point). This was supported by an additional force of 50,000-plus guarding Rome and some 40,000 of Rome's more recent allies (both Italic and Gallic) also stationed in the north, though the Gallic forces (Veneti and Cenomani) must have been based in their own tribal regions. This is not to mention the legions sent to Sicily and Tarentum mentioned above.

Leaving aside issues of the depth of Rome's manpower reserves (see Appendix Four), we must ask ourselves how long it took Rome to muster over 200,000 Roman and allied soldiers, and create the armies that Rome had under their command. Clearly this was not done on the spur of the moment, which begs the question when this vast mobilization took place? Even after the planning stage, the Romans would have needed to communicate their requirements to their outlying citizen colonies throughout Italy and to their allies. These men needed to settle their affairs and travel to muster points. They would then need time to collect in their smaller units, and then in their larger formations. We have no information on how many were veterans and how many were new recruits, so some training and familiarization must have taken place, both on an individual and group level. Given all this, we must assume that this mobilization took place prior to 225 BC to have all these armies ready to move north when the invasion did take place.

In command of the Romans armies were the Consuls L. Aemilius Papus and C. Atilius Regulus. We know nothing of the prior career of the men themselves, but both came from distinguished Consular families with a martial background. The most famous were the Atilii Reguli who had held

Consulship since the fourth century. Caius was a son of the famous Roman Commander M. Atilius Regulus (Cos. 267 and 256 BC), who famously handed himself back to the Carthaginians after encouraging the Senate to reject the peace offer he had been sent to deliver following his capture during the failed Roman invasion of Africa (an act which resulted in his torture and death). Caius' elder brother Marcus had been Consul just two years earlier (in 227 BC). The other man, L. Aemilius Papus, hailed from a distinguished patrician family, whose ancestor (Q. Aemilius Papus) held the Consulship in 282 and 278 and a Censorship in 275 BC.[21] Interestingly, his ancestor was most likely the Roman commander who defeated the Boii at Lake Vadimon in 283 BC. This may not be coincidence, but could account for his election in 225 BC, on the back of a family pedigree in defeating invading Gauls. There is no record of any Aemilii Papi holding a command in the First Punic War and the family appears not to have held the Consulship in the intervening fifty years. Therefore, although we know little of these men's military record to date, both came from established and distinguished military families and would have been seen as sound commanders to face the challenge ahead.

The Gallic Invasion of 225 BC

It was in 225 BC that the Romans' worst fears became a reality, when the Gallic tribes went on the offensive once more. The Gaesatae (and Taurisci) crossed the Alps early in the year and descended into the Po Valley to join their allies, the Insubres and the Boii. Polybius puts their total number at 50,000 infantry and 20,000 cavalry, composed of horse and chariot, though he does not provide a breakdown between the two main tribes and their mercenary contingent.[22] Diodorus provides an inflated figure of 200,000 for the Gallic army.[23] Polybius also states that the defection of the Veneti and Cenomani, who were to the east of the Insubres and Boii (see Map 2), to the Roman cause forced the Boii and Insubres to leave a substantial part of their forces behind to defend themselves against an attack from their rear by these tribes, though Polybius gives no figures. Once again we can see the disruptive impact of tribal disunity on the Gauls and the success of the Roman diplomacy on this front.

We must examine the tactics the Romans used, as they reveal a number of issues connected to the conduct of the war. Despite seemingly knowing that an attack was imminent, the Romans still had one major intelligence problem; namely which route would the attack take? Given the barrier of the Apennines, the Gauls could either choose to attack via the west of the Apennines into Etruria or via the east into Picenum.

In theory, the Romans had an obvious answer to the problem they faced. The two largest armies were those of the Consuls and these could be deployed either side of the Apennines to blunt the initial impact of the Gallic invasion. They would be supported by a praetorian army of allies and a considerable reserve defending Rome itself. Once the direction of the Gallic thrust had been determined, then the other Consular army could swing round and either support the first army or catch the Gauls in a pincer, depending upon various local factors such as the exact terrain and timings.

However, this is not how the Romans deployed, and it was a decision that was to prove costly. At some point early in the year, one of the Consuls, C. Atilius Regulus, had been dispatched with his legions to Sardinia (as seen in Chapter Two). Polybius provides this detail, but does not state the reason why. Zonaras has recorded that a revolt broke out in Sardinia prior to 225 BC, possibly in 227 or 226 BC, as a result of the Romans imposing a permanent governor on the province; one of the new Praetors.[24] This left the Romans with one Consular army and one Praetorian to face the Gallic invasion, which seems curious given the anticipated scale of the threat.

There are several factors that may have underpinned this tactical decision. Firstly, the revolt in Sardinia may have been more serious than our meagre surviving sources state, which would have provided an unnecessary distraction to the coming Gallic campaign and may have even raised issues over potential Punic involvement in a region that had once been part of their empire. Secondly, there would have been merit in blooding an untested army, and potentially an untested commander, especially if overwhelming force was used to ensure that the campaign was a short one. We are not told how many of his four legions Atilius took with him, but we must assume that it was the bulk of them.

The third reason lies in a calculation the Romans seem to have made; they appear to have been convinced that the Gallic invasion would take place to the east of the Apennines and into Picenum. There were sound reasons for such an assumption; it was the natural route from the Po Valley, it bordered the lands of the Boii, it was on freshly conquered lands the Romans had taken from the Gallic tribes in the past half century and it was the route the Gallic forces had used less than a decade before, in the Gallic War of the 230s (as seen in Chapter Three).

Based on such a logical set of assumptions, the Romans duly dispatched the remaining Consul, L. Aemilius Papus, to the Roman stronghold of Ariminum, on the Adriatic coast, as a base to await the Gallic invasion. Polybius expressly states that the Romans were expecting the attack to come via this route.[25] As a precaution, the army of Sabines and Etruscans, commanded by an unknown Praetor, was dispatched to Etruria. The logic behind such a move must have been that the Etrurian route would have been within range of the Consul Atilius Regulus, in Sardinia, and would allow him to finish the campaign on the island and then move across the Tyrrhenian Sea to reinforce the west.

Unfortunately for the Romans, this tactical plan, based though it was on strong logical assumptions, contained two major flaws; namely that the Gallic armies actually invaded via the west of the Apennines, through Etruria, and that Atilius was still campaigning in Sardinia when they invaded. In short, despite all their military intelligence, advance preparations and full-scale mobilization, the Romans placed their weakest force in the path of the Gallic onslaught.

Although we have some sources to support our analysis of the Roman tactics, we have none with which to analyse the Gallic battle–plan. However this is worth a brief analysis, especially as it seemed to catch the Romans completely off-guard and gave the Gauls a major tactical advantage. It is interesting to note the change between the tactics the Gauls used in the 230s and on this occasion, and the possible changes of motivation and personnel. The war of the 230s BC had seemed to be a sequel to the wars of the 280s, namely a desire by the Boii and their allies to regain the lands lost to the Romans in eastern Italy. This attack, however, seemed to have been more intended to destroy Rome itself, more akin to the infamous invasion of the fourth century, which culminated in the capture of Rome and the near collapse of Roman power in Italy (as seen in Chapter Three).

Interestingly, a fragment of Dio contains a report that certain of the Gauls made an oath and had 'sworn not to remove their breastplates until they had mounted to the Capitol.'[26] We have no way of telling whether they did make such an oath, but it is entirely possible that they did and had set out to deliberately emulate their ancestors and attack Rome itself. It is interesting to speculate upon the effects that the Insubres and Gaesatae may have had on Gallic tactics. Less than a decade earlier, the Boii, whom Polybius names as the originators of this Gallic alliance, had been content with just an assault on Rome's eastern flank to regain their lost lands. The Insubres and their mercenary contingent seemed more intent on attacking Rome itself, and ending their power in northern Italy at least, and to that end seem to have opted for the direct route. Thus it seems that Rome, for all their military intelligence, may have been complacent about the exact nature of the threat they faced and were intent on fighting a re-run of the previous wars of the third century and thus, despite everything, had seriously underestimated their enemy.

The Early Campaign and the Battle of Faesulae – Polybian Version

Although we have Polybius' narrative, there are a number of omissions and rushed chronology which pose problems in gaining a full understanding of the early campaigning of the war. Added to this are problems with identification of the location of the first battle and a disagreement between Polybius, Diodorus and Orosius about the number of battles, the victors of each and even their identities. Nevertheless, as Polybius provides our fullest and earliest surviving account, which is considered the accepted version, we must begin with an analysis of the campaign as detailed by him. However, we must not lose sight of the variations presented by our other surviving sources, and these will be discussed later.

The first issue is that we have no details or chronology of Atilius' Sardinian campaign, which seems to have so exposed Rome's western flank. We do not know whether Atilius' campaign became enmeshed in a guerrilla war in the Sardinian interior or whether the Gauls advanced far quicker than Rome was expecting. Secondly, we are not told where the Praetorian army in Etruria was stationed. What is clear is that this Praetorian army was bypassed completely, with the Gallic force moving unopposed through Etruria and towards Rome itself. Polybius provides us with the following:

> The Celts, descending on Etruria, overran the country devastating it without let or hindrance and, as nobody appeared to oppose them,

they marched on Rome itself. When they had got as far as Clusium, a city three days' journey from Rome, news reached them that the advanced force which the Romans had posted in Etruria was on their heels and approaching. On hearing this, they turned to meet it, eager to engage it.[27]

The key question here is how or why the unnamed Roman Praetor allowed the Gallic force to bypass him and move directly on Rome, and why in this position he then gave battle on his own. There are two possibilities to the first question, why the Gallic army passed the Roman Praetor. The first is that he was caught unawares by the Gallic thrust into Etruria and that it took him some time to locate the Gauls and catch up with them, presuming that the Gauls were moving at some speed. It is also possible that, as he was not expecting the arrival of the Gauls, the Roman campaign plan was thrown into disarray and he had to wait for further instructions from the Consul Aemilius Papus before setting off in pursuit.

The second possibility is that this tactic was a deliberate one and that he had been ordered to allow the Gauls free passage, given that his army was smaller, and that he was waiting for the arrival of Aemilius so that they could combine both armies and then give battle from a position of strength. Giving the Gauls free reign to devastate Etruria and march towards Rome was not without risks, but the effects would have been ameliorated by the presence of the Roman reserve force protecting Rome and the swiftness of Aemilius' army's movement from Picenum towards Rome. It is clear that, although the Gallic invasion of Etruria had caught the Romans by surprise, messengers had been swiftly dispatched to both Consuls, in Picenum and Sardinia, to converge on Etruria as quickly as possible. From Polybius' narrative it is clear that Aemilius and his army were closing in from eastern Italy, and it does therefore seem most likely that the Roman plan was for the Praetorian army to shadow the Gallic force and await the arrival of the Consular army of Aemilius before giving battle. However, once again, Roman plans did not take into account the tactics of the Gauls.

For the Gauls, the thrust into Etruria had paid off and they had marched unopposed into the heartland of Roman territory, advancing towards Rome itself. Polybius notes that the Gauls were apparently aware of the shadowing Praetorian army, and we can postulate that they knew that they were being shepherded into a pincer movement with the advancing Consular army from eastern Italy. Their scouts may have alerted them to the positions of both Roman forces. For the Gauls, the plan must have been a simple one: avoid getting caught in the pincer by eliminating the lesser of the two armies, then meeting the Consular army head on. To do this, however, they would need to persuade the Praetorian army to give battle, without waiting for the arrival of the Consular army of Aemilius. Once again the Gauls employed a simple but timeless strategy of a feint; tricking the Roman Praetor into the belief that they had turned tail and fled, disrupting his battle-plan and panicking him into rash action. Unfortunately for Rome and the unnamed Praetor, he fell for this tactic:

> At sunset the two armies were in closed proximity, and encamped for the night at no great distance from each other. After nightfall, the Celts lit their camp-fires, and, leaving orders with their cavalry to wait until daybreak and then, when visible to the enemy, to follow on their track, they themselves secretly retreated to a town called Faesulae and posted themselves there, their intention being to wait for their cavalry, and also to put unexpected difficulties in the way of the enemy's attack. At daybreak, the Romans, seeing the cavalry alone and thinking the Celts had taken to flight, followed the cavalry with all speed on the line of the Celts' retreat.[28]

Obviously fearful that the Gauls had escaped the impending trap, the Praetor then promptly fell into a Gallic one by not waiting for the arrival of Aemilius and giving heedless pursuit, with inevitable consequences:

> On their approaching the enemy, the Celts left their position and attacked them, and a conflict, at first very stubborn, took place, in which finally the numbers and courage of the Celts prevailed, not fewer than six thousand Romans falling and the rest taking to flight. Most of them retreated to a hill of some natural strength where they remained. The Celts at first attempted to besiege them, but as they were getting the worst of it, fatigued as they were by their long night march and the suffering and hardships it involved, they hastened to rest and refresh themselves, leaving a detachment of their cavalry to keep guard round the hill, intending next day to besiege the fugitives, if they did not offer to surrender.[29]

Thus the Roman Army was panicked from its position by the supposed retreat of the Gauls, gave heedless chase and fell into a Gallic ambush; wasting the careful planning and co-ordination that had gone into the Roman battle-plan and once again exposing the Roman weakness when it came to a combined military effort. The Praetorian army composed of Sabine and Etrurian allies had been defeated, with at least 6,000 men killed and the rest corralled on a hilltop.

One problem we have is the location of this battle. Polybius is clear that the Gauls advanced as far south as Clusium, but then apparently retreated as far back north as Faesulae (see Map 5). Polybius' narrative implies that the battle was fought the day after reaching Clusium, which means they would not have been able to march as far north as the only recorded city of Faesulae, approximately eighty miles to the north. There are several possibilities here. The first is that either Polybius or one of the surviving manuscripts of Polybius has given us the wrong name of the battle site, though it is more likely to be one of his copied manuscripts, rather than Polybius himself. If the name is correct, then the next logical possibility is that the Gallic army did actually retreat that far north, rather than stand and fight, and Polybius is contracting the time span this took for dramatic effect.

The next possibility is that there was another town or city by the name of Faesulae near Clusium, or more likely that the name was similar and a mistake has been made. The fourth possibility is that Polybius is conflating two different battles into one; the first at the start of the Gallic invasion near Faesulae, and the second later in the campaign near Clusium. Ultimately, given the time elapsed, we will never know which of these possibilities accounts for this discrepancy and therefore we must still refer to this clash as the Battle as Faesulae for want of a better term, bearing in mind the issues that surround this.

The Gallic Retreat of 225 BC

Fortunately for the Romans the defeat at Faesulae did not becomes a total disaster, and the besieged survivors of the Roman Army were saved thanks to the arrival of the Consul Aemilius Papus and his army, which had marched across the Apennines from eastern Italy. According to the Polybian narrative, Aemilius arrived with his army that very night and camped nearby. Both the Roman survivors of the Praetorian army and the Gauls saw Aemilius' campfires and reacted very differently. According to Polybius, the Roman survivors managed to send messengers through the Gallic cordon of cavalry to Aemilius' camp to alert him to the disaster that had occurred and the location of the survivors.[30]

Unfortunately for us, we are not given enough detail by Polybius to properly reconstruct the dispositions of the three forces: Roman survivors, Gauls and Aemilius. We know that the Gauls had left a contingent of cavalry to guard the hill, but we do not know if the main Gallic army was between the two Roman forces or the hill was between the Gauls and Aemilius. In any event upon hearing the news Aemilius split his force into two, leaving his infantry under the command of his military tribunes, to advance on the Gauls at daybreak. He preceded them with his cavalry towards the hill and the remains of the praetorian army.

The narrative of Polybius gives the impression that he mustered his cavalry and rode out almost immediately, certainly before daybreak, in an attempt to confront the Gallic cavalry and break through to the Roman survivors. Given this description, we must assume that the main Gallic army was not between Aemilius and the hill where the Roman survivors were gathered, but were either behind or to the side of the hill.

We must assume that Aemilius' plan was to drive off the Gallic cavalry guarding the hill and then rejoin his infantry before battle was given with the main Gallic army. Whilst it was a bold move to lead his cavalry personally and rescue the defeated Romans, not being in charge of his army when they faced the main Gallic force would have been unforgivable. As events transpired this was not an issue for Aemilius, as the Gauls took an unusual step and retreated rather than give battle. This is an odd move for several reasons. Firstly, the Gauls had made what seems to have been a lightning fast incursion into Roman territory, heading straight towards Rome itself. Secondly, they had just soundly defeated a Roman Army and had the survivors bottled up on a hilltop. Thirdly, they seemed to still maintain the numerical advantage, certainly over Aemilius' army on its own. Finally, Aemilius' army had only just apparently arrived in the region and must have been marching at a heavy pace for a number of days to get there, whereas the Gaul were fresh from a victory.

Polybius tells us that upon seeing the campfires of Aemilius' army, the Gauls convened a war council that night, when one of the chieftains of the

Gaesatae, Aneroëstus, proposed that the Gauls withdraw rather than fight Aemilius on account of not wanting to risk the large amounts of spoils that they had taken already, 'for it appears that the quantity of slaves, cattle and miscellaneous spoil was enormous.'[31]

This in itself is revealing as it shows the huge devastation that the Gauls had caused during their invasion of Etruria. Furthermore, Polybius tells us that Aneroëstus argued that they should return to their homeland (presumably north of the Alps), deposit their spoils and then return if possible to face the Romans. As always we must question how Polybius, or his source, was privy to the inner workings of the Gallic war council, though it is interesting that he does name the Gallic chieftain behind this. Even if we accept that this account is based on a kernel of truth, what are we to make of this turnaround by the Gauls?

Here we must recall the nature of the Gallic army, composed as it was of two very different types of Gallic tribes. On the one hand there were the two tribes from Gallic northern Italy, the Boii and Insubres, who seem to have been implacably opposed to Rome, realising that they would not be able to co-exist with the Roman Federation and that for one to survive the other must fall. However, the second element were the Gaesatae (and Taurisci), who were mercenaries from north of the Alps. Their motivation was plunder, not a fight for survival, as Rome's reach had not yet passed the Apennines, let alone the Alps. Whilst the Insubres and Boii may have wanted to press on with the war and defeat Rome, and possibly sack Rome itself once more, it seems that for the Gaesatae this campaign had already succeeded in its aims. They had amassed a huge amount of plunder (slaves, cattle and movable goods), all from a more sophisticated civilization and had accumulated far more wealth than they would have achieved in plying their mercenary trade elsewhere in the region.

Given these disparate natures, it is likely that this was the motivation for the sudden *volte-face* of the Gallic army and its decision to refuse battle and strike north once again. In other words, the various Gallic factions fell into dissension once more and the Gaesatae decided to end the campaign on a high and not push their luck by facing the Romans in battle again. Thus the Insubrian and Boian plans for the destruction of Rome and Roman power in Italy seem to have been shattered, and they were left with little choice but to retreat rather than face the Roman Consular army on their own, without their Gaesatae allies. Once again it seems that lack of

Gallic cohesion between the various tribes and factions proved to be their downfall.

The Gauls broke up camp that night and set out north-westwards towards the Etrurian coast, and from there northwards following the coastline, no doubt continuing their pillaging as they went (with rich picking amongst the coastal towns). This allowed Aemilius to rescue the Roman survivors from the hilltop unopposed and integrate them into his own army, after which he set off in pursuit of the Gauls. According to Polybius, Aemilius did not give battle, but wanted to wait for more favourable circumstances.[32]

Although the Gauls must have been wreaking havoc amongst the coastal towns and cities of Etruria, the important aspect from a Roman point of view was that the Gauls were heading away from Rome and its territories. Furthermore, even with the remnants of the Praetorian army integrated into his own, Aemilius must still have faced a numerical disadvantage. More importantly still, the Gauls were heading in precisely the direction of the second Consular army, that of C. Atilius Regulus, who was based in Sardinia. In other word, the retreating Gauls, in their haste to return to their own territories, were inadvertently heading into the jaws of a Roman pincer, between two Consular armies.

Chapter Seven

The Gallic War II –
The Battle of Telamon (225 BC)

I t is only during the Gallic retreat northwards that Polybius reintroduces the second Consul, C. Atilius Regulus. We have no details of his activities in Sardinia, and only know that he was detained long enough to leave eastern Italy under-defended, allowing the Gallic tribes to push through unopposed. We must assume that when the Gallic army did invade western Italy, messengers were sent to him at the same time as Aemilius in the east. Again, Polybius does not provide us with a timescale, but whilst events were transpiring at the Battle of Faesulae, Atilius seemingly ended his campaign in Sardinia (though we are not told with what level of success) and transported his army across the Tyrrhenian Sea to the city of Pisa (see Map 5). Polybius states that Atilius marched south towards Rome, which he must have assumed was the intended objective of the Gallic force. At this point it is clear that he did not know of the events of Faesulae or that the Gauls were heading directly towards him. He naturally sent scouts out ahead of the main force and it was they who first encountered the retreating Gallic army near the city of Telamon (modern Talamone) on the Etrurian coast (see Map 5):

> When the Celts were near Telamon in Etruria, their advanced foragers encountered the advance guard of Caius and were made prisoners. On being examined by the Consul they narrated all that had recently occurred and told him of the presence of the two armies, stating that the Gauls were quite near and Lucius behind them. The news surprised him but at the same time made him very hopeful, as he thought he had caught the Gauls on the march between the two armies.[1]

The Battle of Telamon (225 BC) – Polybian Version

Thus, through a change of circumstance Atilius found his fortunes drastically changed; from having been held too long in Sardinia and missing the Gallic invasion, he now found that he was in prime position to fight and defeat the Gauls, and set his army to give battle. We are fortunate to have a detailed narrative of the battle preserved in Polybius, probably based on a first-hand account from Fabius Pictor (see Appendix One):

> He ordered his Tribunes to put the legions in fighting order and to advance thus at marching pace in so far as the nature of the ground allowed the attack in line. He himself had happily noticed a hill situated above the road by which the Celts must pass, and taking his cavalry with him, advanced at full speed, being anxious to occupy the crest of the hill before their arrival and be the first to begin the battle, feeling certain that thus he would get the largest share of credit for the result.[2]

It seems that Atilius was over-eager to claim the glory of defeating the Gauls for himself and neglected to link up with the army of Aemilius, which was trailing the Gauls. Once again two Roman commanders failed to link up properly and deliver a decisive blow to the Gauls, and utilise the numbers of both armies catching the Gauls in a pincer. Nevertheless, Atilius' decisiveness had allowed him to select his own battle site and occupy the high ground. The first clash of the battle was a light skirmish between an advance force of Gallic cavalry and infantry and Atilius' cavalry on the top of the hill:

> The Celts at first were ignorant of the arrival of Atilius and imagined from what they saw, that Aemilius' cavalry had got round their flank in the night and were engaged in occupying the position. They therefore at once sent on their own cavalry and some of their light-armed troops to dispute the possession of the hill. But very soon they learnt of Caius' presence from one of the prisoners brought in.[3]

Although Polybius gives us no details of this first skirmish between the two sides at Telamon, his narrative does indicate that the Gauls were able to take prisoners and thus ascertain the nature of the threat they faced, and were able to make the appropriate tactical decisions. Thus Atilius seems to have lost some of the initiative:

> [the Gauls] lost no time in drawing up their infantry, deploying them so that they faced both front and rear, since, both from the intelligence that reached them and from what was happening before their eyes, they knew that the one army was following them, and they expected to meet the other in their front.[4]

Whilst the fighting was continuing for the hill between Atilius' cavalry and the Gauls, fortune again favoured the Romans, as Aemilius was now close enough to learn of Atilius' disposition and lend aid:

> Aemilius, who had heard of the landing of the legions at Pisa but had not any idea that they were already so near him, now, when he saw the fight going on round the hill, knew that the other Roman Army was quite close. Accordingly, sending on his cavalry to help those who were fighting on the hill, he drew up his infantry in the usual order and advanced against the foe.[5]

Thus a third force of cavalry entered the battle on the hill, to join Atilius' cavalry and the Gallic cavalry supported by Gallic infantry. Away from the hill, it seems that Aemilius was in fact closer to the main body of the Gallic army than Atilius' main force, which must have been further ahead. Polybius presents us with a detailed disposition of the Gallic force:

> The Celts had drawn up facing their rear, from which they expected Aemilius to attack, the Gaesatae from the Alps and behind them the Insubres, and facing in the opposite direction, ready to meet the attack of Caius' [Atilius'] legions, they placed the Taurisci and the Boii from the right bank of the Po. Their wagons and chariots they stationed at the extremity of either wing and collected their booty on one of the neighbouring hills with a protecting force round it. This order of the Celtic forces, facing both ways, not only presented a formidable appearance, but was well adapted to the exigencies of the situation. The Insubres and Boii wore their trousers and light cloaks, but the Gaesatae had discarded these garments owing to their proud confidence in

themselves, and stood naked, with nothing but their arms, in front of the whole army, thinking that thus they would be more efficient, as some of the ground was overgrown with brambles which would catch in their clothes and impede the use of their weapons.[6]

Despite the Gauls being caught between two Roman armies, the lack of Roman co-ordination and the skirmish on the hill had allowed them time to make adequate dispositions to face both Roman armies with confidence. Facing the north and Atilius' army were the Boii and Taurisci, and to the south and facing Aemilius' army were the Gaesatae and the Insubres.

As before, the initial phase of the battle was between the cavalry of all three armies and focussed on gaining control of the hill, though we do not know the number involved:

At first the battle was confined to the hill, all the armies gazing on it, so great were the numbers of cavalry from each host combating there pell-mell. In this action Caius [Atilius] the Consul fell in the mêlée fighting with desperate courage, and his head was brought to the Celtic kings; but the Roman cavalry, after a stubborn struggle, at length overmastered the enemy and gained possession of the hill.[7]

Thus, the Romans emerged victorious in this initial phase, but lost the Consul Atilius. It is difficult to know what to make of Atilius' tactics. He seems to have made the decisive move to offer battle at Telamon and chose his ground well, but we must question his decision to take the fore with his cavalry on the hill. From the information we have, it does seem that he struck out too far from his main army and made himself a tempting target sat on top of that hill. At first the Gauls were able to attack him in force, capturing prisoners, and thus learn of the nature of the force that awaited them, avoiding any attempt at ambush.

Furthermore, his force seems to have been overwhelmed on that hill, leading to his death in battle. Ultimately, his decision not to link up with the army of his Consular colleague appears to have cost him at least his life, but not the battle; an outcome which was only avoided by Aemilius' timely arrival rather than any co-ordination between the two men.

With the cavalry battle concluded and the Romans victorious on the hill, the main armies moved to engage. Despite the loss of the Consul Atilius

Regulus, it seems that the Romans armies were able to co-ordinate their actions, possibly thanks to the cavalry of the two Roman armies intermingling on the hill. We have no timescale for the lapse between the cavalry battle and the advance of the main armies. Now, however, the Gauls found themselves attacked on two fronts:

> The infantry were now close upon each other, and the spectacle was a strange and marvellous one, not only to those actually present at the battle, but to all who could afterwards picture it to themselves from the reports. For in the first place, as the battle was between three armies, it is evident that the appearance and the movements of the forces marshalled against each other must have been in the highest degree strange and unusual. Again, it must have been to all present, and still is to us, a matter of doubt whether the Celts, with the enemy advancing on them from both sides, were more dangerously situated, or, on the contrary, more effectively, since at one and the same time they were fighting against both their enemies and were protecting themselves in the rear from both, while, above all, they were absolutely cut off from retreat or any prospect of escape in the case of defeat, this being the peculiarity of this two-faced formation. The Romans, however, were on the one hand encouraged by having caught the enemy between their two armies, but on the other they were terrified by the fine order of the Celtic host and the dreadful din, for there were innumerable horn-blowers and trumpeters, and, as the whole army were shouting their war-cries at the same time, there was such a tumult of sound that it seemed that not only the trumpets and the soldiers but all the country round had got a voice and caught up the cry. Very terrifying too were the appearance and the gestures of the naked warriors in front, all in the prime of life, and finely built men, and all in the leading companies richly adorned with gold torques and armlets. The sight of them indeed dismayed the Romans, but at the same time the prospect of winning such spoils made them twice as keen for the fight.[8]

As was custom, the Romans opened with a volley of pila, which seemed to have a particularly devastating effect on the Gaesatae facing Aemilius' army:

But when the javelineers advanced, as is their usage, from the ranks of the Roman legions and began to hurl their javelins in well-aimed volleys, the Celts in the rear ranks indeed were well protected by their trousers and cloaks, but it fell out far otherwise than they had expected with the naked men in front, and they found themselves in a very difficult and helpless predicament. For the Gallic shield does not cover the whole body; so that their nakedness was a disadvantage, and the bigger they were the better chance had the missiles of going home. At length, unable to drive off the javelineers owing to the distance and the hail of javelins, and reduced to the utmost distress and perplexity, some of them, in their impotent rage, rushed wildly on the enemy and sacrificed their lives, while others, retreating step by step on the ranks of their comrades, threw them into disorder by their display of faint-heartedness. Thus was the spirit of the Gaesatae broken down by the javelineers.[9]

With the volleys of pila exhausted, the two sides met head on:

...but the main body of the Insubres, Boii, and Taurisci, once the javelineers had withdrawn into the ranks and the Roman maniples attacked them, met the enemy and kept up a stubborn hand-to hand combat. For, though being almost cut to pieces, they held their ground, equal to their foes in courage, and inferior only, as a force and individually, in their arms. The Roman shields, it should be added, were far more serviceable for defence and their swords for attack, the Gallic sword being only good for a cut and not for a thrust.[10]

It seems, however, that the two sides were evenly matched until the decisive move was made by the Roman cavalry on top of the hill, attacking the Gallic force from the flanks:

But finally, attacked from higher ground and on their flank by the Roman cavalry, which rode down the hill and charged them vigorously, the Celtic infantry were cut to pieces where they stood, their cavalry taking to flight.[11]

Thus it seems that both Consuls had a hand in the tactics that led to the Roman victory; Atilius for recognizing the importance of taking control of the hill top which would give the Romans access to the Gallic flank, and Aemilius for having the presence of mind to send reinforcements to the hill top when it seemed that Atilius had overreached himself and placed his position in jeopardy. In the end, despite the disjointed start to the battle, the Roman emerged totally victorious, with the defeated Gauls trapped between three Roman forces and annihilated. Polybius, supported by other sources, places the total Gallic dead at 40,000, with 10,000 taken prisoner; the most comprehensive Roman victory over the Gauls in Roman history to date.[12] Given that our sources stated that the Gallic forces were 70,000 strong (50,000 infantry and 20,000 cavalry, see above), this must mean that some 20,000 Gauls escaped. Of the Gaesatae chieftains, Concolitanus was taken prisoner and Aneroëstus fled, but committed suicide rather than be taken prisoner.

The Battle of Telamon (225 BC) – Non-Polybian Versions

Although Polybius preserves by far the best account, written less than 100 years later and based on first-hand accounts, a number of other sources provide shorter versions of the campaign, some of which add some interesting details or variations. Both Diodorus and Orosius offer short accounts of the campaign and the Battle of Telamon; both are remarkably similar:

> The Celts and Gauls, having assembled a force of 200,000 men, joined battle with the Romans and in the first combat were victorious. In a second attack they were again victorious, and even killed one of the Roman Consuls. The Romans, who for their part had seven hundred thousand infantry and seventy thousand cavalry, after suffering these two defeats, won a decisive victory in the third engagement. They slew forty thousand men and took the rest captive, with the result that the chief prince of the enemy slashed his own throat and the prince next in rank to him was taken alive.[13]

Battle was joined near Arretium [modern Arezzo]. The Consul Atilius was killed and his 800,000 Romans, after part of their number were cut down fled, even though the slaughter on their side ought not to have panicked them, for historians record that only 3,000 of them were killed.[14]

After this a second battle was fought against the Gauls in which at least 40,000 of them were slaughtered.[15]

Both sources seem to make the same mistake on the Roman numbers, interpreting Polybius' figures for total available manpower as the number of soldiers Rome had in the field, and Orosius seems to believe that all eight hundred thousand Roman soldiers fled the field. Diodorus interestingly has three battles in his campaign; two Roman defeats and a victory. However he states that a Consul (Atilius) was killed in the second battle, which indicates that both sources, or their source, separated the Battle of Telamon into two separate battles; the cavalry action on the hill and the infantry clash, the former of which he believes to have been a Roman defeat. Similarly Orosius has separated the battle into two, with Atilius being killed in a defeat, followed by a victory.

It is interesting to see how the narrative of this battle has evolved over time, with Atilius' action evolving into a Roman defeat, which was then avenged at Telamon, rather than being seen as two parts of the same battle. Ancient historians seemed to have judged Atilius poorly, mostly for being killed in battle, which then discredited his actions on the hill. As it was, it was his tactical move to secure the hill for the Roman cavalry which proved to be the turning point of the battle, securing Roman victory, though he needed Aemilius' force to secure control of the hill, having seemingly overstretched his own position. Despite his short and garbled account, Orosius is the only one to provide us with a figure for the Roman dead; three thousand as opposed to the forty thousand killed on the Gallic side.

The theme of Atilius' role being downgraded as time passed can be seen in the account preserved by Eutropius, who erases him altogether:

> When Lucius Aemilius was Consul, a vast force of the Gauls crossed the Alps; but all Italy united in favour of the Romans; and it is recorded by Fabius the historian, who was present in that war, that there were eight hundred thousand men ready for the contest. Affairs, however, were brought to a successful termination by the Consul alone; forty thousand of the enemy were killed, and a triumph decreed to Aemilius.[16]

Here Eutropius goes out of his way to state that it was Aemilius alone who was responsible for the Roman victory. Florus too has a short account of the war, which although severely lacking in detail, states that it was Aemilius who defeated the Gauls.[17] The only exception to this trend is Pliny, who does not provide detail of the campaign, but does comment on Aemilius and Atilius raising nearly 800,000 men (again a misreading of Polybius, who stated that that number were available, not mobilized.[18] Plutarch comments on the early years of the war without even mentioning either Consul of 225 BC:

> The first conflicts of this war brought great victories and also great disasters to the Romans, and led to no sure and final conclusion. [19]

The figure of 40,000 Gallic dead is a common one throughout all accounts of the battle. Even Jerome preserves the figure in an entry.[20] Dio has a fragment on the Gallic character, which may reveal some small additional detail about the battle:

> The Gauls became dejected on seeing that the Romans had already seized the most favourable positions.[21]

Zonaras, however, preserves an interesting variation on the campaign, no doubt mirroring the original account of Dio:

> The barbarians plundered some towns, but at last a great storm occurred in the night, and they suspected that Heaven was against them. Consequently they lost heart, and falling into a panic, attempted to find safety in flight. Regulus pursued them and brought on an engagement with the rear-guard in which he was defeated and lost his life. Aemilius occupied a hill and remained quiet. The Gauls in turn occupied another hill, and for several days both sides were inactive; then the Romans, through anger at what had taken place, and the barbarians, from arrogance born of their victory, charged down from the heights and came to blows. For a long time the battle was evenly fought, but finally the Romans surrounded the others with their cavalry, cut them down, seized their camp, and recovered the spoils.[22]

Here we have some significant differences. The first notable one concerns the early Gallic campaigns, which ignores the Roman defeat at Faesulae and has the Gauls turning back due to divine omens. Next we have the role of Regulus, who again is relegated to a supporting role, killed fighting the Gallic rearguard, which is interesting as he actually lay in the path of the Gauls and was attacked by an advance contingent of Gallic cavalry, whilst it was Aemilius who was to their rear. Dio again separates the two engagements, this time inserting a number of days between the clashes. During the final battle, again unnamed, both sides occupied opposing hills and then charged at each other, though again the battle is won by the Roman cavalry.

This is a fascinating example of the divergences we see in the ancient sources. If we did not have the account of Polybius, then it would be Zonaras who provided the most detail. We would conclude that there were indeed two final battles to the campaign, separated by a period of time, with Atilius and Aemilius not joining up their forces and Atilius dying in battle first. Given this disparity, it does beg the question how many other accounts of Roman battles and campaigns we have which are similarly skewed towards one version without us even being aware of it.

The Invasion of Gallic Italy (225 BC)

Following the battle, it seems that Aemilius did not rest on his victory. According to Polybius he sent the spoils of the battle to Rome, for his subsequent Triumph, made arrangements to return the recovered plunder the Gauls had taken from Etruria and then pressed on northwards to invade Gallic northern Italy and attack the lands of the Boii themselves. This shows the complete reversal in the relationship between the Romans and the Gauls which had taken place after just the one battle. The victory at Telamon had been so complete, and had seen the cream of the Boii, Insubres and Taurisci tribes and their Gaesatae allies wiped out, that the Romans suddenly felt strong enough to launch an assault on the Gallic lands themselves.

This assault on the Boian lands seems to have been a punishment raid accompanied by massive Roman looting. Polybius states that Aemilius' legions were able to 'pillage to their hearts content'.[23] Nevertheless, there were strong tactical reasons for this assault. As Polybius had previously stated, the Boii and Insubres had left a portion of their force behind to guard their northern flank against Rome's allies, the Veneti and Cenomani. The speed of this invasion built on the element of surprise, following up the news of the total Gallic defeat at Telamon, and would have been a powerful statement to the Boii and the other Gallic tribes, allies and enemies alike, that although the invasion may have rocked Rome and even led to a defeat, Rome was ultimately the militarily superior power in Italy.

Polybius states that Aemilius marched through Liguria on the way to the lands of the Boii (see Map 5). We are not made aware of any specific issues with the Ligurians, but a Gallic invasion of this size into Roman Italy was bound to have stirred them up, given the war fought by Rome in Liguria a decade previously (as seen in Chapter Three). Aemilius skilfully built upon the Roman victory at Telamon by stamping Roman power across northern Italy, bringing the clear implications and message of this victory home to the Gauls in typically forthright Roman fashion. His swift actions here seem to have secured the victory won at Telamon.

Neither Polybius, nor any of the other sources who mention this campaign (Diodorus and Zonaras), provide much detail of the campaign itself and we are not aware of any major battles with the remaining Boian forces. Diodorus provides the only detail of the fighting:

> After this exploit [Telamon] Aemilius, now become proconsul, overran the territory of the Gauls and Celts, captured many cities and fortified places, and sent back to Rome an abundance of booty.[24]

The Boii seemingly avoided any open engagement using their remaining forces and retreated to their cities and strongholds. After spending the rest of the year attacking and pillaging the key Boian towns and forts, Aemilius and his legions returned to Rome in triumph.

The Triumph and role of L. Aemilius Papus

Aemilius returned to Rome to a well-deserved Triumph in 224 BC. His Triumph was adorned with the captives from the defeated Gallic tribes, who were paraded on the Capitol. For the Romans, this must have been a seminal moment, with the Capitol, scene of Rome's defiance in the face of Gallic destruction, being at the centre of the celebration of the defeat of the Gallic tribes. Dio relates the following story:

Aemilius on conquering the Insubres celebrated a triumph, and in it conveyed the foremost captives clad in armour up to the Capitol, making jests at their expense because he had heard that they had sworn not to remove their breastplates until they had mounted to the Capitol.[25]

As stated earlier, we have no way of knowing if this Gallic oath was true or not, but the Romans believed that the Gauls would only have settled for a second sacking of Rome. This Triumph and Aemilius' gesture reinforced the almost ceremonial ending of the Gallic threat to Roman power in Italy, and ultimately to Rome itself. This was the last time that Rome would fear the Gallic threat in Italy.

The Triumph is a good place to assess the crucial role of L. Aemilius Papus, both in this war and in Roman history. As we have already discussed, Aemilius came from a distinguished patrician family with a connection to fighting Gauls. Aemilius' victory at Telamon would have turned him into one of the most celebrated generals of his day and ensured that he was elected to the next available Censorship, in 220 BC (along with C. Flaminius). This appears to have been the end of his military career; following his Censorship, he is only mentioned once again, in 216 BC as part of a special Senatorial financial commission.

However, his fame does not seem to have translated into familial security for the Aemilii Papi, as we have only two references to other members of the family during the Second Punic War and then no trace for the rest of the Republic. We find an M. Aemilius Papus in 210 BC dying whilst holding the obscure religious office of *Curio Maximus*. The other was another L. Aemilius Papus, the son of the Consul of 225 BC, who was a Praetor fighting in the Second Punic War in 205 BC. He rose no higher than Praetor and we find him referred to again dying whilst holding religious office in 172 BC.[26] After this there are no further recorded traces of the family.

This eclipsing of his family, however, should not obscure the achievements of the man himself. On two occasions he had to come to the rescue of his fellow commanders who rushed into battle against the Gallic tribes single-handed, rather than waiting to link up with additional Roman forces, in order to face the Gauls with matching military strength. On the first occasion, at the Battle of Faesulae, he was too late to save the Roman Army from being defeated, but was able to rescue it from annihilation. His arrival was greatly responsible for the Gallic decision to turn away from Rome and return north, albeit aided by dissension amongst the Gallic tribes. Nonetheless, he was originally stationed at Ariminum on the Tyrrhenian coast and had to march across the Apennines to reach western Italy. His timely arrival rescued the situation and prevented a Roman defeat from becoming a disaster.

On the second occasion, he came to the aid of his consular colleague, Atilius Regulus, who had rashly attacked the oncoming Gauls. Although Atilius' tactics were sound, it does seem that he overstretched his forces and placed his cavalry, with himself at the head, in an exposed position, which not only cost the Romans the element of surprise, but caused him to be cut off and ultimately overrun and killed. It was only the timely arrival of Aemilius' cavalry that secured the hill and eventually the victory.

Aemilius' third major contribution was in the Battle of Telamon itself, which was initiated by his colleague but won by him. His actions secured the hill for the Romans, which was to prove vital to the overall result. It was his attack that proved so deadly against the Gaesatae during the battle. We do not know how the two Roman armies communicated, or who took command of Atilius' army after his death, but the overall co-ordination must have fallen to Aemilius, as would the decision and timing of the cavalry attack from the hill on the Gallic flank, which proved the decisive blow.

His fourth contribution came in the swift manner in which he built upon the victory, taking the offensive and invading the Gallic territories in northern Italy. He seems to have travelled through Liguria to ensure their compliance and snuff out any potential rebellion caused by the Gallic invasion. He then invaded the territory of the Boii and devastated the region, putting Rome in the ascendancy. He topped this off with a Triumph in which Gallic prisoners were paraded on the Capitol, laying to rest the ghost of the Gallic sack and the fear of the Gauls.

Unfortunately, Aemilius has faded from the collective historical consciousness, certainly of modern Roman historians. His victories are from a period which is sandwiched between the more noted Punic Wars and suffers from a lack of surviving sources. Nevertheless, we must not let this obscure the man's achievements, both in the short and the long term. It was primarily thanks to him that the Romans were able to defeat one of the greatest Gallic invasions and threats to Roman power in Italy, and could finally gain the ascendancy in the two centuries long-struggle for northern Italy. Given that all future Roman success is built on this foundation,

Rome owed Aemilius a great deal and his place in Roman history should be acknowledged by all.

In contrast stands the figure of C. Atilius Regulus, whose reputation seems to have become deliberately obscured as time passed. Son of a famous father, who also was defeated in battle, Atilius' role in this campaign is a mixed one. To begin with, he was on the island of Sardinia when the Gauls invaded Roman territory via the relatively undefended western flank of Italy. Although the decision may have been the Senate's, his army was still engaged on Sardinia when the invasion happened. It also meant that he would not have been able to come to the aid of Aemilius in eastern Italy had the Gauls invaded there as expected. Perhaps this role played on his mind when he did reach Italy and came face-to-face with the Gallic army. Despite the Gauls heading north, he rushed to engage them, without apparently finding out where his colleague was or making an attempt to link up with him. His choice of battlefield at Telamon seems to have been ideal, including securing the hill overlooking the road on which to ambush the Gauls. However, he seem to have overstretched himself and become isolated with his cavalry, losing the element of surprise and nearly being overrun, which ultimately cost him his life. As we have seen, as time passed, his role in the battle and the war were written out, in favour of his more successful colleague.

The Atilii Reguli seem also to have suffered from a similar obscurity that shrouded the Aemilii Papi. Regulus' older brother Marcus, consul of 227 BC, went on to hold a second consulship in 217 BC, replacing C. Flaminius following his death at the Battle of Lake Trasimene, seemingly adjudged to be a safe pair of hands in a crisis. The only other recorded Atilii Reguli was also in the Second Punic War; another M. Atilius Regulus, possibly the son of the consul of 227 and 217 BC, who held a Praetorship in 213 BC and further minor military roles until 210 BC.[27] After this, there is no trace of the Atilii Reguli again in the Republic, a rapid fall from grace for a family which boasted of four generations of Consuls in the fourth and third centuries. Ironically, as Caius' reputation in defeat was increasingly written out of Roman history, that of his noble father, also defeated in battle, rose as an exemplar of Roman virtue in the face of adversity.

Summary

The year 225 BC saw one of the gravest threats that faced the Republic and ended in one of its greatest victories, not just of the period to date, but of the whole Republic. In just one battle the whole balance of power in Italy, between the Gallic north and the Roman centre and south, swung decisively in Rome's favour; never again would the Gauls invade the Roman Federation.

Yet as we have seen, the Romans once again managed to snatch victory from the jaws of defeat and the campaign saw a number of near disastrous Roman mistakes. Despite expecting the Gallic invasion, they assumed that the Gauls would invade from the north-east and left the north-western flank under-defended. This allowed the Gauls to rampage through Etruria unchecked and advance towards Rome.

Despite deploying their forces intelligently, with two main Consular armies, one Praetorian in reserve and a force to guard Rome itself, on two separate occasions Roman commanders rushed to give battle alone, without waiting to join forces and fight on equal terms. This exposes a flaw which continued throughout the Republic; a desire by Roman commanders to gain personal glory over the good of the state. Such a flaw led to some of the greatest Roman defeats in defending Italy; against Hannibal at Cannae and the Cimbri and Teutones at Arausio.

In both cases, disaster was averted thanks to the calm generalship of one man, L. Aemilius Papus, who arrived on the battlefields having marched his army to link up with his colleagues. On the first occasion, at Faesulae, he was just too late to avert a Roman defeat, but ensured that the Gauls could not march towards Rome without facing stiff opposition. On the second occasion, at Telamon, he was able to salvage the situation and win the battle.

However, unlike the later Roman sources, we must not forget the great victory at the battle of Telamon was not simply the work of one man, but had two architects, both Consuls; L. Aemilius Papus and C. Atilius Regulus. It was Regulus who chose the battleground and the tactics, and it was his battle plan that led to victory, albeit needing Aemilius to execute it after Atilius overstretched his position. Even though the two men were not consciously working together, ultimately they brought victory to Rome, even if Atilius' rashness cost him his life and his place in the history books.

The other notable aspect of the Battle of Telamon is the role the Roman cavalry played. Traditionally, the Roman cavalry are seen as having a subservient, far lesser part in Roman military victories than on this occasion. It was the cavalry which secured the hill at Telamon and it was their intervention, sweeping into the Gallic flank, which secured the Roman victory.

This period also saw the full might of the Roman military machine and the unrivalled potential of the Roman series of alliances in terms of available manpower. According to Polybius, the Romans had the potential to field nearly 800,000 men, should the need arise, though ever mobilizing that many men at zone time would have been practically impossible. Moving away from the accuracy of Polybius' (or Fabius Pictor's) figure, the point Polybius was trying to make is that this period showed the unparalleled potential of the Roman military machine, especially if the Romans were able to end the constant threat on their doorstep from Gallic Northern Italy.

However, despite the fact that the Battle of Telamon and Aemilius' follow-up campaigns had switched the momentum towards Rome, it remained to be seen whether the Roman commanders who followed him could build on this momentum and win the subsequent war for Rome.

Chapter Eight

The Gallic War III – The Roman Invasion of Northern Italy (224–223 BC)

The Roman Invasion of Gallic Italy 224 BC

The Boian Campaign of 224 BC

Given that Proconsular commands were uncommon in this period,[1] command of the war turned to the Consuls of 224 BC, T. Manlius Torquatus and Q. Fulvius Flaccus. For both men this was their second Consulship, indicating again that the electorate, such as it was, chose men with a proven track record. Torquatus had been a Consul in 235 BC and had celebrated a Triumph in Sardinia (as seen in Chapter Two), whilst Flaccus had been a Consul in 237 BC and had campaigned against Gauls and Ligurians (as seen in Chapter Three). Although the pair had been Consuls in separate years, they were partners in the Censorship of 231 BC, which gave them a proven track record of working together, something that perhaps had been lacking the previous year.[2]

With the Gallic invasion crushed, and with Aemilius Papus celebrating a historic Triumph over the Gauls on the Capitol, it seems that the Senate decided to build on this victory and continue the war to its logical conclusion, namely the Roman subjugation of Gallic Northern Italy. This momentous decision and the details of the initial campaign of 224 BC are unfortunately almost entirely lost to us, due to Polybius devoting only a few sentences to it and the other surviving sources preserving only a few meagre details. Nevertheless, what details they do preserve paint an important picture of the campaign this year, which contained a notable milestone, namely the first Roman armies to cross the River Po (see Map 6). Below are the key sources for the campaign this year:

> This success encouraged the Romans to hope that they would be able entirely to expel the Celts from the plain of the Po and both the Consuls

of the next year, Quintus Fulvius and Titus Manlius, were sent against them with a formidable expeditionary force. They surprised and terrified the Boii, compelling them to submit to Rome, but the rest of the campaign had no practical results whatever, owing to the very heavy rains, and an epidemic which broke out among them.[3]

In the following year, the Consuls Manlius Torquatus and Fulvius Flaccus were the first to lead Roman legions across the Po. There they fought with the Insubrian Gauls, killing 23,000 of them and capturing 6,000 more.[4]

The Romans now not only gained the entire territory of the Boii, but also crossed the Po for the first time against the Insubres, whose country they proceeded to ravage.[5]

For the first time, Roman armies crossed the Po and the Gallic Insubres were defeated in a series of battles.[6]

As can be seen, we have few details to work with and those we do have seem somewhat at odds with each other. Despite the lack of details, it seems clear that the Consuls had been tasked with crushing the Gallic tribes that had invaded Roman territory, namely the Boii and Insubres. The invasion and conquest of the Boii was the more expected, as this would take the Romans up to the River Po and would end a long-standing enmity between the two sides. The Boii were clearly never going to accept the territory they had lost to Rome and were always going to be an implacable enemy.

We are not told the size of the Roman armies that were deployed this year, but Polybius labels them as 'formidable'.[7] Of the armies raised the previous year, we know that the praetorian army was heavily defeated, though we have no casualty figures, and are told that the two Consular armies only suffered 3,000 casualties at Telamon. Of the other forces, we can reasonably assume that the reserve force guarding Rome was stood down, though the army of Gallic allies may well have been used during this campaign. Given the numbers of soldiers raised the previous year to defend Italy, the Romans potentially had a huge force at their disposal with which to subjugate Gallic Northern Italy, numbering around 100,000 if not more, though we are not told how many were used for this campaign.

The other key issue we are not told is how the two Consuls were deployed. Working from what little narrative we have, it seems clear that the Romans attacked the Boii first and only then moved on to the Insubres. However, apart from that we have no details of how the two Consuls deployed their armies.

Common practice would assume that two Consular armies were deployed, but whether they acted separately or in concert is not known. It is always possible that the Romans deployed a similar tactic to the previous years, and had one army push into the Boian territory via the west and one the east.

Again we have no details of the Boian campaign, but the two sources that mention them, Polybius and Zonaras, indicate that both Consuls were able to defeat the Boii relatively easily and still have time to deploy across the River Po.[8] Polybius speaks of the Romans surprising the Boii. Given that their armies were crushed at Telamon, and that Aemilius had ravaged their territory the year previously, we get the impression that the Boii were a spent force. It is possible that the Boii had hoped that the Romans would have been satisfied by Aemilius' campaign and not take the offensive again, but the invasion the previous year seems to have stirred up the Romans' emotions around the Gallic sack and given them the imperative never to allow it to happen again.

This, combined with the huge numbers of Romans under arms and the relative Boian weakness, made a Roman war of subjugation almost inevitable. Given the paucity of our sources, we do not hear of any embassies made by the Boii to the Romans seeking terms. If there were, then it is clear that they would have been rebuffed. In any event, the whole of the Boian territory fell in less than year and the Romans now found themselves on the banks of the River Po, facing the Insubres.

An Insubrian Campaign in 224 BC?

With the Boii defeated, it seems the Consuls were authorised to cross the River Po for the first time in Roman history with an army and invade the territory of the Insubres. As can be seen from Map Six, with the Boii conquered and the Cenomani and Veneti allied to Rome, the Insubres were the only major Gallic power south of the Alps who remained hostile to Rome. Thus began the Insubrian campaign of the Gallic War and the first concerted effort to push Roman power (if not territory) in Italy to the Alps.

Unfortunately our surviving sources provide few details of this first and momentous campaign. The details they do provide seem to be at odds with each other (notably between the testimony of Polybius and that of Orosius, which was likely based on Livy):

But the rest of the campaign had no practical results whatever, owing to the very heavy rains, and an epidemic which broke out among them.[9]

There they fought with the Insubrian Gauls, killing 23,000 of them and capturing 6,000 more.[10]

Thus we can see that according to Polybius the two Consuls achieved little of note after crossing the Po due to the heavy rains and an outbreak of disease, and thus returned home without major incident. However, according to Orosius the Consuls fought a major battle against the Insubrians. It must also be pointed out that Polybius never states that the Consuls of 224 BC actually crossed the Po and invaded the Insubrian territory. Thus our nearest chronological source – and a usually reliable one – ends his campaign for 224 BC, possibly with the Consuls still in Boian territory, whilst Orosius (a fifth century AD writer) was adamant that it was these Consuls who first crossed the Po and fought a victorious battle against the Insubrians.

The other surviving sources are little help. Neither Zonaras nor the Periochae of Livy identifies the Consuls of 224 BC as the men who crossed the Po, nor that they won a victory. Neither of their brief accounts can be dated to 224 as opposed to 223 BC with any certainty. It is also pertinent to note that there is no record of a Triumph being granted for either man in the Fasti Triumphales in this year, which is odd given the victory across the Po. This had led many, including Walbank, to speculate whether this invasion and battle actually took place, or whether it was a later annalistic invention, repeated by Orosius.[11]

We do know that the Consuls were out of Rome for a considerable period, owing to the fact that a Dictator had to be elected to hold the Consular elections for 223 BC.[12] We also know that the Consuls did not receive a Triumph for their conquest of the Boii, although this probably had more to do with the lack of a set piece battle. We must also consider that Polybius' account does skip over the campaigns of this year in an effort to recount the more 'interesting' Consulship of Caius Flaminius the following year. The counter to this argument is that there may have been little of interest to report because there were no set piece battles to recount, merely a slow grinding conquest. Polybius' account was also light on detail of Aemilius' campaigns in the Boian territory the previous year.

We are left with the problem that this important first Roman campaign across the Po and the first battle in Insubrian territory is not supported by our closest chronological source. Ultimately it is a matter of personal choice. However, we have Orosius' explicit testimony that it was these Consuls who crossed the Po and fought a battle against the Insubrians. This testimony would have been based on a solid annalist source, probably Livy, and is not explicitly contradicted by Polybius. The lack of a Triumph is curious, but there may have been reasons behind this which we are not made aware of by our few surviving sources. Whilst the numbers certainly look impressive, if they are accurate, it seems that this victory had little wider impact on the war itself.

By the end of 224 BC, the Romans had defeated the Boii, pushed Roman territory up to the Po and had most likely crossed the Po itself and invaded Insubrian territory. The Romans now had clearly set their goal of total domination of all of Italy below the Alps, and it would fall to the Consuls of 223 BC to continue this work. Whilst the Boii had clearly been exhausted by the defeat at Telamon and the campaigns of Aemilius in 225 BC, the Insubrians appeared to have recovered and were ready to face the might of Rome once again.

The Insubrian Campaign of 223 BC

The Consuls of 223 BC were C. Flaminius and P. Furius Philus. Their election represented an interesting change from the previous year, as neither man had been Consul before. We have no explicit details of any military experience prior to their election, though Flaminius is known to us from his Tribunate of 232 BC, when he attempted to railroad the Senate over the matter of land distribution in the *ager gallicus*. We also know that Flaminius was one of the new Praetors for 227 BC and the first official governor of Sicily, though we are not told of any military campaigning. Interestingly, as will be seen shortly by other events in Rome, it seems that Flaminius remained more of a popular choice than a Senatorial one. Nevertheless, the election of two men to their first Consulship to contest this war perhaps indicates the degree of confidence the Romans felt at the way in which the war had turned to their advantage.

However, as Polybius reveals in a more detailed narrative, it seems that this confidence may have been misplaced:

Next year's Consuls, however, Publius Furius and Caius Flaminius, again invaded the Celtic territory, through the country of the Anares who dwelt not far from Massilia. Having admitted this tribe to their friendship, they crossed into the territory of the Insubres, near the junction of the Po and Adda. Both in crossing and in encamping on the other side, they suffered some loss, and at first remained on the spot, but later made a truce and evacuated the territory under its terms.[13]

The campaign opened with a Roman invasion of the Insubrian territories, thrusting north at the confluence of the River Po and the Adda, between what became Placentia (see Map 6). As Walbank points out, we must discount the reference to Massilia as showing the limits of Polybius's knowledge of the geography of the region. As Walbank also says this invasion route would have taken the Romans through Liguria and across the Apennines north of modern Genoa.[14] We have little information on the Anares tribe, but again we can see that the neutral tribes of the region were allying with Rome.

Although the surviving sources do not mention any conflict en-route, the fact that P. Furius was awarded a Triumph for fighting the Ligurians does seem to indicate that the Romans had to engage with them, to some level, during their passage northwards, in a campaign which is lost to our surviving sources. It seems that the campaign by Aemilius Papus in 225 BC had not entirely pacified the region.

It seems that the Insubres were a far greater challenge to Rome than the Boii and managed to force Flaminius and Furius to retreat from Insubrian territory. We are given no further details on these losses or even how they were sustained; possibly a skirmish, rather than a full-scale battle, but it does show the strength of Insubrian resistance.[15] This strength may have been due to the Insubres being forced to leave behind a substantial portion of the fighting forces to defend against a potential attack from the pro-Roman tribes, especially the Cenomani (as seen in Chapter Six). This may well explain why the Boii were so exhausted after Telamon but the Insubres were not.

The Consuls did not retreat southwards back across the Po, but pushed eastwards across the River Oglio (a tributary of the Po) into the territory of the Cenomani, who were recent Roman allies (see Map 6). This raises the possibility of whether the Consuls' campaign was based on a joint invasion of Insubrian territory from the Consular armies to the south and the Cenomanic armies from east. If this was the plan, then it seems that the Insubrians must have learnt of it and struck the Romans as they crossed, to prevent the two armies meeting up, forcing the Consuls to retreat into safe (allied) territory, regroup, and try again.

> After a circuitous march of some days, they crossed the River Clusius [Chiese] and reached the country of the Cenomani, who were their allies, and accompanied by them, again invaded from the district at the foot of the Alps the plains of the Insubres and began to lay the country waste and pillage their dwellings. The chieftains of the Insubres, seeing that the Romans adhered to their purpose of attacking them, decided to try their luck in a decisive battle.[16]

Thus the Consuls invaded the Insubrian territories for a second time, this time from the east with a Consular and an allied army.

Battle of the River Clusius (224 BC)?

We are not given the location for the battle, only that it took place on a river. Walbank has speculated that the river in question was the Clusius (a branch of the Oglio). If this is the case, then it appears that the Insubres moved to meet the Romans fairly quickly after they crossed into their territory, which is not the impression one gets from Polybius' narrative when he talks of the Roman laying waste to Insubrian territory. However, given the earlier clash it does seem that the Insubrians had already mustered their forces to meet the Roman invasion and had clearly adopted a principle of attacking the Romans at the earliest opportunity. Therefore a clash somewhere on the Clusius does seem the most logical. As well as detailing both sides' preparations, Polybius does give us some detail as to the respective numbers of both sides; 50,000 Insubrians and fewer Romans and Cenomani:

> Collecting all their forces in one place, they took down the golden standards called "immovable" from the temple of Minerva, and having made all other necessary preparations, boldly took up a menacing position opposite the enemy. They were about fifty thousand strong. The Romans, on the one hand, as they saw that the enemy were much more numerous than themselves, were desirous of employing also

the forces of their Celtic allies, but on the other hand, taking into consideration Gallic fickleness and the fact that they were going to fight against those of the same nation as these allies, they were wary of asking such men to participate in an action of such vital importance. Finally, remaining themselves on their side of the river, they sent the Celts who were with them across it, and demolished the bridges that crossed the stream, firstly as a precaution against their allies, and secondly to leave themselves no hope of safety except in victory, the river, which was impassable, lying in their rear. After taking these measures they prepared for battle.[17]

The Consuls Flaminius and Furius decided to go into battle against the Insubrians having divested themselves of their allies, lessening their numbers further and with the river at their backs, having cut off any means of escape. At best this was a bold move, at worst foolhardy. Nevertheless, it does seem that the Consuls had made preparations for fighting the enemy:

The Romans are thought to have managed matters very skilfully in this battle, their tribunes having instructed them how they should fight, both as individuals and collectively. For they had observed from former battles that Gauls in general are most formidable and spirited in their first onslaught, while still fresh, and that, from the way their swords are made, as has been already explained, only the first cut takes effect; after this they at once assume the shape of a strigil, being so much bent both length-wise and side-wise that unless the men are given leisure to rest them on the ground and set them straight with the foot, the second blow is quite ineffectual. The tribunes therefore distributed among the front lines the spears of the triarii who were stationed behind them, ordering them to use their swords instead only after the spears were done with.[18]

Walbank again provides an excellent analysis of the validity of the Polybius statements on the Gallic swords and, combined with the archaeological evidence, finds them lacking.[19] Walbank argues that the Gallic sword was of excellent strength, but was more suited for slashing rather than thrusting. Thus if the Romans could get in closer to the Insubres, then they (the Insubrians) would not be able to slash with their swords as effectively.

Polybius gives credit for this tactical innovation to the military Tribunes rather than the Consuls in command, a point Walbank puts down to a biased pro-Senatorial source used by Polybius.[20] It is hard to imagine that the Tribunes would take this upon themselves, or even be allowed to do so, without the prior approval of the Consuls. Nevertheless, despite the precarious position the Consuls adopted, they prepared their troops well to fight the Insubres:

> They then drew up opposite the Celts in order of battle and engaged. Upon the Gauls slashing first at the spears and making their swords unserviceable the Romans came to close quarters, having rendered the enemy helpless by depriving them of the power of raising their hands and cutting, which is the peculiar and only stroke of the Gauls, as their swords have no points. The Romans, on the contrary, instead of slashing continued to thrust with their swords which did not bend, the points being very effective. Thus, striking one blow after another on the breast or face, they slew the greater part of their adversaries. This was solely due to the foresight of the tribunes, the Consul Flaminius being thought to have mismanaged the battle by deploying his force at the very edge of the river-bank and thus rendering impossible a tactical movement peculiar to the Romans, as he left the lines no room to fall back gradually. For had the troops been even in the slightest degree pushed back from their ground during the battle, they would have had to throw themselves into the river, all owing to their general's blunder. However, as it was, they gained a decisive victory by their own skill and valour, as I said, and returned to Rome with a quantity of booty and many trophies.[21]

Polybius does not give the casualty figures for the battle, but we find them in Orosius, who states that 9,000 Insubrians were killed and 17,000 captured.[22] We can see that Polybius does not appear to rate Flaminius' military skills very highly. He is critical of his positioning, leaving no room for tactical manoeuvring to the rear, as is customarily used in manipular tactics. The victory is solely ascribed to the tactical innovation by the military Tribunes and the bravery of the soldiers. Whilst Walbank ascribes Polybius' dislike of Flaminius to a pro-Senatorial source, it is clear that he, and his fellow Consul, took an extraordinary risk in positioning his army as he did. Firstly, they positioned the Roman Army with their backs to the river, which meant in the event they were turned the entire army would be massacred, as happened at some of Rome's greatest defeats such as Lake Trasimene and Arausio (the former being commanded by Flaminius himself).[23]

This was supported by the destruction of the bridges across the river, meaning that no one would be able to escape such a defeat. Thirdly, the Consuls sent their Cenomani allies to the other side of the river, reducing their numbers further and negating the whole point of co-ordinated action with their allies. Thus Polybius had some justification for his belittling of Flaminius' abilities. Against this must be weighed the tactical innovation the Consuls introduced to adjust the Roman fighting style to neutralise the Gallic method of warfare, which seems to have been highly successful. In denying the Gauls the room to slash, they blunted the initial Gallic attack and drove them back, inflicting heavy losses on the Insubres. As well as this, the Roman Army knew that it had nowhere to retreat to and that being turned would result in a massacre, which could only serve to make the Romans fight harder.

Another point to note is that Polybius has completely neglected the other Consul, P. Furius Philus (as does Walbank). We are given no details as to how he conducted himself during the battle or even the campaign as a whole. However, this is not the greatest of Polybius' omissions. In the other surviving sources which detail this campaign, one event looms large, perhaps larger than the battle itself, and this is a letter sent by the Senate to the Consuls prior to the battle, ordering them not to engage the enemy but to return to Rome.

The Recall of the Consuls

The origins of this unusual incident lie in numerous strange portents and omens which were reported throughout Italy, which later sources describe in ever-increasing detail, as can be seen by both Zonaras and Plutarch.[24] These portents were apparently leapt on by Flaminius' enemies in the Senate, many of whom would not have forgiven his for his conduct during his Tribunate of 232 BC (as seen in Chapter Three and Appendix Three) and his land distribution policy, and argued that the Consuls' election was invalid due to these ill omens (albeit after the event). The Senate apparently sent a letter to the Consuls ordering them not to engage the enemy, in the face of such ill omens, and return to Rome, where it would be judged whether they had been elected Consul inauspiciously. The later the surviving source, the more emphatic this illegality of election becomes:

> On account of these portents and also because some declared that the consuls had been illegally chosen, they summoned them home. The consuls received the letter, but did not open it immediately, since they were just on the point of beginning the war; instead, they joined battle first and came out victorious. After the battle the letter was read, and Furius was for obeying promptly; but Flaminius was elated over the victory and kept pointing out that it showed their election to have been proper, and he insisted that in their jealousy of him the nobles were even misrepresenting the will of the gods.[25]

> ...for he remembered his (Flaminius') former controversies with the Senators, which he had waged war when a Tribune of the Plebs and later as Consul, in the first place about his Consulship, which they had tried to annul.[26]

> He [Flaminius] had been made Consul without the confirmation of the auspices, and though both gods and men had sought to recall him for the very battle line, he had not obeyed.[27]

> ...and the priests who watched the flight of birds at the time of the consular elections insisted that when the consuls were proclaimed the omens were inauspicious and baleful for them. At once, therefore, the Senate sent letters to the camp, summoning the Consuls to return to the city with all speed and lay down their office, and forbidding them, while they were still Consuls, to take any steps against the enemy. On receiving these letters, Flaminius would not open them before he had joined battle with the barbarians, routed them, and overrun their country.[28]

To Zonaras (and Dio), there were questions of illegality, whilst by Plutarch's time the Consuls were clearly elected despite poor auspices being observed. One hardly needs to point out the flaw with Plutarch's account; namely why, if these ill omens were observed at the time, the election was allowed to stand and both Consuls were allowed to take command and not recalled until they had invaded Insubrian territory? Livy's two accounts reflect the inconsistencies that still circulated about this incident; firstly, the Senate tried to annul the election, and secondly, Flaminius was elected without confirmation of the auspices. Zonaras' account is far the more likely, that such a rash of ill omens gave Flaminius' enemies in the Senate the excuse to recall him before he had a chance to gain military glory.

There is another surviving source portraying a different picture of Flaminius: the first century AD poet Silius Italicus, who has several odd references to Flaminius and his campaign in his work the Punica, the most relevant ones of which are:

The tribe of the Boii had formerly been attacked by an army under Flaminius; and then he had gained an easy triumph and crushed a fickle and guileless people.[29]

…he [Flaminius] cried in fury: 'Was it thus that you saw me rushing to battle against the Boii, when the great peril of that fearsome horde came against us, and the Tarpeian rock feared a second siege?'[30]

When Flaminius conquered and slew Gargenus, king of the Boii, he had fitted to his own head this famous trophy that no hand could mutilate, and proudly he bore it in all his battles.[31]

…his prowess had been witnessed by brave Flaminius, when with better fortune he fought the Celtic armies and crushed them.[32]

Here we have an interesting twist to the evolution of the image of Flaminius. Far from being the Consul who fought against the auspices or lost at Lake Trasimene, he is the hero who saved Rome from the Boii, crushing the Gauls and defeating a Boian king in battle. Italicus seems to have merged a number of events of this war into one in the form of Flaminius. It was he, not Aemilius Papus, who saved Rome from the Boii, and it was he who killed a Boian general in battle. This last point is an interesting one as we have no other reference to a Gargenus. This could be a reference to the Consul of the following year, M. Claudius Marcellus, who killed a Gallic chieftain in single combat, though the names are different (see below). We can see that Italicus has little apparent interest in historical accuracy, but merely wants to build Flaminius up in order to make his death at the hands of Hannibal more dramatic, and to him all Gauls are Boian. Nevertheless, it is curious to see Flaminius evolve into a tragic hero in Roman poetry, whilst the histories increasingly make him a villain.

The other interesting aspect of the portrayal of this whole incident is the role of Flaminius' colleague, Furius. By Plutarch's time Furius has dropped out of the picture altogether and it is solely about Flaminius. However, there is nothing to suggest that Furius engendered such animosity in the Senate, but the recall would have ruined his career by association. Building on this last point, it is interesting that Zonaras notes that both Consuls refused to read the letter before the battle, but by Plutarch's account it is solely Flaminius who does so. If both Consuls had been tipped off about the letter's contents, as was likely, by allies within the Senate, or even by the messenger, then neither would have been eager to commit treason by directly disobeying a Senatorial order; better to do so by the sin of omission, and pre-empt Admiral Lord Nelson and his famous use of his blind eye to a recall signal some 2,000 years later. Interestingly, Plutarch does refer to Furius in another of his biographies, and here he opposed Flaminius prior to the battle, rather than co-operate in this disobedience:

> The Consul, Caius Flaminius, was daunted by none of these things, for he was a man of a fiery and ambitious nature, and besides, he was elated by great successes which he had won before this, in a manner contrary to all expectation. He had, namely, although the Senate dissented from his plan, and his colleague violently opposed it, joined battle with the Gauls and defeated them.[33]

For both Consuls, the stakes in the battle were even higher as they would have to read the recall letter following the battle and return to Rome, leaving them just this one chance at military glory. Was this the reason that they took such risks with their disposition, or perhaps a contributing factor? We must always remember our earliest surviving source, Polybius, who himself is not unduly positive about Flaminius, has no reference to this incident at all. This is curious to say the least. We can see from the surviving sources that the story becomes more rigid as the years passed, though Livy reflects both traditions. Flaminius' disastrous defeat at the hands of Hannibal at Lake Trasimene would not have helped Roman posterity's view of him. Nevertheless, the absence of this incident in our earliest surviving source means we must treat this recall letter with some caution.

The Truncated Insubrian Campaign of 223 BC

After the battle it seems that the solidarity between the Consuls disappeared. With the battle won, they could answer the recall to Rome, but according to Zonaras (Dio), differences appeared between the men on the timing of their return:

> Consequently he [Flaminius] refused to depart until he had settled the whole business in hand, and he said he would teach the people at home, too, not to be deceived by relying on birds or anything of the sort. So he was anxious to remain where he was, and strove to detain his colleague, but Furius would not heed him. However, since the men who were going to be left behind with Flaminius feared that if left by themselves they might suffer some disaster at the hands of their opponents and begged him to remain for a few days longer; he yielded to their entreaties, but did not take any active part. Flaminius travelled about laying waste the country, reduced a few forts, and bestowed all the spoils upon the soldiers as a means of winning their favour.[34]

It seems that Furius was set to split the Roman Army and return home immediately, leaving Flaminius in the Insubrian territory to continue the war, though again we must exercise caution when dealing with a later source, by which time Flaminius' name was thoroughly blackened. To a more suspicious mind, this story smacks of one which Furius himself would have spread on his return to Rome as to why he did not return immediately; namely that Flaminius did not wish to return immediately and that he did not wish to split and weaken the army. To any student of the late Republic, there are a number of themes which are common to that period, namely a Consul being recalled by political enemies in the Senate and a general not being able to take action due to his soldiers' wishes.

These common late Republican themes may well explain why the story was seized on and embellished by late Republican writers, whilst Polybius, who hailed from a different era of the Republic, ignores them completely.

Whatever the truth, the important aspect from a military point of view is that the Consuls were unable to build upon their victory at the River Clusius and, possibly mirroring events from the year before, withdrew from the territories across the Po, with the Insubrians defeated in battle but still active in the war. On this occasion, however, the Roman campaign had been marred by political infighting amongst the Roman elite, which despite the victory at the River Clusius cost the Romans the momentum that such a success should have brought.

The one crucial aspect that is missing from the details of this year's campaign is a timescale for these events. We are not told how much time occurred between the start of the campaigning season and the Battle of Clusius or exactly how long it took Flaminius to conduct his punitive expedition against the Insubres before the Consuls returned home. Nevertheless, given the narrative we must assume that the campaign was curtailed early in the campaigning season, giving the Insubres time to regroup once more.

The Triumphs of the Consuls

A postscript to these events came when the Consuls returned home to Rome, as detailed by Zonaras and Plutarch, who again preserve differing accounts:

> At length the leaders returned home and were charged by the Senate with disobedience; for Furius also incurred disgrace because of the anger felt against Flaminius. But the populace, in its zeal for Flaminius, opposed the Senate and voted them a Triumph. After celebrating this, the Consuls laid down their office.[35]

> Therefore, when he [Flaminius] returned with much spoil, the people would not go out to meet him, but because he had not at once listened to his summons, and had disobeyed the letters, treating them with insolent contempt, they came near refusing him his triumph, and after his triumph, they compelled him to renounce the Consulship with his colleague, and made him a private citizen.[36]

Once again we can see two different versions of the same event. In Zonaras (based on Dio), both Consuls were charged by the Senate for disobedience and refused Triumphs for their victory at the River Clusius. However, it seems that Flaminius appealed to his popularity with the people of Rome, who voted him and Furius Triumphs, against the Senate's wishes.[37] They then laid down their office. In Plutarch, however, this story has evolved to being the people refusing to meet Flaminius and nearly refusing him a Triumph, and then compelling him to lay down his Consulship. The obvious omissions in Plutarch's account are the role of the Senate and the presence of Furius.

The reality is that both men were awarded Triumphs for the Insubrian campaign, despite its ultimate shortcomings. What is interesting is the nature of the Triumphs they were awarded, as can be seen below from the translated inscriptions of the Triumphal Fasti:

223/2 C. Flaminius C.f. L.n., Consul, over the Gauls, 6 id.Mart. (10 March)

223/2 P. Furius Sp.f. M.n. Philus, Consul, over the Gauls and Ligurians, 4 id.Mart. (12th March)

The most striking aspect is that Flaminius was voted a Triumph over the Gauls whilst his colleague, who is mostly absent from our sources, was voted a Triumph over the Gauls and the Ligurians. The key question is why did Furius receive a Triumph over the Ligurians whilst Flaminius did not? We must remember here that the Triumph was voted for by the people, against the Senate's wishes, and so must have reflected what Flaminius wanted. If there were Ligurians at the Battle of River Clusius, then surely both Consuls would have triumphed over them. There seems to be only one logical conclusion; namely that P. Furius Philo conducted a separate campaign against the Ligurians, most likely at the start of the campaign as the Consuls pushed northwards towards the River Po. This campaign, which must have been a short one, has been omitted from our surviving sources. We have no idea of scale, but it seems more likely that this was a local pacification to ease their route to the north of Italy. With the Triumphs celebrated, the Consuls renounced their office, though again we have no timescales for when this happened, only that the Triumphs were celebrated first. It fell to the Consuls of the following year to continue the prosecution of the Insubrian campaign and oversee its completion.

Chapter Nine

The Gallic War IV – The Battle of Clastidium (222 BC) and Subsequent Campaigns (222–218 BC)

The Insubrian Campaign of 222 BC

Thus the Insubrian War dragged on into another year and saw a third set of Consuls take command. The Consuls of 222 BC were M. Claudius Marcellus and Gn. Cornelius Scipio Calvus. Again neither man had held the Consulship before and nothing is known of their military record prior to their election.

Insubrian Preparations for War and Peace

However, before the new Consuls could take the field, the Insubres sent ambassadors to Rome to sue for peace. We have no way of knowing whether the offer was genuine or whether the Insubres were buying time to rebuild their strength. It is of course possible that both elements were present and the Insubres were seeing if they could find agreeable terms and maintain their independence, whilst simultaneously preparing for the next Roman campaign. Here again we find divergent accounts in our surviving sources:

> Next year the Celts sent ambassadors begging for peace and engaging to accept any conditions, but the new Consuls Marcus Claudius and Cnaeus Cornelius strongly urged that no peace should be granted them.[1]

> Other consuls, Claudius Marcellus and Cnaeus Scipio, chosen in their stead, made an expedition against the Insubres; for the Romans had not granted this people's request for peace.[2]

> Now it has been said that, although the Gauls made many conciliatory proposals, and although the Senate was peaceably inclined, Marcellus tried to provoke the people to continue the war. However, it would seem that even after peace was made Gaesatae renewed the war.[3]

For Polybius and Zonaras (Dio), the Insubres offered terms of peace which were refused by Rome, at the Consuls' urging. This is hardly surprising given that the Consuls would want a career-defining campaign and the Senate would want to avenge the Gallic invasion, and saw the opportunity to end the Gallic threat to Roman Italy once and for all. In Plutarch's account, however, the Senate seemingly accepted the Insubrian offer of peace and a peace was made, which was then broken by the Gaesatae on the Gallic side, with the Consul Marcellus having tried the same thing. Given the circumstances and the clear testimony of Polybius, it is extremely doubtful that peace was made or even considered on the Roman side.

It seems that the Insubres had a similar view to the Romans in terms of this being a defining war to the finish, and that the ambassadors the Insubres sent to Rome were not the only ones they sent out. Other ambassadors were apparently sent to the Rhone to recruit a fresh army of Gaesatae to bolster their numbers. On this occasion we do not know what was offered, but the prospect of plunder was always attractive and the Romans had annexed the Boii and crossed the Po, bringing in their sphere of control far closer to the Gaesatae. In any event, both Polybius and Plutarch agree that an army of 30,000 Gaesatae crossed the Alps and joined the Insubres. We are not given the Insubrian numbers, but Plutarch states that they were greater than the Gaesatae, which puts the total Gallic forces at over 60,000. According to Polybius, this was done in secret and they were held in reserve. waiting to counter the expected Roman thrust.[4]

The Early Campaigns to the Siege of Acerrae

Once again the Consuls took to the field, although we are not given the size of the army they took with them. In all our surviving sources the narrative swiftly moves onto the Roman siege of the Insubrian stronghold of Acerrae. We are not told the route the Consuls took, though we must assume they followed that of the Consuls of the previous year, albeit without the campaigning in Liguria. More importantly, we are not told why the Romans opened their campaign with a siege of Acerrae. This seems to be a change to the tactics of the previous year and it appears as though the Insubrians tempered their natural enthusiasm to give battle and held back. Although neither Polybius nor Plutarch give a location for Acerrae, later sources place it on the banks of the River Addua and equate it with the village of Gera near Pizzighettone (see Map 6).[5]

We must assume that the Consuls crossed the Po, and with no force coming to meet their thrust set upon reducing the Insubrian strongholds, perhaps hoping to force them into battle. Whilst no surviving source provides details of any actions prior to the siege of Acerrae, Zonaras does have the following statement: 'At first the consuls carried on the war together, and were in most case victorious.'[6]

This does seem to indicate the siege of Acerrae was not the opening shot of the campaign, but the latest in a number of engagements. Perhaps the most interesting aspect is the use of the words most commonly translated as 'in most cases'. This indicates that there were occasions in this opening campaign where the Consuls were not successful. With no enemy to fight in open battle, we must assume that the Consuls undertook the destruction of a number of Insubrian strongholds, some with more success than others. In the case of Acerrae, we do know that both Consuls took command and seemingly used their entire army.

If their plan was to force the Insubrians into open battle by trying to break the siege, it failed, as a combined Insubrian–Gaesatae force flanked the Consuls, crossed the Po in force and attacked the town of Clastidium (modern Casteggio) in the territory of the Anares, a recent Roman ally (see Map 6).[7] According to Plutarch, the invading Gallic force numbered 10,000.[8]

The Battle of Clastidium (222 BC)

When the Consuls learned of this incursion, they decided to divide their forces. The bulk of the Roman Army remained with Cornelius Scipio continuing the siege of Acerrae, whilst Marcellus took two-thirds of the cavalry and 600 light infantry and set off after the Gauls who had crossed the Po. Given the numbers involved, it is clear that the Roman priority was the siege of Acerrae, but they could not allow the Gauls to plunder the territory of Roman allies unchecked. Marcellus therefore took the fastest and most mobile elements of the Roman Army and set off to counter the Gallic force.

We have three principal surviving accounts of the battle that ensued, which again differ significantly in terms of emphasis. On the one hand we have the narrative of Zonaras, which paints it as a glorified skirmish with little detail. Next we have Polybius himself, who details a sizeable battle.

Finally we have Plutarch, who paints a grand narrative of an epic clash pitting a small Roman force against a barbarian horde:

At first the consuls carried on the war together, and were in most case victorious; but soon, learning that the allied territory was being plundered, they separated their forces. Marcellus made a quick march against those plundering the land of the allies, but found them no longer there; he then pursued them as they fled, and when they made a stand, overcame them.[9]

On the Consuls learning of this, Marcus Claudius set off in haste with the cavalry and a small body of infantry to relieve the besieged if possible. The Celts, as soon as they were aware of the enemy's arrival, raised the siege and advancing to meet them, drew up in order of battle. When the Romans boldly charged them with their cavalry alone, they at first stood firm, but afterwards, being taken both in the rear and on the flank, they found themselves in difficulties and were finally put to rout by the cavalry unaided, many of them throwing themselves into the river and being swept away by the current, while the larger number were cut to pieces by the enemy.[10]

When Marcellus learned of this, he left his colleague at Acerrae with all the heavy-armed infantry and a third part of the cavalry, while he himself, taking with him the rest of the cavalry and the most lightly equipped men-at-arms to the number of six hundred, marched, without halting in his course day or night, until he came upon the ten thousand Gaesatae near the place called Clastidium, a Gallic village which not long before had become subject to the Romans. There was no time for him to give his army rest and refreshment, for the Barbarians quickly learned of his arrival, and held in contempt the infantry with him, which were few in number all told, and, being Gauls, made no account of his cavalry. For they were most excellent fighters on horseback, and were thought to be especially superior as such, and, besides, at this time they far outnumbered Marcellus.

Immediately, therefore, they charged upon him with great violence and dreadful threats, thinking to overwhelm him, their king riding in front of them. But Marcellus that they might not succeed in enclosing and surrounding him and his few followers, led his troops of cavalry forward and tried to outflank them, extending his wing into a thin line, until he was not far from the enemy. And now, just as he was turning to make a charge, his horse, frightened by the ferocious aspect of the enemy, wheeled about and bore mostly forcibly back. But he, fearing lest this should be taken as a bad omen by the Romans and lead to confusion among them, quickly reined his horse round to the left and made him face the enemy, while he himself made adoration to the sun, implying that it was not by chance, but for this purpose, that he had wheeled about; for it is the custom with the Romans to turn round in this way when they make adoration to the gods. And in the moment of closing with the enemy he is said to have vowed that he would consecrate to Iupiter Feretrius the most beautiful suit of armour among them.

Meanwhile the King of the Gauls espied him, and judging from his insignia that he was the commander, rode far out in front of the rest and confronted him, shouting challenges and brandishing his spear. His stature exceeded that of the other Gauls, and he was conspicuous for a suit of armour which was set off with gold and silver and bright colours and all sorts of embroideries; it gleamed like lightning. Accordingly, as Marcellus surveyed the ranks of the enemy, this seemed to him to be the most beautiful armour, and he concluded that it was this which he had vowed to the god. He therefore rushed upon the man, and by a thrust of his spear which pierced his adversary's breastplate, and by the impact of his horse in full career, threw him, still living, upon the ground, where, with a second and third blow, he promptly killed him. Then leaping from his horse and laying his hands upon the armour of the dead, he looked towards heaven and said: O Iupiter Feretrius, who beholdest the great deeds and exploits of generals and commanders in wars and fightings, I call thee to witness that I have overpowered and slain this man with my own hand, being the third Roman ruler and general so to slay a ruler and king, and that I dedicate to thee the first and most beautiful of the spoils. Do thou therefore grant us a like fortune as we prosecute the rest of the war.

His prayer ended, the cavalry joined battle, fighting, not with the enemy's horsemen alone, but also with their footmen who attacked them at the same time, and won a victory, in its sort and kind, was remarkable and strange. For never before or since, as we are told, have so few horsemen conquered so many horsemen and footmen together.

After slaying the greater part of the enemy and getting possession of their arms and baggage, Marcellus returned to his colleague.[11]

In addition to our three major accounts we have a range of other references to the battle:

After this, the Consul Claudius annihilated 30,000 Gaesatae; he himself went in to the front line and killed their king Virdomarus.[12]

Nor must we separate from these examples the memory of M. Marcellus. Such vigour of courage was in him that by the Po he with a few horsemen attacked the king of the Gauls, who was surrounded by an enormous host, and straightway slew him, stripped him of his arms and dedicated them to Iupiter Feretrius.[13]

Claudius Marcellus, having unexpectedly come upon some Gallic troops, turned his horse about in a circle, looking around for a way of escape. Seeing danger on every hand, with a prayer to the gods, he broke into the midst of the enemy. By his amazing audacity he threw them into consternation, slew their leader, and actually carried away the spolia opima in a situation where there had scarcely remained a hope of saving his life.[14]

A few years after, a battle was fought with the Gauls within the borders of Italy, and an end put to the war, in the consulship of Marcus Claudius Marcellus and Gnaeus Cornelius Scipio. Marcellus took the field with a small body of horse, and slew the king of the Gauls, Viridomarus, with his own hand.[15]

Consul Marcus Claudius Marcellus killed the leader of the Gallic Insubres, Vertomarus, and returned with the supreme booty.[16]

Marcus Marcellus vanquished Virdomarus, the leader of the Gauls, in individual combat.[17]

We also have the inscription of his Triumph from the *Acta Triumphales*:

222 / 1 M. Claudius M.f. M.n. Marcellus, proconsul, over the Insubrian
Gauls and the Germans, 1st March – he brought back the spolia opima
after killing the enemy leader, Virdomarus, at Clastidium

Thus we can see that we have a range of views on the Battle of Clastidium.
To most later Roman sources this is a major Roman victory, a classic example
of Roman martial prowess when facing a numerically superior enemy, and
one of only three occasions when a Roman commander claimed the *spolia
opima*; this was the one of the most revered Roman trophies of war, whereby
a commander stripped the armour of an opposing commander whom he had
killed in single combat. Marcellus was only the third Roman commander
ever to win the *spolia opima*; the others being Romulus, the legendary
founder of Rome, and A. Cornelius Cossus (in either 436 or 428 BC).[18]

Yet aside from the tales of heroism and valiant single combat, we must
ask ourselves what do we know about the battle and what ultimately was
its significance? We know that a smaller Roman force, comprised mostly of
cavalry, defeated a far larger Gallic force. Plutarch places it at 10,000, whilst
Orosius has it as high as 30,000. We know that the Consul Marcellus killed
a Gallic chieftain Virdomarus (though there are a number of variations to
the name).

In terms of its location, it seems that the battle was nearer the Po than
the settlement of Clastidium. Both Zonaras and Polybius state that the
Gauls were not at Clastidium when Marcellus arrived, but had broken off
their attack. Polybius states that the Gauls were driven into a river, which
accounts for the high number of Gallic casualties, and Valerius Maximus
writes that the battle took place on the Po, which was some eight miles north
of Clastidium. Determining how the battle came about is even more of a
challenge. In Zonaras, the Gauls have broken the attack on Clastidium and
fled with Marcellus in pursuit. The Gauls then made a stand, presumably
when they reached the Po. In Polybius, it is the other way around and the
Gauls broke the attack of Clastidium to march north to meet the advancing
Romans.

Perhaps the most intriguing is the reference found in Frontinus, who
speaks of Marcellus stumbling upon the Gauls by accident, blundering into
their midst whilst looking for a means of escape, thus throwing the Gauls
into confusion. He was then able to face and kill their chieftain and won
the day almost by accident. This is a wonderful variant tradition amidst all
the Plutarchian rhetoric of heroic Roman valour, which leaves no surviving

trace elsewhere. In tone it is similar to the account of Zonaras, who has the clash as little more than a skirmish, or Polybius, who neglects to mention the *spolia opima*.

Whether it was intent or accident that brought the two sides together, it is clear that a smaller Roman force, composed of mostly cavalry, was able to rout a far larger Gallic force of infantry and cavalry. The death of their chieftain at the hands of the Consul was a contributory factor, as was the Gallic army being forced into the Po as they retreated. What is interesting is the tactics that Marcellus seems to have adopted to counter the fact that he was significantly outnumbered and lacked infantry. Polybius speaks of him being able to attack from the front, flank and rear, almost surrounding them, despite being significantly outnumbered (though we are not told the total number of cavalry in Marcellus' force). This is supported by a line in Plutarch's account:

> But Marcellus, that they might not succeed in enclosing and surrounding him and his few followers, led his troops of cavalry forward and tried to outflank them, extending his wing into a thin line, until he was not far from the enemy.[19]

Marcellus apparently strung his cavalry out into a long thin line, not allowing the Gauls to outflank him, but in fact enabling him to nearly encircle the more tightly-packed Gallic force. Given how thin this line of Roman cavalry must have been when so stretched, it is unlikely that they would have been able to withstand a full-blown Gallic assault, as Plutarch describes, so it does favour Marcellus being the one who took the offensive. This line of analysis does perhaps shed light on the whole success of Marcellus' battle plan. When faced with a force of far superior numbers and with only a force of cavalry at his disposal, it seems that he took the principle that attack was the best form of defence and surprised the Gauls by charging at them, aiming for the Gallic chieftain, with the intent of quickly decapitating the opposing force before they could make their superior numbers tell. Taken by surprise, and with their leader killed, the Gauls were seemingly thrown into confusion, and faced with the Romans attacking on a broad front they fell back and were driven into the river, turning a rout into a slaughter.

Thus it seems that Marcellus adopted a high-risk strategy which paid off. This seems to have been a characteristic of the man and his generalship, which ended in an ill-judged scouting mission during the Second Punic

War (208 BC) when he and his then Consular colleague were ambushed by Numidian horsemen and killed. On this occasion his gamble paid off, handsomely as it turned out, and allowed him to go down in Roman military history as the third man to claim *spolia opima*. Had he not been able to kill the Gallic chieftain, his cavalry force way well have been worn down by the superior Gallic numbers and annihilated.

However, we must still tackle the issue of what this battle achieved in terms of the overall campaign? To do this we need to put aside talk of *spolia opima* or the surviving sources' glowing accounts of Roman heroism in the face of overwhelming odds. We must remember that the Gallic thrust across the Po was at best a diversionary tactic to try to draw the Romans away from the siege of Acerrae, which was the main Roman focus of the war. Although it may have started out as a secondary campaign, it seems that the effects of Clastidium – the death of a Gallic leader and a large number of his men – became the tipping point of the Insubrian campaign.

It is important to note that Clastidium was seemingly the last full-scale battle of the Insubrian War. We do not know how many men the Insubrians had in total, or what their losses from Telamon and the battles of 224 and 223 BC were. However, we do know that once again the Insubrians needed Gaesatae mercenaries in order to continue the fight against Rome. It is here that the identity of the Gauls fighting at Clastidium becomes important. If it was purely the Gaesatae contingent, as Polybius claims, then Marcellus destroyed the Insubrians' reinforcements, along with their commander, and thus reduced the Insubrians to the state they had been at the end of 223 BC, with a limited offensive military capacity and limited manpower. This seems to have been the key effect of the Battle of Clastidium; it finished off the Insubrians as an offensive military force.

The Final Campaign – From Acerrae to Mediolanum

With Marcellus absent, the other Consul, Gn. Cornelius Scipio Calvus, continued the siege of the important Insubrian stronghold of Acerrae. We know nothing about this Insubrian stronghold other than it was a walled settlement and held a large supply of Insubrian corn. It seems to have been the Insubrians' second most important settlement. Zonaras describes it as 'favourably placed and well walled'.[20]

Nevertheless, the city soon fell to Scipio, who used it as a Roman base for the rest of the campaign. With the loss of Acerrae, the Insubrians fell back to their capital Mediolanum (modern Milan), itself built on the ruins of an Etruscan city, Melpum, which the Gauls destroyed in 396 BC. It seems that a substantial number of Insubrians escaped the fall of Acerrae, possibly quitting the city before it fell with the intention of carrying the fight on at Mediolanum. According to Polybius, Scipio did not allow them time to regroup, pressed hard on their retreat and followed them to the gates of the city itself. [21]

However, it seems that Scipio had overstretched his forces giving chase to these survivors. It is important to note that he only had a third of the total force of cavalry and few light troops, given that they were with Marcellus across the Po. Harrying the fleeing Insubrians to Mediolanum, he did not have sufficient forces to lay siege to the city there and then and the Insubres did not rise to the bait and come out to face him; that is until he withdrew to return to Acerrae and collect the rest of the Roman Army:

> Gnaeus followed close on their heels, and suddenly appeared before Mediolanum. The Gauls at first did not stir, but, when he was on his way back to Acerrae, they sallied out, and made a bold attack on his rear, in which they killed a considerable number of the Romans and even forced a portion of them to take to flight, until Gnaeus, calling back the forces in advance, urged the fugitives to rally and withstand the enemy. After this the Romans, on their part obeying their Consul, continued to fight vigorously with their assailants, and the Celts after holding their ground for a time, encouraged as they were by their momentary success, were shortly put to flight and took refuge on the mountains. [22]

Scipio had managed to avert a disaster and defeated the defenders of Mediolanum outside the city. Again, we have some difference of opinion in our surviving sources as to how exactly Mediolanum fell:

> Gnaeus, following them, laid waste the country and took Mediolanum itself by assault, upon which the chieftains of the Insubres, despairing of safety, put themselves entirely at the mercy of the Romans. [23]

> And setting out from that point, they subdued Mediolanum and another town. After these had been captured the rest of the Insubres also made terms with them, giving them money and a portion of the land. [24]

Marcellus returned to his colleague who was hard put to it in his war with the Gauls near their largest and most populous city. Mediolanum was the city's name, and the Gauls considered it their metropolis; wherefore they fought eagerly in its defence, so that Cornelius was less besieger than besieged. But when Marcellus came up, and when the Gaesatae, on learning of the defeat and death of their king, withdrew, Mediolanum was taken, the Gauls themselves surrendered the rest of their cities, and put themselves entirely at the disposition of the Romans. They obtained peace on equitable terms.[25]

Afterwards, in conjunction with his colleague, he cut to pieces a numerous army of the Gauls, stormed Milan, and carried off a vast booty to Rome. Marcellus, at his triumph, bore the spoils of the Gaul, fixed upon a pole on his shoulders.[26]

Among the many town of the Insubrians whom he [Marcellus] force to surrender, he captured the flourishing city of Milan.[27]

Again we can see either a pro or an anti-Marcellus stance in a number of our surviving accounts. According to Polybius, Scipio was the man who captured Mediolanum, on the other extreme we have Plutarch who has Marcellus rescuing Scipio (presumably from the attack detailed above) and taking Mediolanum, Orosius omits Scipio entirely. In truth it seems that Mediolanum did not fall until Marcellus had rejoined Scipio, but whether it was Scipio himself who defeated the Insubrians outside Mediolanum or had help from Marcellus is difficult to determine. According to Polybius, it was Scipio on his own, according to Plutarch it was with Marcellus' help, and Polybius does omit Marcellus completely from the final event of the Insubrian campaign.

Plutarch's account of the fall of the city is interesting. If we use this to flesh out Polybius' briefer narrative, it seems that Scorpio's defeat of the Insubres outside Mediolanum did not bring about the fall of the city immediately. However, whilst the Roman were preparing for a siege of the city, news of Clastidium reached the defenders. If there was a significant Gaesatae contingent still defending the city, reports of the destruction of their army along with the death of their chieftain were the final straws for them, and the Gaesatae once again deserted their Gallic allies and left the city to fend for itself. Given the loss of what may have been a substantial number of the city's defenders, coupled with Scipio's victory earlier, it seems that this desertion was the final straw and the Insubrians surrendered their capital. According to Zonaras, one other (unknown) stronghold was taken, following which the Insubres surrendered.[28]

In just four years (225–222 BC), the Romans had turned a potentially disastrous Gallic invasion of Roman Italy into a victorious war of subjugation, which saw the Boii and the Insubres utterly defeated and northern (Gallic) Italy fall to Rome. With the Insubrian surrender, Marcellus and Scipio returned to Rome, where Marcellus was voted a Triumph over the Insubres and the Germans (Gaesatae).

We must exercise caution in thinking that this Roman victory was the final act in the Gallic Wars between Rome and the Gauls of northern Italy. It is clear that it was this war that decisively turned the tide in Rome's favour, from being fearful of Gallic invasion to extending hegemony over the Cisalpine region. However, hegemony did not mean conquest. The Boii and Insubres had been defeated and the other large tribes of the region, the Cenomani and Veneti, had become Roman allies voluntarily (see Map 6).

In line with Roman practice, the Boii and Insubres would have ceded territory to Rome, as Zonaras confirms in the case of the Insubres, but would have been left alone to their own affairs once Roman armies had withdrawn. Although neither tribe would ever be able to threaten a full-scale invasion of Roman Italy again, we would be naive to assume that they took living under Roman suzerainty well or would not take up arms again after having had time (a generation) to recover from their losses. As it turns out, both the Insubres and the Boii went to war with Rome again, in the 190s BC, in the aftermath of the Second Punic War, stirred up by Roman setbacks during the war (see Appendix Five).

The Campaigns of 221 and 220 BC

Polybius ends his Gallic War narrative with the defeat of the Insubres and, after a digression on general Greek and Roman relations with Gauls, eagerly moves his narrative onto preparing for the Second Punic War. However, it is clear from the meagre details preserved in our other surviving sources that Rome pushed on with the momentum gained in the Boian and Insubrian campaigns to extend their strategic grip on northern Italy. Given the fact that Rome had mobilized a huge number of men who were now veterans of several years' worth of campaigning, and had acquired a taste for victory in northern Italy, it is easy to understand why many in the Senate would want to push on and build on the platform these victories had brought, not least the incoming Consuls.

The Campaign of 221 BC – The Istrian War

The Consuls of 221 BC were P. Cornelius Scipio Asina and M. Minucius Rufus. Again, neither man had been Consul before, and we have no details about any prior military experience. It is interesting to note that this was the second year in a row that we see a Cornelius Scipio as Consul. With the Ligurians, Boii and Insubres subdued, and the Cenomani and Veneti as allies, it seems that the Senate turned its gaze to the north-east and the peninsula of Istria (see Map 7). We only have handful of references to the Istrian campaign of 221 BC:

> Later Publius Cornelius and Marcus Minucius made an expedition in the direction of the Ister and subdued many of the nations there, some by war some by capitulation.[29]

> In the consulate of Marcus Minucius Rufus and Publius Cornelius, war was made upon the Istrians, because they had plundered some ships of the Romans, which were bringing a supply of corn, and they were entirely subdued [30]

> Then a new enemy, the Histri, raised themselves up to fight. The Consuls Cornelius and Minucius subdued them although after the loss of much Roman blood.[31]

Given how little remains, it is not difficult to see why the campaigns of this year are usually overlooked.[32] Yet despite the lack of detail, there are some important issues to consider. Each of the three sources above provides us with an interesting detail. Eutropius provides us with the *causus belli*, or at least the excuse: raids on Roman shipping, similar to the reasons given for the First Illyrian War (as seen in Chapter Four). It is highly unlikely that the raids started this year and we must assume that piracy from Istria had been a long-standing problem. It seems that the Senate was once again in a bullish mood and that it, and this year's Consuls, would have been looking to extend Roman power in this region. The piracy gave them a familiar excuse to go to war. It cannot be a coincidence that the tribes of Istria formed the next link in the chain of tribes of northern Italy, from the Ligurians in the west to the Veneti in the east, who had been subdued by force or allies to Rome (see Map 6).

Appian however provides a different perspective on this campaign and links it to events in Illyria:

> While the Romans were engaged in a three years' war with the Gauls on the River Po, Demetrius, thinking that they had their hands full, set forth on a piratical expedition, brought the Istrians, another Illyrian tribe, into the enterprise, and detached the Atintani from Rome. The Romans, when they had settled their business with the Gauls, immediately sent a naval force and overpowered the pirates.[33]

Thus, for Appian, the Istrian campaign is not the penultimate act of the Gallic War but the opening act of a Second Illyrian War (see Chapter Eight). In either event, strategically speaking this was another bold move for Rome. The previous campaigning had been in north-western Italy. However, Istria formed an important link, not just extending the zone of Roman influence further east, but securing a geographically compact peninsula which jutted into the Adriatic and formed another link between Rome's allies in northern Italy and her zone of control in Illyria. If the pirates of Illyria had been subdued, then it made strategic sense to secure the other key points of the Adriatic coastline.

The meagre details that survive give us both the outcome – the subjugation of a number of tribes, by either force or alliance (from Zonaras) – and the cost, with Orosius claiming that 'much Roman blood was spilt'. This clearly indicates that the Romans met fierce resistance and perhaps suffered military setbacks. No Triumphs are recorded for this campaign, but the details of the Triumphs between 222 and 197 BC are lost to us. However, all sources are agreed that this campaign secured the Istrian peninsula to Roman control.

The Campaign of 220 BC – The Alpine Campaign

Remarkably, we have even fewer details for the campaign of 220 BC. The Consuls for this year were C. Lutatius Catulus and L. Veturius Philo. Again, neither man had held the Consulship before, nor have we details of any prior military experience. We only have one line of one source detailing their campaigning this year, from Zonaras, but again it is an important campaign, both in itself and in terms of the continuing Roman thrust into northern Italy:

> Lucius Veturius and Caius Lutatius went as far as the Alps, and without any fighting won over many people.[34]

The Senate sanctioned a further campaign against the tribes of northern Italy, taking the sphere of Roman control right up to the Alps. Frustratingly, we have no details of which tribes capitulated and allied to Rome, but given the fate of the Boii and the Insubres the fact that they did not resist is hardly surprising. The key aspect is that again, even though the threat from the Boii and Insubres had passed, the Senate continued to expand Rome's sphere of control in north-eastern and north-western Italy, utilising the obvious geographic boundaries, the Alps to the north and the Adriatic coast to the east.

The Foundation of Placentia and Cremona and the War of 218 BC

We are not told of any campaigning in this region in 219 BC due to the Senate turning its attention to the east and the deteriorating situation in Illyria (as seen in Chapter Ten). However, not even the outbreak of a second war with Carthage in the west (see Chapter Eleven) ended the campaigning against the Gallic tribes, who once against went into conflict with Rome in 218 BC. Early in 218 BC, the Romans took a further step to consolidate their control of the region by founding the new colonies of Placentia and Cremona, to secure the River Po.[35] Polybius provides us with the following:

> While occupied in enrolling the legions and making other preparations they were pushing on the project of establishing in Cisalpine Gaul the colonies on which they had decided. They took active steps to fortify the towns, and ordered the colonists, who were about six thousand in number for either city, to be on the spot within thirty days. The one city they founded on this side of the Po, calling it Placentia, the other, which they named Cremona, on the far side.[36]

The colonies served two purposes; not only did they provide an additional defensive screen between the Gallic and Roman territories, but they could act as forward bases for future Roman offensives into Gallic territory.[37] Naturally enough, the tribes of the region took exception to this and, as Polybius states, bolstered by the impending war between Rome and Carthage, were emboldened enough to rise up against Rome once more. On this occasion, Polybius states that the Boii led the revolt, having recovered from their defeats of seven years earlier, and were joined by the Insubres. This seemed to catch the Romans off-guard, distracted as they were by the preparations for war in Spain, allowing the Boii and Insubres to overrun the two colony sites:

> …they overran the lands which the Romans had allotted to their colonies and on the settlers taking to flight, pursued them to Mutina, a Roman colony, and there besieged them. Among those shut up there were three men of high rank who had been sent to carry out the partition of the country, Caius Lutatius, a former Consul, and two former Praetors. On these three requesting a parley with the Boii, the latter consented, but when they came out for the purpose they treacherously made them prisoners, hoping by means of them to get back their own hostages.[38]

Rome responded by dispatching one of the Praetors, L. Manlius (Vulso), with a legion to face the Boii and Insubres. Unfortunately for Rome, Manlius seems to have walked into trap in a forest and was heavily defeated in an unnamed battle:

> When the Praetor Lucius Manlius, who with his troops was occupying an advanced position in the neighbourhood, heard of this, he hastened up to give help. The Boii had heard of his approach, and posting ambuscades in a certain forest attacked him from all sides at once as soon as he reached the wooded country, and killed many of the Romans. The remainder at first took to flight, but on getting to higher ground rallied just enough to give their retreat an appearance of order. The Boii following at their heels shut this force too up in the place called Vicus Tannetis. When the news reached Rome that the fourth legion was surrounded by the Boii and besieged, they instantly sent off the legions destined for Publius under the command of a Praetor to its assistance, ordering Publius to enrol other legions from the allies.[39]

When news came that the envoys were prisoners and Mutina and its garrison in jeopardy, L. Manlius, the praetor, burning with anger, led his army in separate divisions to Mutina. Most of the country was uncultivated at that time and the road went through a forest. He advanced without throwing out scouting parties and fell into an ambush, out of which, after sustaining considerable loss, he made his way with difficulty on to more open ground. Here he entrenched himself, and as the Gauls felt it would be hopeless to attack him there, the courage of his men revived, though it was tolerably certain that as many as 500 had fallen. They recommenced their march, and as long as they were going through open country there was no enemy in view; when they re-entered the forest their rear was attacked and great confusion and panic created. They lost 700 men and six standards. When they at last got out of the trackless and entangled forest there was an end to the terrifying tactics of the Gauls and the wild alarm of the Romans. There was no difficulty in repelling attacks when they reached the open country and made their way to Tannetum, a place near the Po. Here they hastily entrenched themselves, and, helped by the windings of the river and assisted by the Brixian Gauls, they held their ground against an enemy whose numbers were daily increasing.[40]

It seems that the Boii and Insubres were still capable of defeating an unwary Roman commander. Despite the relatively light number of losses, a Roman commander being ambushed in a forest and losing legionary standards does have echoes of the infamous defeat in the Teutoburg Forest, some two centuries later. More important than the losses was the fact that this revolt and defeat forced the Romans to disrupt their preparations for the war in Spain and diverted valuable resources. Another Praetor (C. Atilius Serranus) had to be dispatched with a larger force, originally destined for Spain:

…when the intelligence of this sudden outbreak reached Rome and the Senate became aware that they had a Gallic war to face in addition to the war with Carthage, they ordered C. Atilius, the praetor, to go to the relief of Manlius with a Roman legion and 5,000 men who had been recently enlisted by the consul from among the allies. As the enemy, afraid to meet these reinforcements, had retired, Atilius reached Tannetum without any fighting.[41]

It seems that the arrival of Atilius rescued Manlius and the survivors of his army, and forced the Boii and Insubres to retreat once more. We do not hear of any further fighting, though whether this is due to our surviving sources, eagerness to move onto the Punic War or a retreat by the Gallic tribes (possibly awaiting events in the Punic War) is not known. However, Livy does report that in 217 BC Atilius was still in the region with two legions, which he than transferred to the Consul C. Flaminius, prior to the Battle of Lake Trasimene.[42] Thus we can see that even if there was no further open conflict, Rome still needed to maintain the legions in the region to ensure its compliance.

From this point further Gallic campaigns become entangled with the invasion of Italy by the Carthaginians under the command of Hannibal. Nevertheless, this short campaign does show that despite the scale of the victories in the preceding years, a number of anti-Roman Gallic tribes remained implacably opposed to Rome and its northern expansion and would continue to resist as long as possible. Despite Rome gaining the upper hand in the Gallic Wars, these conflicts were far from ended.

Part IV

The Consequences of Expansion (225–218 BC)

Chapter Ten

Roman Expansion in the East – The Second Illyrian War (219 BC)

Having spent the previous five years waging war in northern Italy against the Gauls, Rome suddenly broke off its campaigning and turned their attention once again to Illyria, which they had only secured some ten years previously (as seen in Chapter Four). To see what prompted the change in Rome's military focus, we must review events in Greece and Illyria in the intervening period.

Illyria and Greece in the 220s BC

The principal event in Greece during the 220s was the Cleomenic War (229–222/1 BC) in the Peloponnese, between Sparta under King Cleomenes III and the Achaean League. Whilst the details of this war fall outside of the remit of this work, the war was an attempt by Cleomenes to restore Spartan supremacy in the Peloponnese, having tried to restore the Spartan system to its classical shape.[1] The war, however, dragged in a number of the other powers of the Hellenistic world, either overtly or otherwise, and in part became a proxy war between the great powers of Macedon and Ptolemaic Egypt.

Macedon itself was recovering from the death of its king, Demetrius II, in 229 BC (killed in battle whilst facing an invasion of the Dardani tribe, who had invaded and ravaged Macedon). As Demetrius' son, Philip V, was too young to rule, the regency feel to a cousin, Antigonus III. Antigonus swiftly restored the situation in Macedon, defeating the Dardani and taking the title of King for himself.[2] Proving to be an able general and diplomat, he soon restored Macedonian dominance over Greece, establishing alliances in the south with the Achaean League and in the west with Epirus. His alliance with the Achaean League led him to intervene on their side in the war against

Sparta, which was receiving support from King Ptolemy III of Egypt. The Cleomenic War culminated in Antigonus' victory over Cleomenes in 222 BC at the Battle of Sellasia (the same year as the Roman victory at Clastidium)[3]. Antigonus' victory, however, was cut short when he died in battle fighting against another invasion of Illyrian tribesmen in 221 BC, being replaced on the throne by the young Phillip V.

The recovery of Macedon in this period had only indirect implications for Rome at this point. Although the launch of their first Illyrian campaign predated the death of Demetrius II, the campaign's conclusion had coincided with a sudden decline in Macedon's fortunes. This allowed the Romans to gain a foothold on mainland Greece, in a region traditionally coveted by the kings of Macedon. Paradoxically, the recovery of Macedon under Antigonus coincided with Rome being fully engaged with a tribal invasion of their own in Italy, during the Gallic War. Although Antigonus' military attention was focussed on the Peloponnese, he did reach out diplomatically to the Illyrian region, and in particular allied himself to Demetrius of Pharos, Rome's erstwhile ally in the region. In fact, Polybius reports that Demetrius fought with Antigonus at the Battle of Sellasia in 222 BC against Sparta, along with a force of 1,600 Illyrians.[4] Clearly, Rome's inattention had allowed Macedon to attempt to challenge (albeit diplomatically) Rome's newly-established hegemony in the region.

Rome's focus on the Gallic War also seems to have had an impact of Demetrius himself, who seems to have taken the opportunity to distance himself from Roman overlordship; not just via his alliance with Antigonus. Demetrius had made his fortune by betraying his previous overlords, the Ardiaei, by allying himself to Rome. His reward after the First Illyrian War was rule of the independent island of Pharos, bolstered by some additional territories on the mainland and a watching brief as Rome's representative in the region. However, at some point in the intervening decade, Demetrius had gone further than this and became ruler of the Ardiaei themselves, as a fragment of Dio reveals:

Demetrius, encouraged by his position as guardian of Pinnes and by the fact that he had married the latter's mother Triteuta after Teuta's death, was not only proving oppressive to the natives, but was also ravaging the territory of the neighbouring tribes.[5]

When this happened is undated, as is Teuta's death. There is no reference to this happening as part of the original Roman peace settlement of 228 BC. All that is mentioned is that Teuta was removed as regent for the young Ardiaean king Pinnes, and sent in exile. The Romans would have wanted Demetrius to watch over the Ardiaei to ensure that they caused no further trouble in the region, but it seems that Demetrius took this one stage further and established himself as the de-facto ruler of the Ardiaei.[6]

Using this new powerbase and having secured an alliance with a resurgent Macedon, it appears that Demetrius was intent on establishing a new regional power with himself at its head. The surviving sources all paint a picture of Demetrius' expansion in Illyria, at Rome's expense:

> It so happened that at that time in Illyria Demetrius of Pharos, oblivious of the benefits that the Romans had conferred on him, contemptuous of Rome because of the peril to which she was exposed first from the Gauls and now from Carthage, and placing all his hopes in the Royal House of Macedon owing to his having fought by the side of Antigonus in the battles against Cleomenes, was sacking and destroying the Illyrian cities subject to Rome, and, sailing beyond Lissus, contrary to the terms of the treaty, with fifty boats, had pillaged many of the Cyclades.[7]

While the Romans were engaged in a three-years war with the Gauls on the River Po, Demetrius, thinking that they had their hands full, set forth on a piratical expedition, brought the Istrians, another Illyrian tribe, into the enterprise, and detached the Atintani from Rome.[8]

> But the ruler of the Ardiaeans, Demetrius, as has been stated above, was not only proving oppressive to the natives, but was also ravaging the territory of the neighbouring tribes; and it appeared that it was by abusing the friendship of the Romans that he was able to wrong them.[9]

As Walbank points out, we must beware Roman propaganda in these matters,[10] but it does seem that Demetrius was intent on governing Illyria for himself, and possibly Macedonian rather than Roman interests. He seems to have been slowly but surely overturning all the provisions of the Roman peace treaty of 228 BC. The independent tribes and cities whose freedom was guaranteed by Rome were being attacked and brought under the Ardiaean sphere of influence once more, and Ardiaean pirate ships were again operating in the Adriatic with apparent impunity, with commensurate losses to Italian traders. Walbank has presented the argument over whether Demetrius was bound by a treaty obligation between Rome and Teuta, but that treaty obligation would have been for any ruler of the Ardiaei and not simply one individual.[11] Perhaps the most intriguing note is that of Appian's, who states that Demetrius brought the Istrian tribes under his control. This raises interesting questions over the Roman campaign in Istria of 221 BC (as seen in Chapter Seven).[12]

As in all such cases, it is impossible to fully determine what was going through Demetrius' mind when it came to his actions. Rome would never allow such a blatant challenge to their newly-won dominance in Illyria and the Adriatic to stand, especially from one of their own allies. Whilst it is clear that Rome's full attention was engaged in the Gallic War, it was equally clear that after 225 BC Rome had the upper hand in the war and would emerge not only victorious, but stronger than ever. Polybius' account is clearly looking forwards to the Second Punic War, but even in the late 220s such a war was not a certainty, and there was no clear indication that it would break out when it did. Perhaps the key factor that emboldened Demetrius was the support he had from Antigonus of Macedon. It appears that he had changed from being a Roman client ruler to a Macedonian one, and perhaps he was counting on this to protect him from Roman intervention. At this point even Rome would have thought twice about going to war against Macedon over control of Illyria.[13]

Unfortunately for Demetrius, events turned against him. By 221 BC the Romans had won the Gallic War and again had armies of battle-hardened veterans and experienced commanders. The piratical attacks on Italian shipping would have created immense pressure on Senators to act and, worst of all, his patron, Antigonus III of Macedon, died whilst fighting an invading Illyrian tribe.[14] His replacement was a 17-year-old, Philip V, who promptly turned his attention south, not west, and led a coalition of Greek states in a war against the Aetolian League and Sparta, known as the Social War (220–217 BC). Thus Demetrius had lost his sponsor and Macedon had diverted its attention to the south, giving Rome another window of opportunity.

The Roman Decision for War (219 BC)

The surviving sources are split on how they report the outbreak of the Second Illyrian War. For Polybius, Roman eyes are on the impending conflict with Carthage and the war was a strategic decision to secure their eastern flank before going to war with Carthage in the west. For Dio and Zonaras, as soon as the Consuls of 219 BC heard of Demetrius' actions they summoned him to Rome to explain himself, and when he ignored them they declared war:

> Consequently, the Senate, adapting their measures to this supposition, decided to secure their position in Illyria.[15]

> The Romans, in view of those proceedings and of the flourishing fortunes of the Macedonian kingdom, were anxious to secure their position in the lands lying east of Italy, feeling confident that they would have time to correct the errors of the Illyrians and rebuke and chastise Demetrius for his ingratitude and temerity.[16]

> As soon as the Consuls, Aemilius Paullus and Marcus Livius, heard of this, they summoned him before them. When he paid no heed, but actually proceeded to assail their allies, they made a campaign against him in Issa.[17]

Appian has a completely different chronology for the war, which is so interesting a variation that we must examine it separately. Both sets of accounts contain interesting differences. Dio and Zonaras seem to bring an immediacy to proceedings, with the Senate acting the moment that it received news of Demetrius' activities. This narrative seems to ignore the build-up of Demetrius' activities and the wider context, but could be referring to a particular act by Demetrius, which was a tipping point for the Senate to intervene; perhaps the Ardiaean fleet moving beyond Lissus.

Polybius placed the war in the context of the epic Second Punic War which he knew came so soon after. For him, the Senate had a limited window of opportunity to act, between the Gallic Wars and the Second Punic War. Whilst events in Spain surrounding the Carthaginian attack on the Roman ally of Saguntum were of obvious concern to the Senate (see Chapter Nine), at this point war with Carthage was far from certain; many flashpoints had arisen and been defused over the preceding two decades without resulting in a second war. The key to understanding the outbreak of this war is to consider both the long- and short-term factors. It must have been clear to the Senate for a number of years that Demetrius was slipping out of their control; from becoming the de-facto ruler of the Ardiaei to fighting for Antigonus at the Battle of Sellasia. Whilst the Gallic War was raging, it is clear that Rome was not in a position to do much about it militarily, especially with Antigonus as Demetrius' patron.

However, victory at the Battle of Clastidium in 222 BC proved to be the apogee for Rome in the war, with military action outside Italy a viable option from that point onwards. The question we must ask ourselves is why it took Rome until 219 BC to act? It is possible that the Senate was talking to Demetrius before this point in the hope of bringing him back to Rome's fold. It is also possible that they wanted to avoid military action against the man which they had appointed to look after their affairs unless it was absolutely necessary; a clear demonstration of the failure of their light touch policy of 'governing' their protectorate. The Senate may well have been hoping to avoid a potential clash with Antigonus of Macedon or becoming entangled in a larger war with Macedon.

By 219 BC, however, a number of factors were now in Rome's favour; Antigonus was dead and his young successor was entangled in a war in Greece, northern Italy had been subdued and if the situation in Spain did become more serious, then it was best to strike now rather than later. There may well have been a particular *causus belli* which forced the Senate to act against their erstwhile ally. The naval limitations on the Ardiaei had been much trumpeted by Rome throughout Greece, and so Demetrius' breaching of them would bring an especial loss of face. Any attacks on Italian shipping would also bring domestic pressure to bear on the Senate. Faced with this accumulation of factors, it appears that the Senate summoned Demetrius to appear before them and explain himself. Demetrius felt bold enough to ignore the order and went on the offensive, leading to the declaration of war on him by the Roman people and the start of the Second Illyrian War.

Roman and Demetrian Objectives in the War

We must ask ourselves what Demetrius' tactics were? By 219 BC he had very visibly distanced himself from Rome, and antagonised them, yet his patron

Antigonus was dead and he of all people knew that the Ardiaei could not withstand a Roman military attack. It does seem strange that he seemingly refused the offer to appear before the Senate and explain himself, and either try to stall for time or give enough ground for to the Senate to avoid the need for war. If he had hoped that his Macedonian ties would aid him he was to be sorely mistaken, as Philip V did nothing to come to his aid and remained focussed on leading the war against the Aetolian League.

With Rome committed to war and Macedon remaining neutral, perhaps his only hope was to avoid a set piece confrontation with Rome and try to draw them into a protracted war, and hope that factors elsewhere came to his aid; in the form of either the Macedonians or the Carthaginians. Polybius does report that Demetrius made preparations to withstand sieges of key strongholds in the region. In his favour, he had experienced the Roman method of fighting first-hand during the first war and had aided them in facilitating the surrender of a number of these locations without a fight. To this end he fortified the town of Dimale, near Apollonia (see Map 7), whilst he himself withdrew to his home town of Pharos:

> While this was taking place Demetrius, getting wind of the Romans' purpose, at once sent a considerable garrison to Dimale with the supplies requisite for such a force. In the other cities he made away with those who opposed his policy and placed the government in the hands of his friends while he himself, selecting six thousand of his bravest troops, quartered them at Pharos.[18]

Nevertheless, it is clear from the outset that the Romans were the vastly superior force, both in terms of numbers and military ability. This is not to say that the war did not hold certain risks for them. Whilst fighting Demetrius held little danger for them directly, they needed to avoid being drawn into a larger war with Macedon, in whose traditional area of influence they were operating, and they needed a quick victory, having to keep one eye on the situation in Spain (as seen in Chapter Nine).

The Campaign of 219 BC

The Consuls of 219 BC were L. Aemilius Paullus and M. Livius Salinator. For both men this was their first Consulship, and as is usual for this period we are not aware of any prior military experience for either man, but it would be fair to assume that both had seen action in a junior capacity during the Gallic War. Throughout his narrative Polybius only refers to Aemilius Paullus operating in Illyria, with no mention of Livius Salinator. However, it is clear from other sources that not only did Livius have a command during the war, but the *de viris illustribus*, admittedly a much later source, states that he won a Triumph for his campaign, though we now possess no details whatsoever.[19] Why Polybius omits Livius from his narrative of the war so completely is unknown. What we do know is that Aemilius chose to attack the Demetrian forces at their strongest point, the fortress of Dimale, which was said to be impregnable:

> The Roman Consul, on reaching Illyria with his army and observing that the enemy were very confident in the natural strength of Dimale and the measures they had taken for its defence, there being also a general belief that it was impregnable, decided to attack it first, wishing to strike terror into them. Having given instructions to his officers and erected batteries in several places he began to besiege it. By capturing it in seven days, he at one blow broke the spirit of all the enemy, so that from every city they at once flocked to surrender themselves unconditionally to Rome.[20]

Again, unfortunately, we do not possess any details of this successful Roman siege, which was conducted in a remarkably short period and which would throw important light on Roman siege tactics during the third century. Nevertheless, Aemilius' tactics proved remarkably successful. He deliberately selected the enemy's supposed strongest fortification and reduced it so quickly, and one imagines with so much accompanying destruction, that it sent a stark message to the other towns and strongholds that were allied to Demetrius; no one was safe from the wrath of Rome. Polybius reports the wholesale surrender of other key Demetrian strongholds. Thus with just one short siege, Rome had unravelled Demetrius' strategy for a protracted, drawn-out war of sieges, whilst meeting the key Roman requirement for a short war.

With the fall of Dimale and the surrender of a number of other strongholds, it seems that Demetrius was isolated on Pharos, onto which Aemilius moved next. It appears that Aemilius was a skilled and innovative tactician. Not only did he storm Dimale in seven days, but he completely outwitted Demetrius and took the stronghold of Pharos in an even shorter time. On this occasion we have the details recorded in Polybius, which involved drawing Demetrius out of his well-fortified stronghold and luring him into an ambush:

> Having accepted their submission and imposed suitable conditions on each he sailed to Pharos to attack Demetrius himself. Learning that the city was very strong, that a large force of exceptionally fine troops was assembled within it and that it was excellently furnished with supplies and munitions of war, he was apprehensive that the siege might prove difficult and long. In view of this, therefore, he employed the following impromptu stratagem. Sailing up to the island at night with his whole force he disembarked the greater part of it in certain well-wooded dells, and at daybreak with twenty ships sailed openly against the harbour which lies nearest to the town. Demetrius, seeing the ships and contemptuous of their small number, sallied from the city down to the harbour to prevent the enemy from landing.[21]

Aemilius had drawn Demetrius into his trap, with the latter being tempted out of a well-fortified position to attack what he thought was an easy target.

With Demetrius having been drawn out of the city, Aemilius then sprung his trap at the Battle of Pharos:

> On his encountering them the struggle was very violent, and more and more troops kept coming out of the town to help, until at length the whole garrison had poured out to take part in the battle. The Roman force which had landed in the night now opportunely arrived, having marched by a concealed route, and occupying a steep hill between the city and the harbour, shut off from the town the troops who had sallied out. Demetrius, perceiving what had happened, desisted from opposing the landing and collecting his forces and cheering them on started with the intention of fighting a pitched battle with those on the hill. The Romans, seeing the Illyrians advancing resolutely and in good order, formed their ranks and delivered a terrible charge, while at the same time those who had landed from the ships, seeing what was going on, took the enemy in the rear, so that being attacked on all sides the Illyrians were thrown into much tumult and confusion. At the end,

being hard pressed both in front and in the rear, Demetrius' troops turned and fled, some escaping to the city, but the greater number dispersing themselves over the island across country.[22]

And having learned in advance that he was lying secretly at anchor somewhere in the vicinity of the landing-places, they sent a part of their ships to the other side of the island to bring on an engagement. When the Illyrians, accordingly, turned against these, thinking them to be alone, the main force sailed in at leisure, and after pitching camp in a suitable place, repulsed the natives, who, in their anger at the deception, had promptly attacked them.[23]

In just one day Aemilius lured Demetrius into a deadly ambush and destroyed his forces outside Pharos. Apparently, with just these two brief campaigns he won the war for Rome. Whilst we are not told how he took the fortress of Dimale, his Pharos campaign shows a tactical astuteness combined with a willingness to innovate, which comprehensively outwitted his opponent. The Battle of Pharos was accompanied by the fall of the city:

Aemilius, the Roman Consul, took Pharos at once by assault and razed it to the ground, and after subduing the rest of Illyria and organizing it as he thought best, returned to Rome late in summer and entered the city in triumph, acclaimed by all, for he seemed to have managed matters not only with ability, but with very high courage.[24]

Demetrius fled Illyria following the battle and sought refuge at the Macedonian court of Philip V. Without him, the nascent Ardiaean Empire he had been rebuilding collapsed once more, showing the weakness of empires built around one figure. Demetrius became a trusted advisor to the young Macedonian king and seems to have had a hand in the later alliance between Philip and Hannibal in 215 BC. According to Polybius the treaty between the two included clauses freeing all the Roman allies in the Illyrian region and returning Demetrius' possession to him once more:

...that the Romans shall no longer be masters of Corcyra, Apollonia, Epidamnus, Pharos, Dimale, Parthini, or Atitania: and that they shall return to Demetrius of Pharos all his friends who are in the dominions of Rome.[25]

Unfortunately for him, not only were the Romans able to keep control of their Illyrian protectorate, but Demetrius himself was killed in 214 BC attacking the city of Messene in the Peloponnese, whilst in command of a Macedonian army. Variant traditions can be found in our surviving sources which have Demetrius returning to Illyria and being killed by the Romans.[26]

Polybius' narrative gives all the credit for winning in the war in such a short timescale to Aemilius Paullus. This was perhaps an attempt to emphasise the great lineage of the later L. Aemilius Paullus, who defeated Macedon at the Battle of Pydna in 168 BC. However, as we have seen from other sources, not only was Livius Salinator commanding during the war, but he too apparently won a Triumph for his actions. What role he played in these events remains lost to us. Given his military action, we must assume that the war was wider than just these two campaigns; Dimale and Pharos, and that not all Demetrian strongholds surrendered immediately.

Yet it is clear that the war was won in a remarkably short timescale, even given the disparity of resources between the two sides. For the Romans, this had been the perfect campaign; Demetrius had been defeated and driven from Illyria, the revival of the Ardiaean Empire had been crushed and the war was over before it could affect matters in Spain or allow Philip V of Macedon to become involved. If there was one negative aspect, it was that Demetrius himself had not been captured, but had become an advisor to Greece's superpower, Macedon, a situation that would only stoke tensions between these two rivals.

The Second Illyrian War – The Appian Variation (221–219 BC)

Whilst the other surviving sources indicate a short sharp war, apparently with a limited focus, the account that survives in Appian's fragmentary work on the Illyrian Wars paints an entirely different picture. The account is usually dismissed as being a garbled and misunderstood version of the events depicted in other sources, but it is worth analysing in its own right, especially given the clear omissions found in sources such as Polybius.

> While the Romans were engaged in a three years' war with the Gauls on the River Po, Demetrius, thinking that they had their hands full, set

forth on a piratical expedition, brought the Istrians, another Illyrian tribe, into the enterprise, and detached the Atintani from Rome. The Romans, when they had settled their business with the Gauls, immediately sent a naval force and overpowered the pirates.

The following year they marched against Demetrius and his Illyrian fellow culprits. Demetrius fled to Philip, king of Macedonia, but when he returned and resumed his piratical career in the Adriatic they slew him and utterly demolished his native town of Pharus, which was associated with him in crime.[27]

For Appian, or perhaps his source, the war was not a short one, nor was it focused on a handful of sieges. Appian has Demetrius spreading his influence on a far wider scale than is found in any other source, and allied with or controlling the pirates of Istria, thus extending his influence across the whole of the Adriatic. The Istrian campaign of 221 BC is found in a number of other sources; notably in the Periochae of Livy, Zonaras, Orosius and Eutropius, the latter of which mentions their piratical activities.[28] We must be clear that none of these brief notes link them to Demetrius and it could well be that Appian mixed up separate campaigns.

However if Appian has not made a mistake then there is a logic behind what he says. Although the Romans were operating in northern Italy, the suddenness of the lurch to the north-east, is an unusual one, given that all previous campaigns were in the north-west. We must therefore ask was there any special reason behind this campaign, especially as it took precedence over bringing Demetrius to heel? Extending his powerbase up the Adriatic coast to a fellow community of pirates would have been in keeping with Demetrius, and the Romans may have been worried that even if the Istrians were not formally linked to Demetrius that he was attempting to extend his powerbase there, when they acted as they did.

For Appian, the Istrian expedition is the opening campaign in the Second Illyrian War. According to Appian the following year (220 BC) the Romans moved on Demetrius, but he fled to Philip V, something the other sources place in 219 BC, after the Battle of Pharos. Only Zonaras preserves any mention of the activities of the Consuls of 220 BC, and they are campaigning in the Alpine region.[29] However, this does not rule out other Senatorial commanders or a delegation being sent to Demetrius, who then flees. No explanation is given to why Demetrius gives up without a fight, but then faced with the might of Rome it could have been discretion being the better part of valour, especially if he hoped to gain additional support from Philip V.

The third year of Appian's Illyrian War (219 BC) has Demetrius returning to Illyria, after the Romans had left, which saw him face Rome in combat, as in the other sources, but with the added twist that he was killed whilst fighting Rome, possibly at the Battle of Pharos. This death in battle comes despite other sources placing him at Philip V's court until 214 BC, when he was killed leading a Macedonian army in the Peloponnese. The exception to this is Zonaras, who also has Demetrius returning to Illyria, after an undetermined time, and then being arrested and executed by the Romans.[30]

Appian's account, despite its brevity, has three notable elements not found elsewhere. Firstly, there is the inclusion of the Istrian War, which could well have been associated with Demetrius. Secondly, there is the year where he flees to Philip and then returns the next year, which seems unlikely, but is not contradicted elsewhere. Thirdly, there is Demetrius dying in battle with Rome in 219 BC, which is clearly contradicted by a range of other sources, who state that he lived on to 214 BC. This may not be a case of Appian making a mistake but by his day there being a variant tradition circulating amongst the histories about this war, as perhaps seen by Zonaras, and presumably Dio, who also reports a similar fate for Demetrius. In any event it certainly provides us with a fresh account of the war and may even throw more light on events of 221 BC and possibly 220 BC.

The Settlement and Aftermath

Unlike the end of the First Illyrian War, we have few details as to the settlement the Romans made in Illyria following this war. The only explicit reference comes from Appian: 'They spared the Illyrians on account of Pinnes, who again besought them to do so.'[31] We do not know how old Pinnes was by 219 BC, but he must have been approaching adulthood and perhaps took sole charge of the Ardiaei, especially with Rome having such difficulties with his guardians. Perhaps one reason for the silence of the sources on this settlement is that the Romans merely reinstated their earlier settlement, with the notable omission of Demetrius. It is also probable that the Romans were in a hurry to settle their affairs in Illyria in order to concentrate on the brewing crisis in Spain (see Chapter Nine). Polybius, later in his narrative, does refer to Demetrius leading a contingent of pro–Macedonian naval forces, of ninety ships, past Lissus, and thus breaking the treaty with Rome:

> …when Scerdilaïdas, together with Demetrius of Pharos, sailed from Illyria with a fleet of ninety boats and passed Lissus, thus breaking the treaty with Rome. They touched first at Pylos and made some attacks on it which failed. Demetrius now with fifty of the boats started for the islands, and sailing through the Cyclades pillaged or levied blackmail on some of them. [32]

This is interesting as it is a variation on the naval element of the Roman settlement following the first war. Other than this, however, we must assume that the settlement of Illyria remained the same. We must also assume that Rome reinstated their alliances, however informal, with the cities and tribes of the region, and thus resumed their protectorate over a swathe of territory on the Adriatic coast and Illyrian interior.

Back in Rome, both Consuls celebrated Triumphs for this war, but both seem to have fallen foul of accusations of corruption in relation to the booty seized during the war. Of the two, Livius Salinator was found guilty, having been condemned by thirty-four of the thirty-five tribes.[33] This did not stop him being elected to a second consulship, in 207 BC, and a Censorship in 204 BC. His colleague Aemilius Paullus was also tried but found not guilty and won a quicker second consulship, in 216 BC. However, he was killed fighting at the infamous Roman defeat at the Battle of Cannae.

Summary

This seemingly short war highlighted both the strengths and weaknesses of Roman foreign policy, especially when compared to other great Mediterranean powers such as Macedon. As with the first war, Rome was able to take advantage of a change of Macedonian ruler to reassert their claim to suzerainty over a portion of Illyria. Unfortunately, this war also showed the weakness of Rome's first post-war settlement, which unravelled in just a decade and required further intervention. Unlike the annexation of the islands of Sardinia and Corsica, or north-western Sicily, Rome did not directly choose to rule the region or appoint a fresh magistrate to administer it, but chose to wield influence by proxy, in this case Demetrius of Pharos. Whilst this may have been a sound tactic in terms of not burdening themselves with the mechanics of direct rule or alarming the other states of mainland Greece by directly annexing territory, Rome's settlements of Illyria did highlight a weakness of their foreign policy and one which was to plague them for the next 100 years. Whilst Rome could win wars through military force, without direct rule of the particular region, these post-war settlements were open to being undermined, either from within (Demetrius) or without (Antigonus).

In military terms, however, the Second Illyrian War was another major success. We are only given details of two campaigns and both are accredited to L. Aemilius Paullus, rather than his colleague M. Livius Salinator. Yet both generals ensured that Rome was not drawn into a protracted series of sieges or, even worse, a wider conflict with Macedon. Even if Philip V had had the desire to intervene militarily on Demetrius' side, the campaign was over (if we follow the standard sources) before he would have had time to disengage from his ongoing Greek wars and march westwards.

Some mention needs to be made of the role of the Ardiaei themselves. All too often, the focus of these two Illyrian Wars is centred on the individuals who led the opposition to Rome; Teuta and Demetrius. Yet both waged war on Rome as head of the Ardiaei, building on the rapid expansion of the Ardiaei under Agron. Whilst the Ardiaei were never a major enemy of Rome, they were clearly able to mobilize significant ground and naval forces, which combined with the collapse of Epirus did, for a short while, present them with an opportunity to turn themselves into a regional power. Unfortunately for them however, the Romans also saw the opportunity that the collapse of Epirus presented and had far greater military resources to command. Nevertheless, under King Pinnes and his successors, the Ardiaei maintained their role as a regional power and returned once again to fight the Romans for a third time (see Appendix Five).

Yet, despite this swift military success, Rome's attention was again to focus elsewhere, this time to the west and the Carthaginians and what was intended to be a war in Spain. Once again, Rome had secured her position in the Adriatic in the short term; however their long-term position was another matter. Rome's position in Illyria was a clear strategic issue for Macedon, who had long been the hegemonic power in the region. Rome's victory in the first war was followed by a loss of focus, with the outbreak of the Gallic War in Italy. On this occasion it was matters arising in Spain (and soon Italy itself) which diverted Rome's attention. Macedon itself was again undergoing a transitional period, between kings, but soon had a young, ambitious and militarily talented monarch on the throne, in the form of Philip V. Furthermore, Demetrius of Pharos, the exiled Ardiaean ruler, was now an exile at the royal court and would provide both the motive and opportunity for a Macedonian intervention in Illyria.[34] Thus, in these respects the Second Illyrian War stabilised Rome's position in the short term, but did little to address the longer-term issues and if anything made further conflict in the region and war with Macedon more likely. War with Macedon broke out just five years later in 214 BC (see Appendix Four), though Philip V was already campaigning in non-Roman Illyria as early as 217 BC.[35]

Chapter Eleven

Carthaginian Expansion in Spain and the Roman Response (225–218 BC)

Just as the settlement the Senate had implemented in the east, in Illyria, had broken down within a decade, so it also proved to be the case in the west in Spain.

Carthaginian Expansion under Hasdrubal 225–221 BC

With Roman involvement in Spain limited in theory by the Ebro Treaty and in practice by the Gallic invasion of central Italy, the Carthaginian commander Hasdrubal had a free hand to continue with the expansion of the Carthaginian Empire, by both force and diplomacy. Unfortunately, as we do not possess any Punic sources, we are left wholly in the dark about Hasdrubal's activities in the years following the so called Ebro Treaty. Naturally enough, the few sources which do survive for this period either concentrate on the Gallic War in Italy or are eager to 'fast forward' their narrative to 218 BC.

Nevertheless, we must not take this silence to assume that Hasdrubal did not continue his campaigns of expansion, especially now that he was free from the threat of Roman interference. Both the existence of the treaty and Rome's involvement with the Gallic War were a clear indication that Rome would not be coming to the aid of any Spanish tribes or cities south of the Ebro (with the possible exception of Saguntum), who thus would have to face the Carthaginians without any outside help. This can only have helped Hasdrubal in his campaigns and diplomacy.

It is interesting to speculate what effect, if any, the events in Italy had on Hasdrubal's strategic thinking. News that the Gauls had invaded central Italy must have been soon followed by reports of the great Roman victory at Telamon. Whilst the subsequent Roman campaigns in northern Italy, of 226–219 BC, would have kept them occupied, and thus away from Spain, it would have been increasingly clear to Hasdrubal and the Carthaginian Senate, that, far from collapsing, Roman power was in fact increasing. With Roman influence (rather than territory) now extending to the Alps, it must have been on Hasdrubal's mind that it would not be that long before the Senate turned its attentions back to Spain. However, it must be stressed that this does not mean that war between the two great western powers, over the Spanish issue, was inevitable. Whatever tactical thinking was in Hasdrubal's mind, his involvement came to a sudden end in 221 BC when he was assassinated in Spain by a Celtic slave, though the exact details are disputed:

> This digression has led us away from the affairs of Spain, where Hasdrubal, after governing the country for eight years, was assassinated at night in his lodging by a certain Celt owing to wrongs of a private nature.[1]
>
> One of his household slaves plotted against him, and he was slain after he had held the command for nine years.[2]
>
> A barbarian whose master he had put to death murdered him in broad daylight, and when seized by the bystanders he looked as happy as though he had escaped.[3]

Hasdrubal's rule in Spain met an equally violent end as that of his father-in-law, Hamilcar, but this time through murder rather than dying in battle. Nevertheless, during his period in command he had built on Hamilcar's foundations and not only secured the Carthaginian Empire in Spain, but expanded it, through both conquest and diplomatic means. An equally impressive achievement was his securing of a treaty with Rome, which on the face of it not only secured the nascent empire from Roman interference, but produced an agreement (whether tactic or explicit) that all of Spain, south of the Ebro, fell into Carthage's sphere of influence. Furthermore, it is apparent that he had taken steps to ensure a smooth transition of power of the Spanish command in the event of his death, which not only secured Carthage's position, but that of the Barcid family. His choice of successor was his second in command, and cavalry commander, who, more importantly was the son of Hamilcar, and thus his brother-in-law, a man by the name of Hannibal.

Carthaginian Expansion under Hannibal 221–219 BC

Up until this moment, this study has deliberately avoided all mention of Hannibal, as his ancient and modern reputation has an unfortunate tendency to overshadow other events and factors behind them. However, with his rise to the command of the Carthaginian Empire in Spain, we must now confront this issue.

Throughout Roman history, Hannibal represented the ultimate 'bogeyman' and the histories (both ancient and modern) are full of symbolic moments in his life; whether it be the oath of enmity towards Rome which his father Hamilcar supposedly made him swear, to his crossing of the Alps with elephants. Yet we must step away from these dashes of historical colour and sensationalistic biography and analyze him in the same manner as we have both Hamilcar and Hasdrubal.

Hannibal had seemingly accompanied his father and brother-in-law to Spain, and by the time of Hasdrubal's death was commander of the Carthaginian cavalry and so was well versed in battle. As with Hasdrubal, we are told that Hannibal was acclaimed commander by the Carthaginian army in Spain, a decision which was ratified by the Carthaginian Senate and people. Appian presents an interesting variation of this acclamation of Hannibal:

> Now the army proclaimed Hannibal, although still very young, yet greatly beloved by the soldiers, their general, and the Carthaginian Senate confirmed the appointment. Those of the opposite faction, who had feared the power of Hamilcar and Hasdrubal, when they learned of their death, despised Hannibal on account of his youth and prosecuted their friends and partisans with the old charges. The people took sides with the accusers, bearing a grudge against those now prosecuted, because they remembered the old severities of the times of Hamilcar and Hasdrubal, and ordered them to turn into the public treasury the large gifts that Hamilcar and Hasdrubal had bestowed upon them, as being enemy's spoils. The prosecuted parties sent messengers to Hannibal asking him to assist them, and admonished him that, if he should neglect those who were able to assist him at home, he would be thoroughly despised by his father's enemies.[4]

We are not told what actions, if any, Hannibal took next regarding his opponents in Carthage, but this does lay bare internal opposition to the

Barcid faction and their continued monopoly on the Spanish command. Nevertheless, Hannibal was confirmed as the Carthaginian commander in Spain and immediately set off on a fresh series of expansionist campaigns. This is understandable, given that he would want to quickly prove that he was able to fill the role at such a young age and silence any critics at home. Polybius provides us with details:

> Hannibal on assuming the command, at once set forth with the view of subduing a tribe called the Olcades, and arriving before their most powerful city Althaea, encamped there and soon made himself master of it by a series of vigorous and formidable assaults, upon which the rest of the tribe were overawed and submitted to the Carthaginians. After exacting tribute from the towns and possessing himself of a considerable sum, he retired to winter quarters at New Carthage. By the generosity he now displayed to the troops under his command, paying them in part and promising further payment, he inspired in them great good-will to himself and high hopes of the future.[5]

We do not know when in 221 BC Hannibal took command, but he immediately set off on campaign against the Olcades and had subdued them in time to return to winter quarters. Livy provides some additional information about the Olcades:

> He began by invading the Olcades, a tribe who were within the boundaries but not under the dominion of Carthage. [6]

> Cartala, a wealthy city and the capital of the tribe, was taken by storm and sacked; the smaller cities, fearing a similar fate, capitulated and agreed to pay an indemnity. His victorious army enriched with plunder was marched into winter quarters in New Carthage. Here, by a lavish distribution of the spoils and the punctual discharge of all arrears of pay, he secured the allegiance of his own people and of the allied contingents.[7]

The campaign was against a localised enemy who already fell within the boundaries of the Carthaginian sphere of influence, making it an excellent choice for a short, sharp campaign in what time remained of the 221 BC campaigning season. As both Polybius and Livy note, not only was Hannibal able to cement his reputation and thus secure his position as commander in Spain, he was also able to gather a large amount of booty to distribute to his army and possibly his allies back in Carthage. With this under his belt, he set off on a fresh campaign in 220 BC. Both Polybius and Livy devote passages to these campaigns:

> Next summer he made a fresh attack on the Vaccaei, assaulted and took Hermandica at the first onset, but Arbacala being a very large city with a numerous and brave population, he had to lay siege to it and only took it by assault after much pains.[8]

> At the beginning of spring he extended his operations to the Vaccaei, and two of their cities, Arbocala and Hermandica, were taken by assault. Arbocala held out for a considerable time, owing to the courage and numbers of its defenders. [9]

Hannibal was again able to subdue another of the native Spanish tribes. Unfortunately for him, the other tribes of the region seem to have once again taken the change of Carthaginian command as the ideal opportunity to band together and try to drive the Carthaginians back. Whilst he was campaigning against the Vaccaei, an alliance of the other tribes, a mixture of those yet unconquered and remnants of the defeated tribes, launched an attack on the Carthaginians. Polybius and Livy preserve accounts of the battle:

> Subsequently on his return he unexpectedly found himself in great peril, the Carpetani, the strongest tribe in the district gathering to attack him and being joined by the neighbouring tribes, all incited to this by the fugitive Olcades, and also by those who had escaped from Hermandica. Had the Carthaginians been obliged to meet all this host in a pitched battle, they would assuredly have suffered defeat; but, as it was, Hannibal very wisely and skilfully faced about and retreated so as to place the River Tagus in his front, and remained there to dispute the crossing, availing himself of the aid both of the river and of his elephants, of which he had about forty, so that everything went as he had calculated and as no one else would have dared to expect. For when the barbarians tried to force a crossing at various points, the greater mass

of them perished in coming out of the river, the elephants following its bank and being upon them as soon as they landed. Many also were cut down in the stream itself by the cavalry, as the horses could bear up better against the current, and the mounted men in fighting had the advantage of being higher than the unmounted enemy. Finally, Hannibal in his turn crossed the river and attacked the barbarians, putting to flight a force of more than one hundred thousand.[10]

...the fugitives from Hermandica joined hands with those of the Olcades who had abandoned their country - this tribe had been subjugated the previous year – and together they stirred up the Carpetani to war. Not far from the Tagus an attack was made upon Hannibal as he was returning from his expedition against the Vaccaei, and his army, laden as it was with plunder, was thrown into some confusion. Hannibal declined battle and fixed his camp by the side of the river; as soon as there was quiet and silence amongst the enemy, he forded the stream. His entrenchments had been carried just far enough to allow room for the enemy to cross over, and he decided to attack them during their passage of the river. He instructed his cavalry to wait until they had actually entered the water and then to attack them; his forty elephants he stationed on the bank. The Carpetani together with the contingents of the Olcades and Vaccaei numbered altogether 100,000 men, an irresistible force had they been fighting on level ground. Their innate fearlessness, the confidence inspired by their numbers, their belief that the enemy's retreat was due to fear, all made them look on victory as certain, and the river as the only obstacle to it. Without any word of command having been given, they raised a universal shout and plunged, each man straight in front of him, into the river. A huge force of cavalry descended from the opposite bank, and the two bodies met in mid-stream. The struggle was anything but an equal one. The infantry, feeling their footing insecure, even where the river was fordable, could have been ridden down even by unarmed horsemen, whereas the cavalry, with their bodies and weapons free and their horses steady even in the midst of the current, could fight at close quarters or not, as they chose. A large proportion were swept down the river, some were carried by cross currents to the other side where the enemy were, and were trampled to death by the elephants. Those in the rear thought it safest to return to their own side, and began to collect together as well as their fears allowed them, but before they had time to recover themselves Hannibal entered the river with his infantry in battle order and drove them in flight from the bank. He followed up his victory by laying waste their fields, and in a few days was able to receive the submission of the Carpetani.[11]

Both Polybius and Livy (probably using the former) provide us with a number of 100,000 for the combined tribal armies which attacked Hannibal, though as always we must treat these numbers with caution. But it is clear that Hannibal won a major victory and broke the back of the remaining resistance in south-eastern Spain. Polybius and Livy end their sections by stating that all of Spain south of the Ebro had fallen to Carthage (whether by formal conquest by having paid homage). Despite their various efforts, it is clear that the Spanish tribes were being worn down by the constant Carthaginian campaigning, slowly picked off tribe after tribe. When the tribes were able to unify their efforts and challenge the Carthaginians en-masse, it seems that this merely led to a far greater set piece defeat. At the heart of the Carthaginian success lay an extraordinary series of three commanders, Hamilcar, Hasdrubal and Hannibal, all close family members (whether by blood or marriage) and all pursing a coherent and constant strategy of Carthaginian (and Barcid) expansion.

However, we must always treat with caution claims that all of Spain south of the Ebro had fallen to Carthage. In terms of the eastern Spanish seaboard this may have been a reflection of the truth, but we are not clear how far this Carthaginian Empire stretched into the Spanish interior, to the north and west. By later Roman times, these tribes fought fiercely for their independence, with nearly two centuries of warfare. Yet it is clear that Carthage dominated Spain's eastern seaboard, through direct rule or tribute. We do not know how many towns or settlements lay outside of their direct control, but by far the most significant was Saguntum.

Carthaginian Expansion and the Siege of Saguntum (219 BC)

Hannibal's campaign against the alliance of native tribes took place during 220 BC. The year that followed saw an escalation of the Carthaginian campaign, which resulted in the clash which many must have anticipated: war with Rome. We know the event that was used as the excuse for a second war between Carthage and Rome; the Carthaginian attack and capture of Saguntum. What we don't know, and will never know for certain, is why it happened?

Saguntum lay to the south of the Ebro, the de-facto demarcation line between Roman and Carthaginian influence. Saguntum was an anomaly, and perhaps designed to be so by the Romans, as it had some form of alliance with Rome. For the last 2,000 years historians have debated the exact nature of this treaty, with views ranging from everything from informal friendship to formal alliance.[12] Ultimately we must accept that, based on the current surviving evidence, we will never be able to ascertain the exact nature of the relationship between Rome and Saguntum. Nevertheless, the motives behind the relationship are clearer to discern. The Saguntines must have hoped that the ties to Rome would guarantee their independence from the ever-growing Carthaginian Empire.

For the Romans, the ties with Saguntum had two advantages, one immediate and one which had greater potential. In terms of the immediate factors, Rome now had an outpost in Carthaginian territory, which was well-placed to report to Rome on Carthaginian activities, as well as afford opportunities for Roman officials to visit and use as a base of operations should they wish. Saguntum forms part of a chain of Roman outposts which ringed their Italian Empire, from Massilia in Gaul to the Cenomani and Venetia in Gallic Northern Italy, their allies in Illyria and even their possessions in western Sicily. Saguntum was the most westerly outpost of Roman influence. However, Saguntum also afforded the Romans a potential reason to intervene in Carthaginian affairs. A disagreement, whether real or contrived, could easily erupt between Saguntum and their more dominant neighbour, which Rome could use to their advantage and back their ally. This does not mean that the Romans were treaty-bound to intervene, merely that they had the potential to do so should they wish.

According to Polybius it seems that the Saguntines had sent emissaries to alert Rome to Hannibal's victories against the tribal alliance led by the Carpetani and the implications for increased Carthaginian control over the eastern Spanish seaboard.[13] Naturally, the Saguntines would have been alarmed by this expansion of Carthaginian control and what it held for them and would have been seeking reassurances from the Roman Senate that

Rome would act on their behalf if need be. Again, it needs to be stressed that we don't know the terms of the alliance between Saguntum and Rome, and more specifically whether the Romans were pledged to defend Saguntum from Carthaginian attack; and even if they were, whether they would honour it. All this must have been in the Saguntines' minds when they sent their emissaries to Rome.

Polybius states that the Senate had paid little attention to the Saguntines in previous years, but that on this occasion they sent a Senatorial delegation to Spain to investigate.[14] We know of two members of the delegation: Q. Baebius Tamphilus and P. Valerius Flaccus,[15] the latter a former Consul of 227 BC. By the time they reached New Carthage, however, the Carthaginians were already at war with Saguntum.

All the sources we have for this conflict, and the events it led to, date from later periods and are all Roman or pro-Roman. By then the war and the myths surrounding Hannibal and his eternal enmity for Rome were well set in the historical canon. The standard narrative is that Hannibal was merely awaiting an opportunity to go to war with Rome, as were his predecessors, and that this was his sole aim. Whilst it may be true that another war between Carthage and Rome was always likely, we must try at least to view events from the perspective of the time.

According to Appian, the war between Carthage and Saguntum came about as a result of a dispute between Saguntum and a neighbouring tribe, the Turbuletes, who seem to have been Carthaginian clients.[16] Appian follows the belief that this quarrel was engineered by Hannibal as a reason to intervene. What is clear is that Hannibal referred the matter back to the Carthaginian Senate, who authorized him to intervene against Saguntum. What is unclear is the chronology behind these events and the dispatch of a Roman Senatorial delegation to New Carthage. Was it purely to investigate Carthaginian expansion or was it to deal with this dispute between a Roman client and a Carthaginian one? The whole issue is muddied further by Polybius' undated reference to internal dissension within Saguntum itself, which the Romans had apparently previously intervened in:

> …in his answer to the legates affected to be guarding the interests of the Saguntines he accused the Romans of having a short time previously, when there was a party quarrel at Saguntum and they were called in to arbitrate, unjustly put to death some of the leading men.[17]

Modern commentators have taken this to refer to the existence of two key factions within the Saguntine elite, one pro-Carthaginian, and one pro-Roman. These factions are easy enough to visualize and replicated divisions seen across the Mediterranean world, when small cities were faced with a far larger power on their doorstep, as often seen in Greece. Some of the elites saw co-operation or collaboration as the only way to maintain their independence, whilst others saw opposition and alliance with a rival power as the best option. What is clear is that at some point previously (and unrecorded elsewhere, aside from this reference in Polybius), dissension between these factions had led to civil strife within Saguntum itself, so much so that the Romans had to send a delegation to restore pro-Roman dominance. This does suggest that the pro-Carthaginian faction had been in the ascendancy. Unfortunately, we have no date for this Roman intervention, but most commentators argue that it was in the previous few years (c.223–220 BC).[18]

It is tempting to see Hannibal's hand in these in internal dissensions. If Saguntum was a 'Roman thorn in his side' then it would have been to his advantage to encourage and assist the pro-Carthaginian elements of the Saguntine elite to seize control and possibly repudiate the treaty with Rome, thus bringing them fully into the Carthaginian fold without the need for bloodshed or confrontation with Rome. It is also possible that this dispute needed no outside agitation to turn into violence. It is equally tempting to argue that if Hannibal's' ploy to subvert Saguntum had indeed been blocked by Roman intervention, then he determined to deal with Saguntum in a more direct manner and thus engineered the dispute with their neighbours, the Turbuletes. It must also have been in Hannibal's mind that, despite the Ebro Treaty, Rome had intervened in Saguntum, albeit not militarily, and that they had removed the pro-Carthaginian elements.

Given the paucity and one-sidedness of our surviving ancient sources, it is clear that we will never know what the motivations or machinations were which lay behind these events. What we do know is that Hannibal, with the apparent blessing of the Carthaginian Senate, launched an attack on Saguntum. Both Polybius and Appian refer to Hannibal crossing the Ebro.[19] Of the two, Appian clearly states that Hannibal crossed the Ebro to attack Saguntum, which is nonsense, as Saguntum lies 100 miles to the south of the Ebro, but Appian must be repeating the tradition that Hannibal clearly violated the Ebro Treaty and thus caused the war. More interesting is Polybius' oblique reference to the Ebro:

The Romans protested against his attacking Saguntum, which they said was under their protection, or crossing the Ebro, contrary to the treaty engagements entered into in Hasdrubal's time.[20]

Polybius does not directly attach the crossing of the Ebro to the attack on Saguntum, but seems to be listing them as two separate factors, both of which showed that Hannibal was clearly (to Roman minds at least) at fault for the subsequent war. However, nowhere else is it mentioned that Hannibal had crossed the Ebro or even gone near it until war with Rome had been declared. Some modern commentators have argued that Hannibal followed up the defeat of Saguntum with a march across the Ebro, but there is no clear evidence he crossed the Ebro until after the Roman declaration of war.[21]

Perhaps the most notable feature about the Carthaginian campaign against Saguntum was its length. All too often ancient accounts gloss over the campaign itself in their haste to reach the subsequent Punic War. Yet the Carthaginian attack on Saguntum turned into a protracted siege of the city, which lasted for eight or nine months (depending on the source), indicating the strength of the city's defences and perhaps its size and importance. Livy called it the richest city south of the Ebro, located about a mile (seven stades) from the sea, and centre of a land and naval trading network, making it a prize for the Carthaginian Empire in its own right.[22]

We are told that the city was protected by strong defensive walls with a number of towers. There are also references to a harbour, but given the location of the city itself, a mile from the sea, we must assume that this was separate from the city. We have no references to the Saguntines having the equivalent of the Athenian 'long walls' which connected the inland city of Athens to the Piraeus harbour.

Polybius dismisses the campaign with the following sentence: 'At length after eight months of hardship and anxiety he took the city by storm.'[23] Livy however, provides a lengthy and detailed account of the siege of Saguntum, though we are not certain from where this account originated. Eutropius provides figures for the size of the Carthaginian besieging force at Saguntum of 50,000 infantry and 20,000 cavalry.[24] Livy puts the figure even higher, at 150,000.[25]

Given what must have been a massive disparity in the size of the two forces, the Saguntines wisely seem to have retreated behind their city walls and prepared for a siege, leaving the Carthaginians to ravage the Saguntine territory around the city. Presumably one of the first targets for the Carthaginians must have been the Saguntine harbour. Even Livy's detailed account does not refer to an attack on the harbour, but does mention that the harbour was in Carthaginian hands whilst the city itself was still being laid siege to.

Livy tells us that Hannibal opted to attack the city from three separate points, utilising the flat ground to approach the walls with his battering rams. These attacks were beaten off by the defenders firstly with a barrage of missiles and then by sorties from the city.[26] This resulted in heavy casualties for both sides, one of which was Hannibal himself, who apparently took a javelin in the thigh, an injury which forced the initial assault to be abandoned.

With quick victory denied to them, the Carthaginians continued the siege, using battering rams against the city walls. Livy reports that there were a number of successes with walls and towers being brought down, but that the Saguntines were able to utilize the rubble to prevent the Carthaginian forces from entering the city. On the occasions when the Carthaginians penetrated through these gaps, the Saguntines were able to marshal their resources and drive them back out, and used the subsequent respite to rebuild the defensive wall.[27] This process seems to have been repeated at different portions of the city wall.

Livy notes that Hannibal's attention to the siege was distracted by a threatened revolt by the newly-defeated tribes of the Oretani and the Carpetani, in response to their troops being levied into Carthaginian service. Aside from the threatened revolt, this is a fascinating insight into the Carthaginian recruitment policy in Spain. It is clear that the experience of both fighting Rome, with her superior allied manpower reserves, and their own treacherous mercenaries had convinced the Carthaginian commanders of the need to follow Rome's lead and enrol defeated enemies. It seems that within a year of defeating the Oretani and Carpetani, they were being levied to fight in Carthage's armies. A key difference here lay in the nature of the defeated enemy and the control exerted by the dominant power. Rome defeated and enrolled the tribes of Italy who came from societies of a similar developmental level. In contrast, Carthage was enrolling freshly-defeated tribesmen into its armies. Furthermore, Rome's domination of Italy came through a series of one-to-one treaties with each defeated tribe, rather than carving out an obvious land empire, and thus revolts seem to have been more common in Spain than in Italy. Nevertheless, the Carthaginians were making great strides in finding a solution to their manpower deficiencies. In this instance, it seems that swift action by Hannibal, who broke away from the siege with a smaller force and marched on the Oretani and Carpetani, ended any potential revolt.[28]

With the siege continuing, it seems that slowly but surely the Carthaginians made progress in demolishing the walls of Saguntum and securing portions of the city. With defeat looming, it appears that the Saguntines opened negotiations for peace, but were apparently met with harsh proposed conditions from Hannibal, which were rejected by the Saguntine elite:

> The conditions were that restitution should be made to the Turdetani, all the gold and silver should be delivered up, and the inhabitants should depart with one garment each and take up their abode wherever the Carthaginians should order them.[29]

Nevertheless, after eight months of siege the inevitable happened and the Carthaginians, upon knocking down a tower, were able to secure a breach and pour into the city, finally capturing it. The fall of Saguntum was accompanied by a slaughter of all adult males and enslavement of the women and children. Livy dates the fall of Saguntum to the latter part of 219 BC, as Hannibal withdrew his forces back to New Carthage for the winter.[30] The siege of Saguntum highlights two important factors. Firstly, that the Carthaginians apparently took eight months to capture an isolated provincial city, that had been cut off from the coast. Whilst the bravery of the defenders and the strength of their defences must have been factors, we must equally look at deficiencies in the Carthaginian tactics and composition of the army. In open battle, the Carthaginian army seemed to be in its element, but in siege warfare less so. The second obvious factor is that throughout the siege, the Saguntines stood alone, receiving no help from their erstwhile ally, Rome.

The Exhaustion of Diplomacy and the Storm from the East (219–218 BC)

It is all too commonly assumed, both in subsequent ancient sources and by many modern commentators, that the attack on Saguntum was a clear declaration of war against Rome and made war inevitable, as it breached either or both of the Ebro Treaty and the alliance between Saguntum and Rome. However, as stated earlier, an attack on Saguntum itself does not seem as though it could have been a breach of the Ebro Treaty given the Ebro lay 100 miles to the north. At the heart of this problem lies the unclear relationship between Rome and Saguntum and how this fitted in with the Ebro Treaty (as detailed in Chapter Five). Not only are our surviving ancient sources unclear on the details of the treaty and the timings of the alliance with Saguntum, but they are all written long after the event, and in a period when the attack on Saguntum was 'obviously' the cause of the Second Punic War.

Speculation aside, we will never have a clear answer to this question. Nevertheless, the key aspect to take away from this is that we must not assume that an attack on Saguntum would automatically lead to war between Carthage and Rome. Florus maintains a section which seems to refer to the Roman dilemma:

> The Romans are most scrupulous in their observation of treaties; and so, on hearing of the siege of an allied city, mindful of the treaty which had been signed by the Carthaginians, they did not immediately rush to arms, but preferred first to lodge a complaint in a legal form.[31]

This proved to be the case, as during the whole of the eight to nine month siege the Roman Senate did not send military aid to Saguntum, nor did they declare war on Carthage. Instead, we have a record of several diplomatic missions sent by the Roman Senate both to Hannibal in Spain and the Carthaginian Senate in Africa. We have differing accounts of these Senatorial missions in Polybius and Livy. In Polybius, a Senatorial delegation arrived at New Carthage at the beginning of the campaign, perhaps as Hannibal was mobilizing his army. After meeting with Hannibal, they moved on to the Carthaginian Senate itself. Livy seems to place a Senatorial delegation arriving during the siege of Saguntum. On this occasion they did not meet Hannibal, owing to him instructing them not to travel for their own safety, as there was a revolt of the Spanish tribes. He does not say where the Romans were travelling from or to, but we must assume that they docked in New Carthage with the intention of travelling towards Saguntum, where Hannibal was based. Having failed to meet Hannibal, they too then moved onto Africa to speak to the Carthaginian Senate.

Livy fleshes out his account with a detailed description of speeches given in the Carthaginian Senate, especially by Hanno, a noted opponent of the Barcid faction. As is common, we have no way of knowing whether Livy, or one of his sources, is making these speeches up to add some colour to his accounts or whether they did indeed survive and were transmitted via an intermediate historian or documents seized from the destruction of Carthage. However, the content of this speech is deeply pro–Roman, with the Romans apparently demanding, and Hanno proposing agreement with, the following terms:

That a commission be at once despatched to Rome to inform the Senate of our compliance with their demands, and a second to Hannibal ordering him to withdraw his army from Saguntum and then surrendering him to the Romans in accordance with the terms of the treaty, and I also propose that a third body of commissioners be sent to make reparation to the Saguntines.[32]

Are we to believe that Rome demanded the handing over of Hannibal and formal submission by the Carthaginian Senate to Rome? Given the respective balance of power in the 230s BC, this might have been the case, but the situation in 219 BC was somewhat different, with Rome faced by a resurgent Carthaginian Empire in Spain. Certainly Rome was in a stronger position in 219 BC than it was in 226 BC when it concluded the Ebro Treaty, on account of their victory over the Gallic tribes of northern Italy. Ultimately, however, the Carthaginian Senate rejected the Roman terms (whatever they might have been), which left the next course of action with the Roman Senate.

Throughout 219 BC, Rome's primary focus had been closer to home and the war in Illyria, fought to re-establish control of the buffer zone on their eastern flank (as seen in Chapter Ten). Although the war ultimately proved to be a quick one, this was not immediately obvious from the outset and

Rome too could have easily become entangled in a protracted series of sieges. There was also the matter of Macedon to consider, as Rome was at war with a ruler who was at times a Macedonian client. The one thing Rome could not afford was a simultaneous war against the two other superpowers of the central and western Mediterranean (Carthage and Macedon). Therefore, unlike Florus, who seems to believe that Rome delayed any action in Spain out of the desire to observe legal process and treaty obligations, there were some very hard military and diplomatic reasons why a war with Carthage was not rushed into and why Saguntum was left to its fate.

In Livy's narrative, the latest diplomatic mission to Carthage returned to Rome on the same day as news of the fall of Saguntum. Livy's account also has the dramatic flourish, seen in other Roman sources, where the Romans believe the Carthaginians are now flooding across the Ebro, in clear violation of the treaty. Again, this seems to be the result of a later lack of clarity over where Saguntum was in relation to the Ebro and a desire to paint the Carthaginians as clear violators of the treaty, and therefore justify Rome going to war.

The truth of the matter is that Rome went to war because they wanted to, not because they were forced to. It is unclear whether the Carthaginians were even violating the Ebro Treaty by attacking Saguntum, and there is no evidence they did cross the Ebro before war was declared. Even if a treaty was violated, this is nothing compared to the cold, hard-thought processes that must have gone through the minds of the Roman Senate when debating their actions. Few would have even been to Saguntum let alone cared about its actual fate. As Astin states, there is an apparent paradox in that 'Rome declared war because of the fall of a city which she had conspicuously failed to help.'[33]

Far more important would have been what the act represented: a resurgent Carthage, which no longer feared Rome or had to bow to Rome's demands. Most in the Senate would have been men who served in the First Punic War and been in the Senate in the 230s BC, when Rome had simply decreed Carthaginian fate and had only to threaten war to have Carthage back down. There must have been many who had heard reports of Carthaginian expansion in Spain, but not really conceptualized what this meant, especially in terms of the changing balance of power between Rome and Carthage. In 226 BC, the clear threat had been the Gauls, the Ebro Treaty had been a necessity and Spain a distraction from the Gallic War to come.

By 218 BC, however, the situation had changed again; the Gauls had been defeated comprehensively and northern Italy was now securely under Roman rule (direct or indirect). Control of certain of the Illyrian territories had been resecured and relations with Macedon had not obviously deteriorated. With all these other matters settled, the Senate had time to turn their attention to the west. In reality, Saguntum itself didn't matter, which is why the Senate left it to its fate; but what it represented did matter. With the fall of Saguntum, Rome had no allies left south of the Ebro, and although there was no indication that Hannibal would be planning on crossing the Ebro (given that huge swathes of inland Spain lay unconquered), there must have been many who saw that Carthage was a clear rival once more and that if war had to come, it was best sooner rather than later. Roman armies had been at war every year since 226 BC, creating a huge reserve of veteran soldiers and a cadre of battle-tested officers.

Thus the Roman Senate determined on war with Carthage, to be fought in Spain, or so they believed. The people were summoned and duly voted for war. The Consuls of 218 BC were P. Cornelius Scipio and Ti Sempronius Longus. Scipio was assigned Spain as his province, whilst Longus received Sicily and Africa; the former for offence and the latter for defence. Rome found itself in their second major war within a decade. Their rivals for control of Italy had been defeated, now they faced their rival for control of the wider western Mediterranean. Within four years, Rome also found itself at war with Macedon, their rival for control of Illyria and ultimately Greece, setting off seventy years of warfare which would lead to Roman supremacy over the Mediterranean.

Conclusion – The Grand Strategy of the Roman Republic?[1]

Having reviewed the evidence, there can be no doubt that the twenty years between the end of the First Punic War and the beginning of the Second Punic War were critical for the development of the Roman Republic and its nascent empire. It is also clear that if we are talking in strategic terms, then Rome was operating at least two different strategies, one for Italy and one outside of Italy. Whilst Rome was clearly in an expansionist frame of mind outside of Italy, paradoxically, for the majority of this period, Rome was on the defensive within Italy itself. In the Gallic Wars of the 230s and the 220s, Rome sat back and awaited the attack of the Gallic tribes. This defensive strategy seems to have been born out of two factors; the seriousness of the threat posed and the historic legacy of the fourth century sack of Rome.

In this period the one true threat to the continued existence of the Roman Republic and its growing empire was not Carthage, who occupied the periphery of the Roman world, but the Gauls of Northern Italy, who lay only a few days' march from Rome itself. Whilst we will never know the true intent and objectives of the Gallic invasion of 225 BC, but given its scale (the use of tribes from both sides of the Alps) and the direct path the invasion took, it does seem that the Gauls had determined to destroy Roman power in Italy before the Romans continued their own expansion northwards into Cisalpine Gaul.

The obvious target was the city of Rome itself, which had been successfully (from the Gallic point of view) sacked in the fourth century. If Rome could have been attacked and destroyed this would clearly have thrown Rome's whole federation into disarray, and would have led to a number of her allies deserting her. We have no way of knowing whether Rome would have been able to withstand such an attack, but throughout the later Republican and Imperial period the city itself was never noted for being able to withstand sieges, as seen in Rome's many later civil wars. We also have no way of telling whether Rome's alliances would have held firm. The Carthaginians adopted a similar tactic a decade later, which did result in some defections in the south of Italy, notably Capua, but then Rome itself was left untouched.

Given the seriousness of the Gallic threat to Rome, the key question is why did the Romans not take the offensive, as they had done in every other theatre of war? The answer to this must lie in a combination of the sheer scale of the task that faced them and the psychological damage inflicted by the Gauls with the fourth century sack of Rome. The other peoples of Italy which Rome had subdued in the preceding century were all of an equivalent magnitude, such as the Samnite Federation, or were weaker, such as the cites of Magna Graecia (southern Italy). The Gallic tribes of northern Italy, however, were more numerous and could field a larger army than Rome, and had the ability to summon reinforcements from across the Alps.

This raises another important issue, one of perception. To modern eyes, Italy is a coherent entity south of the Alps. However in this period, Italy ended north of the Apennines, beyond which was the vastness of Gaul, stretching from the Oceanus Britannicus (English Channel) to the Apennines, bypassing the Alps as a natural barrier. Thus, Rome potentially faced an endless tide of Gallic tribes form the vast geographical region that they understood as Gaul. The other potential factor at work here is the psychological impact to the collective Roman psyche caused by the defeat at the Battle of Allia and the Sack of Rome (c.390–386 BC), which was forever ingrained in Roman memory. Up to this point, no enemy had inflicted such a defeat on Rome and any mention of the Gauls must have conjured up images of these previous humiliations, making Romans understandably more cautious than they were in dealings with the other races of the Mediterranean world.

However, what is clear is that Rome in this period did not simply sit back and ignore the situation. Whilst there seems to have been no question of a military thrust across the River Po and into the heartland of Cisalpine Gaul, Rome seems to have had two additional strategies, one diplomatic and one military, to reduce the threat they faced. Firstly came the diplomatic efforts to gain allies amongst the tribes across the Po; which paid off to some extent when the Venti and the Cenomani allied with Rome in the 220s. Secondly came the military strategy of subduing Liguria, which lay on the western flank of both the Roman Federation and Cisalpine Gaul. This Rome could accomplish without taking on the full might of the tribes which occupied the Po Valley. Nevertheless, both of these sub-strategies did little to counter the danger of a full-scale invasion by a large alliance of tribes. In fact, although Rome had some success in gaining allies from across the Po (and who wouldn't take part in any subsequent invasion), their numbers were more than made up by the influx of tribes from across the Alps.

The cornerstone to this defensive strategy would have been good intelligence, to give the Romans time to mobilize their formidable manpower resources and know from which direction an attack was coming from: east or west of the Apennines. The Gallic invasion of 225 BC showed both the strengths and weaknesses of this strategy. Due to the mobilization of tribes within Cisalpine Gaul and the crossing of tribes from beyond the Alps, word reached Rome in time and they were able to muster a massive army in response. Unfortunately, they seem to have expected the main trust to come to the east of Apennines, as in the 230s, and seem to have left the western route more lightly guarded. This blunder exposed the western flank of the Roman Federation and potentially exposed Rome itself.

Central to this whole period is the Battle of Telamon, which stands as one of the greatest victories in Rome's history. The importance of this battle does not just lie in the victory itself, but its impact and consequences. Thanks to the brilliance of the Consul L. Aemilius Papus (who clearly needs acknowledging as a great Roman general), a massive Gallic invasion was wiped out in a single battle. What also seems to have been defeated that day was the 'myth' of Gallic invincibility. Rome's worst fear of a Gallic invasion, seemingly intent on again attacking Rome itself, had been realised, but then defeated by strength of arms and in just one battle.

Aemilius' other masterstroke was to immediately take the offensive, launching what was to be an unprecedented assault on the tribes of Cisalpine Gaul. It must be questioned whether Aemilius had the authority to launch such an attack; his orders must have been simply to defeat the Gallic invasion. Nevertheless, he successfully reckoned that the time was right to finally go on the offensive, having destroyed so much of the Gallic fighting strength, and press home Rome's advantage before the tribes had time to recover.

Thus the Battle of Telamon led to Rome abandoning the defensive strategy they had adopted towards the tribes of Cisalpine Gaul and saw the region being viewed as Rome would any other, and a new offensive strategy being employed. The battle also signalled a turning point in the history of the Romano-Gallic relationship, with Rome ending the threat of Gallic invasions (from Cisalpine Gaul at least) and bringing the region under Roman domination, if not direct rule. From this point onwards, Roman

Consuls regularly campaigned against tribes of Cisalpine Gaul, thus ending one on the greatest and gravest threats to Roman security.

Outside of Italy however, Roman strategy was another matter altogether, and Rome was clearly not on the defensive. Once the evidence, such as it is, is examined, Rome's dealings with the wider Mediterranean world cannot be reduced to simply having one offensive strategy, but reveals a complex and shifting pattern of strategies. What can perhaps be seen is that there is a clear pattern behind these different strategies, based on zones of influence. It has often been argued that the later Roman Empire adopted a strategy based on a series of zones of control based on geographical proximity,[2] with the regions nearest to Italy being under direct control (as provinces), buffered by client states, followed by nominally independent regions with looser ties to Rome (such as economic) and then the regions free from Roman influence. We can see an early variation of this strategy in play in this period.

At the heart of the Roman Republic lay central and southern Italy, which was a curious mix of areas of direct control (with citizen populations) and those of indirect control (those tied to Rome by treaty). Outside of Italy lay Cisalpine Gaul (northern Italy), an area of indirect control (following 225 BC) and the islands of Sicily, Sardinia and Corsica, which were provinces under direct Roman control. To the east lay the Roman protectorate of Illyria, a group of client states and races under indirect control, while Rome had economic and some cultural ties to the rest of Greece and the wider Hellenistic system. Outside of Italy, to the north and the far west, in Gaul and Spain, were cities such as Saguntum and Massilia, which had loose ties to Rome, via treaties of friendship, but acted as unofficial outposts of Roman interest.

It is interesting to examine reasons behind the different strategies adopted in each area. One clear factor at play here is that of geography. The three islands, which were Rome's first provinces, were each geographically well-defined and had no borders with other states, thus limiting Roman exposure to wider hostile regions. This may explain the difference between Rome's strategies towards Sicily, used as a springboard for an invasion of Italy in the 300s, and Illyria, a springboard for an invasion of Italy in the 280s. One became a province, the other a cluster of client states.

Another important factor in Rome's strategy towards the regions outside of Italy was that of security. Within the prior fifty years southern Italy had been invaded by the Syracusans and Epirotes, both looking to add the region to their developing empires. Carthage also posed a clear and credible threat, with control of large swathes of Sicily and the islands of Sardinia and Corsica. If Rome wished to remain in control of southern Italy, these springboards for invasion needed to be secured. Whilst the islands were geographically isolated enough to be turned into provinces, the same could not be said of Illyria. Direct control would mean sharing borders with a whole range of Illyrian tribes, not to mention offending the cultural sensitivities of the rest of Greece, by directly annexing a swathe of Greek territory. Not only would Rome alienate and alarm a number of potential allies in the region, such as the principal political leagues, but would be an overt challenge to the long-established dominance of Macedon in the region, whose own borders lay on the other side of Illyria.

This brings us to the vexed question of motivation. Over the years a number of theories have been argued for what motivated Rome to an expansionist policy, whether it be defensive imperialism, a social and political structure that encouraged warfare or economic motivations? It does appear that a perceived desire for security was an important factor here. In this period Rome developed an outer buffer zone of provinces and regions under domination which protected the core Italian heartland. To the south lay Sicily, to the east Illyria, to the west Sardinia and Corsica (and to some extent Liguria) and to the north Cisalpine Gaul.

This is not to say that the various noble families which made up the Senate had a coherent policy here. This is ably demonstrated in the *volte-face* over Sardinia and Corsica between 241 and 238 BC. Originally the islands were returned to Carthage, but then annexed just a few years later. Furthermore Rome helped Carthage in the early years of the Mercenary War and then declared a Second Punic War just a few years later.

It is also apparent that the Romans' horizons expanded in this period, in their search for new threats. This is evident in their policy towards the Carthaginians in Spain. Control of Sardinia, Corsica and Sicily gave the Romans a secure buffer zone from any real or imagined Carthaginian threat, yet the Senate, or a faction within it, still felt it necessary to send a delegation to Spain to investigate Carthaginian expansion. On this occasion the delegation seemed satisfied that there was no threat. By 226 BC, however, the Senate was alarmed enough about the threat from the Gauls that they needed to secure a treaty with the Carthaginians over Spain, potentially limiting their northern expansion; though the border did tacitly acknowledge the vast majority of Spain as Carthaginian.

It cannot be said that these strategies which the Senate implemented brought about the security that they apparently felt they needed. In many respects, this only achieved some measure of success in the north with the tribes of Cisalpine Gaul, and then only due to the victories on the battlefield which began with Telamon. The Roman settlement in Illyria unravelled within a decade and brought Rome closer to conflict with the regional hegemon, Macedon, by clearly crossing into their zone of influence. To the west, Roman attempts to limit Carthaginian expansion had clearly failed, with the Barcid family carving out an empire that not only rebuilt Carthaginian resources, but made her stronger than ever. In the near west, the supposedly limited annexations of Sardinia and Corsica dragged Rome into decades, if not centuries, of guerrilla warfare with the natives, whilst to the south the acquiescence of the client kingdom of Syracuse was dependent upon the personal loyalty of its ruler.

Nevertheless, it is clear that this period was a crucial one for the development of the Roman Republic. The Gallic threat from northern Italy was ended and Rome acquired its first provinces and took its first step across the Adriatic into the wider Greek and Hellenistic world. Both these latter actions set Rome down a path that would inevitably draw her into further expansion and further conflicts. However, the success that Rome was to enjoy was not inevitable and further conflicts with the rival powers of Carthage and Macedon would take Roman warfare and expansion into realms undreamed of by the Roman Senate and people of Rome in this period.

Appendix I

The Sources

Any study of this crucial period is constrained by the limited number of surviving sources we have for these years. This period falls between a break in the books of Livy, which restart in 218 BC, again showing how this period suffered in the later ancient and medieval worlds in comparison to the Second Punic War. Nevertheless, we cannot fully understand the history of this period if we do not have an understanding of the sources we must rely on and the ones we have lost.

Surviving Sources

Key Sources

Polybius – Histories *(second century BC)*
Of all of our surviving sources, the most notable is Polybius and the sections of his *Histories* which survive. Writing in the mid-second century BC, his *Histories* are the earliest surviving source for this period (writing only 100 years after) and contain many details not found elsewhere. However, on events in the 230s, such as the wars against the Boii and Ligurians, and the Roman embassy to the Aetolians, the detail is lacking, if not omitted altogether. Polybius' *Histories* are also important as they predate the shaping of an official version of Roman history in the late Republican and early Imperial period, and the civil strife cause by the Gracchan Tribunates. The end of Book One and the beginning of Book Two provide us with a crucial framework for events in this period, especially concerning the Gallic War of the 220s and the Battle of Telamon. These are best used in conjunction with Walbank's commentary.

Zonaras – Epitome of History *(twelfth century AD)*
John Zonaras was a Byzantine chronicler who compiled an abridgment (epitome) of the *Histories* of Cassius Dio. He preserves a number of details

about this period which either supplement Polybius or are unique to these accounts. His provides the only surviving narrative for the Boian and Ligurian campaigns of the 230s.

Lesser Sources

Appian – Illyrian Wars, Punic Wars, Spanish Wars *(second century AD)*
Appian was a second century AD Greek scholar from Alexandria, who wrote a series of works charting the various wars the Romans fought, separated geographically. Although they contain a number of anachronisms the *Spanish* and *Illyrian Wars* provide useful additional information on this period, as does his *Punic Wars*. The anachronisms, such as Saguntum being north of the Ebro, do mean that the details need to be treated with caution.

Cassius Dio – History of Rome *(third century AD)*
Cassius Dio was a Roman senator, of Greek birth, who served under the Serveran dynasty of the late second and early third centuries. He wrote a history of Rome from its origins to AD 229 in eighty books, most of which only survive in fragments. Book Twelve covers the period in question and survives thanks to Zonaras' abridgment.

Cornelius Nepos – De Viris Illustribus *(first century BC)*
Cornelius Nepos was a first century BC scholar, and friend of Cicero, who wrote many works, including a series of short lives of famous Greeks and Romans, many of which still survive. These include lives of Hamilcar and Hannibal.

Diodorus – Library of History *(first century BC)*
Diodorus of Sicily's (Siculus) work took the form of a universal history of the ancient world from its earliest day down to his time. Although much of it has been lost, his later chapters on Roman history provide a wealth of previously unknown details, including the Carthaginian campaigns in Spain.

Eutropius – Breviarium of Roman History *(fourth century AD)*
Flavius Eutropius was a fourth century AD writer who compiled an abridged version of Roman history using earlier sources. For the period in question he relied heavily on the now lost books of Livy. Despite its brevity, it occasionally provides detail not recorded elsewhere in surviving sources, such as the visit of Hiero, Tyrant of Syracuse, to Rome in 237 BC

Florus – Epitome of Roman History *(second century AD)*
Lucius Annaeus Florus wrote a short abridgement (epitome) of Roman
Republican history. Despite its brevity, he preserves accounts for a number
of the wars of the period and gives us an insight into the narrative histories
that are now lost.

Frontinus – Stratagems *(first century AD)*
Sextus Julius Frontinus was a Roman Senator and military commander of
the first century AD. He wrote a number of technical treaties, including one
on military stratagems, which collected large numbers of excerpts of military
history from other writers. Again, on occasion these provide additional
details for events not well covered by our surviving narrative sources.

Justin – Epitome of Pompeius Trogus *(200–400 AD)*
Marcus Iunianius Iustinus wrote a short abridgement (epitome) of the
Hellenistic History written by Pompeius Trogus, an Augustan historian. He
preserves many events not recorded in other surviving sources, such as the
Roman embassy to the Aetolians in the 230s BC. When he was writing is not
known, but estimates range between AD 200–400.   .

Orosius – Seven Books against the Pagans *(fifth century AD)*
Paulus Orosius was a Christian writer of the fifth century AD, who produced
an abridged history of the ancient world which preserves a number of
interesting accounts of Roman history. Book Four covers the period in
question and provides detail not recovered elsewhere in surviving sources,
such as casualty figures for battles, including Telamon. Fear has produced a
fine new translation to accompany this.[1]

Plutarch – Life of Marcellus, Life of Fabius *(first/second century AD)*
Plutarch was a Greek scholar of the late first/early second century AD,
originally from Chaeronea. His best known works are the parallel lives, a
series of biographies of famous Greek and Roman statesmen. His *Life of M.
Claudius Marcellus* preserves an account of the Battle of Clastidium and the
later Gallic campaigns, details of which can also be found in his *Life of Q.
Fabius Maximus*.

Silius Italicus – Punica *(first century AD)*
Tiberius Catius Asconius Silius Italicus was a Roman nobleman and poet. His only surviving work is the *Punica*, a 12,000 line poem about the Second Punic War. His work contains details about the individuals of the period not recorded elsewhere by surviving sources.

Strabo – Geography *(first century BC/first century AD)*
Strabo was a Greek who travelled widely in the ancient world, including settling at Rome for a period during the late Republic. His Geography details the various races and countries of the ancient world and provides background to the period, including a section on Illyria.

Valerius Maximus – Memorable Deeds and Sayings *(first century AD)*
Valerius Maximus was a Roman scholar of the early Empire, who wrote many works, one of which was his nine books of *Memorable Deeds and Sayings*, which was a large collection of facts preserved from other works. He sometimes provides additional details for events not well covered by other surviving narrative sources.

Unknown – De Viris Illustribus *(unknown)*
This anonymous work contains a large number of short biographies of famous figures from the ancient world. Although they are brief, on many occasions they preserve facts not recorded elsewhere by surviving sources.[2]

Unknown – Periochae of Livy *(unknown)*
Despite the loss of Livy's grand narrative history of the Republic, for events between 241 and 218 BC, we do have a surviving collection of summaries of his lost books. We have little idea when they were summarized or by whom, but they condense Livy's narrative into a series of headlines for events that took place each year. Even reduced to such a format, they still provide us with valuable information for the period.

Lost Sources for the Period
As well as a brief survey of the surviving sources, it is important to understand the ones that have not survived from antiquity which would have been of most use. Vast numbers of ancient sources, Greek, Roman and Punic, have been lost to us but would have been available to the ancient sources which do

still survive. The best modern work showing the scope of Roman material we have lost is the *Fragments of the Roman Historians*.[3] Below are just a selection of the key sources we have lost for this period.

Roman Sources

Fabius Pictor – History of Rome *(third century BC)*
Of the many lost histories of Rome, it is Q. Fabius Pictor's that is the most keenly felt. Not only was his *History* the first written by a Roman (albeit in Greek), but he took part in the Gallic Wars of the 220s and thus would have been able to provide us with a first-hand account of the period. His work was used by an unknown number of later historians. According to Eutropius, it was Fabius who provided the figure for total available Roman manpower which Polybius preserves.[4]

Cincius Alimentus – History of Rome *(second/first century BC)*
L. Cincius Alimentus was a Roman Senator who took part in the Second Punic War and was captured by Hannibal. He wrote a history of Rome from its foundation to his own time, and would have included a first-hand account of the Second Punic War.

Claudius Quadraginus – History of Rome *(first century BC)*
Q. Claudius Quadrigarius wrote a *History of Rome* in twenty-three books, from the Gallic sacking to the time of Sulla. We know he was used by Livy in compiling his history.

Coelius Antipater – History of the Second Punic War *(second century BC)*
L. Coelius Antipater wrote a history of the Second Punic War in seven books, which was used by later historians including Livy. He is known to have used the works of Silenus, a companion of Hannibal.

Livy – History of Rome from the Foundation of the City *(first century BC)*
Livy's 142 books of Roman history from the foundation of the city to the time of Augustus provided a year-by-year account of the key events in Rome and her wars. Unfortunately, Books Eleven to Nineteen, which covered the third century, and Book Twenty, which covered the inter-Punic War period, did not survive from antiquity. Various abridged versions of these books do survive, such as the *Periochae*, but these are limited in detail. Many of the

later annalist works, such as Eutropius and Orosius, are believed to have been heavily based on Livy's history.

Pompeius Trogus – Historiae Philippicae *(first century BC)*
Cn. Pompeius Trogus was a Roman scholar who was a contemporary of Livy, and who wrote numerous works, one of which was a forty-four book history of the ancient world, focussing on the regions of the ancient world which had formed the Macedonian Empire. An epitome of this work survives by Justin (see above) and contains useful facts and events not recorded elsewhere.

Valerius Antias – History of Rome *(first century BC)*
Antias wrote a history of Rome from its foundation to the time of Sulla (at least) in at least seventy-five books. Again we know he was used by Livy.

Carthaginian Sources
The obvious problem we face with our canon of surviving sources is that they are all either Roman or Romano-Greek. However, this was not always the case. As befitted its status as a major civilization of the ancient world, Carthage had a flourishing literary scene, including a number of histories written from the Punic perspective. Naturally, the destruction of the city of Carthage in 146 BC destroyed all of the city's collection of literature, though many may instead have been looted. Nevertheless, prior to the destruction, Punic histories seem to have been disseminated, certainly in Sicily and Italy. Polybius himself used a number of these Punic histories, but unfortunately none of these works survived the fall of antiquity.

Philinus – History of the First Punic War *(third century BC)*
Polybius refers to this work by the Punic historian Philinus, which would have been a fascinating account juxtaposing the traditional pro-Roman accounts. It is also believed that Fabius Pictor and Diodorus both used this work.[5]

Hannibal – Inscriptions *(third century BC)*[6]
Hannibal himself had an inscription of his campaigns set up at the Temple of Hera in Cape Lacinium, in both Punic and Greek, in 205 BC, as quoted by both Polybius and Livy. The text of his treaty with Philip V is also preserved by Polybius. Whether he wrote anything himself is unclear.
Silenus – Campaigns of Hannibal *(third/second century BC)*

He was a companion of Hannibal, from Sicily, who accompanied him on his Italian campaigns and wrote a history of them. We know that Polybius certainly made use of them

Sosylus – Campaigns of Hannibal *(third/second century* BC*)*
He was a Spartan freedman of Hannibal who accompanied him on his Italian campaigns and wrote a history of them. We know that Polybius certainly made use of them.

Appendix II

Kings, Consuls and Triumphs

King Lists

Kings and Queens of the Ardiaei[1]
Given our lack of sources, the precise years for the reigns of these rulers is difficult to determine.

Pleuratus	c.260 – c.250 BC
Agron	c.250 – c.231 BC
Teuta (Regent)	c.231 – 227 BC
Demetrius (Regent)	c.227 – 219 BC
Pinnes	c.231 – 217 BC
Scerdilaïdas (Regent/King)	c.218 – 207 BC
Pleuratus II	c.207 – 182 BC
Genthius	c.182 – 168 BC
167 BC	Ardiaean monarchy abolished by Rome

Kings and Queens of Epirus
Pyrrhus	306 – 302 and 297 – 272 BC
Alexander II	272 – 242 BC
Pyrrhus II	255 – 237 BC
Ptolemy	c.237 – 234 BC
Deidamia	c.234 – 233 BC
c.233 BC	Epirote monarchy abolished
167 BC	Epirus destroyed by Rome

Kings of Macedon
Antigonus II	276 – 239 BC
Demetrius II	239 – 229 BC
Antigonus III	229 – 221 BC
Philip V	221 – 179 BC
Perseus	179 – 168 BC
167 BC	Macedonian monarchy abolished by Rome

Carthaginian Generals in Spain

Hamilcar Barca	237–229 BC
Hasdrubal	229–221 BC
Hannibal	221–201 BC

Roman Consuls and Triumphs 241-218 BC

241	A. Manlius Torquatus Atticus (2)	Triumph – Faliscii
	Q. Lutatius Cerco	Triumph – Faliscii
240	C. Claudius Centho	
	M. Sempronius Tuditanus	
239	C. Mamilius Turrinus	
	Q. Valerius Falto	
238	Ti. Sempronius Gracchus	
	P. Valerius Falto	
237	L. Cornelius Lentulus Caudinus	
	Q. Fulvius Flaccus	
236	P. Cornelius Lentulus Caudinus	Triumph – Liguria
	C. Licinius Varus	
235	T. Manlius Torquatus	Triumph – Sardinia
	C. Atilius Bulbus (2)	
234	L. Postumius Albinus	
	Sp. Carvilius Maximus	Triumph – Sardinia
233	Q. Fabius Maximus Verrucosus	Triumph – Liguria
	M. Pomponius Matho	Triumph – Sardinia
232	M. Aemilius Lepidus	
	M. Publicius Malleolus	
231	M. Pomponius Matho	
	C. Papirius Maso	Alban Triumph – Corsica
230	M. Aemilius Barbula	
	M. Iunius Pera	
229	L. Postumius Albinus (2)	
	Cn. Fulvius Centumalus	Triumph – Illyria
228	Sp. Carvilius Maximus (2)	
	Q. Fabius Maximus Verrucosus (2)	

227	P. Valerius Flaccus	
	M. Atilius Regulus	
226	M. Valerius Messalla	
	L. Apustius Fullo	
225	L. Aemilius Papus	Triumph – Gauls
	C. Atilius Regulus	
224	T. Manlius Torquatus (2)	
	Q. Fulvius Flaccus (2)	
223	C. Flaminius	Triumph – Gauls
	P. Furius Philus	Triumph – Gauls and Ligurians
222	M. Claudius Marcellus	Triumph – Gauls
	Gn. Cornelius Scipio Calvus	
221	P. Cornelius Scipio Asina	
	M. Minucius Rufus	
220	M. Valerius Laevinus	
	Q. Mucius Scaevola	
	C. Lutatius Catulus	
	L. Veturius Philo	
219	L. Aemilius Paullus	
	M. Livius Salinator	
218	P. Cornelius Scipio	
	Ti. Sempronius Longus	

Appendix III

The Re-emergence of the Tribunate of the Plebs?

W hilst the primary focus of this work has been on the military aspects of Republic history in this period, there was a notable domestic political issue which arose, partly as a result of the Gallic War of the 230s BC. Attempting to reconstruct domestic Roman political matters in the third century is made significantly more difficult by the absence of Livy's books 11–20 (the second pentad), which combined with our other lost sources leaves a hole in the domestic political narrative between 293 and 218 BC.

Nevertheless, the late 230s saw a clash between a Tribune by the name of C. Flaminius and the Senate over the issue of the distribution of lands captured from the Senones during a previous Gallic War. Much has been made of this clash, especially in terms of overtones of the late Republic and clashes between Tribunes and the Senate, post-133 BC. To properly understand this clash, however we need a brief sketch of the history of the Tribunate of the Plebs and its role in Roman domestic politics.

The Tribunate and the Early Republic (494–287 BC)

The office of the Tribunate of the Plebs was created in the early days of the Republic (in 494 BC) and was unique in that it was not an official office of state but was the name given to the chosen representative of only a section of the Roman populace, such as it was at that time. The office was for the representatives of the Plebeian order, but unfortunately we have no clear idea of just who the Plebeian order were in fifth century Rome. When dealing with the early years of the Republic we have the odd problem that we have a number of clear narrative accounts, principally Livy, Dionysus and Diodorus, but each was written 500 years after the events they depict. Furthermore,

Rome itself did not develop native historians until Fabius Pictor in the third century BC (over 200 years later), leaving us with fundamental problem of how much trust we place in what we are being told.

Nevertheless, it is clear that the Tribunate played an important role in the 'Dark Age' of the Republic, spearheading the clash between the Plebeian order, who were urban in their nature, and the ruling Patrician elite represented by the Senate. This clash is known as the Struggle of the Orders and lasted throughout the early Republic.[1] As the early Republic developed, the Tribunate evolved in a number of stages. From 493–471 BC the office was an unofficial one, possibly without fixed elections or numbers of holders. From 471–457 BC there were fixed elections and four or five Tribunes elected annually. From 457 BC this number was increased to the traditional ten Tribunes being elected each year. The office was suspended, along with all Roman magistracies, during 451–450 BC (the period of the Decemvirate), but when it was re-established in 449 BC it was done so on an official basis, as an office of the Roman Republic, albeit a junior one and limited to Plebeians only. The other key restrictions were that their power was limited to within the scared boundary of the city itself (the Pomerium). The office also gained powers to legislate for the Plebeian order (the *plebiscitum* rather than the *legem*) and some limited judicial powers.[2]

The years 449–366 BC saw the remit of the office expand as the Plebeian order gradually became more intermarried with the Patrician elite. It also saw the role of Tribunician legislation expand, with the Senate beginning to use Tribunes to legislate on wider matters for expedience.[3] The year 367 BC saw the culmination of a campaign headed by two Tribunes C. Licinius Stolo and L. Sextius Sextinus Lateranus, which saw legislation passed opening up the Consulship to members of the Plebeian order and thus accelerated the merging of the Patricians with the elite of the Plebeian order merging into one Senatorial aristocracy.[4] Thus the Tribunate developed a mixed nature, being both a junior office of state held by young members of the aristocracy and an office of opposition held by ordinary Plebeians.[5] The years that followed saw a continued evolution in the powers of the Tribunate, with their legislative power gaining a wider footing in 339 BC, culminating in the Lex Hortensia of 287 BC giving the laws they passed (*plebiscita*) full and equal legal standing.[6]

The Tribunate and the Middle Republic (287–133 BC)

Following the Lex Hortensia of 287 BC, studying the Tribunate becomes problematic, for two interlinked reasons. The first is that for the period 293–218 BC we do not have the relevant books of Livy and thus our narrative of Tribuncian events is suddenly cut off. We only know the identities of twelve Tribunes in this whole period, despite there being ten a year, and most of these cannot be securely attested to a specific year. Added to this is the work of Polybius, whose narrative tends to ignore any Tribunician activities and whose famous portrait of Roman domestic politics in this period (in Book Six) portrays a golden age of domestic political harmony.

Many have taken this silence in our sources as an accurate portrayal of Republican politics in this period, whereby the various offices of state, and in particular the Senate and the people (and especially the Tribunes), worked in a harmonious fashion. To them the Lex Hortensia ended the so–called 'Struggle of the Orders', between the Patricians and Plebeians, and ushered in a new period of domestic harmony, only broken by the Tribunate of Ti. Sempronius Gracchus in 133 BC. This is certainly a school of thought which existed in the late Republic, which saw domestic strife originating in 133 BC (as can be seen in the works of Appian, Cicero and Sallust).[7]

However, we must ask ourselves whether this was an era of harmony or an era of silence? The moment the narrative of Livy resumes, in 218 BC, we have numerous examples of Tribunes expanding the remit of their office or clashing with more senior Republican officials. As far back as the 1960s, Taylor produced an examination of the Tribunate in the years between the end of the Second Punic War and the Tribunate of Ti. Sempronius Gracchus (201–133 BC).[8] In it she listed the numerous (at the time) high profile clashes between Tribunes and the Senate or Consuls, including several occasions where Tribunes threatened the Consuls with imprisonment or actually did restrain them for a time. These clashes have been subsequently overshadowed by the Tribunates after 133 BC, but clearly show that when we do have a detailed narrative source for domestic politics, such as Livy, we find the Tribunate being used in a manner similar to that of earlier periods.

The Tribunate of C. Flaminius (232 or 228 BC)[9]

This neatly brings us to the Tribunate of C. Flaminius, which sits towards the end of this period of 'silence'. Unusually, it is Polybius who provides us with an account of Flaminius' activities as Tribune:

> Five years after this alarm, in the consulship of Marcus Aemilius Lepidus, the Romans divided among their citizens the territory in Gaul known as Picenum, from which they had ejected the Senones when they conquered them. Caius Flaminius was the originator of this popular policy, which we must pronounce to have been, one may say, the first step in the demoralization of the populace, as well as the cause of the war with the Gauls which followed.[10]

Polybius' account is an interesting one, which clearly hints at the author knowing far more than he wrote. Much has been made of his phrase which translates as 'we must pronounce to have been, one may say, the first step in the demoralization of the populace', which many have taken as a reference to the chaos and bloodshed caused by the Tribunate of Ti. Sempronius Gracchus in 133 BC which also involved a law distributing the public land (*ager publicus*), albeit under far different circumstances.

Polybius' oblique reference to the issues that seemingly lay behind the passing of this law is entirely in keeping with his depiction of a harmonious Roman domestic political scene (especially given his Greek audience). As already detailed (in Chapter Six), the law can be seen in the context of preparations for a further Gallic War, by strengthening the border region between the Roman Federation and Gallic Northern Italy, planting additional military colonies as border posts.

It seems to have been the manner in which this law was passed which caused the controversy. Whilst Polybius may have been reticent about revealing the details, the commentators of the later Republic onwards had no such qualms. Key amongst the men who followed (and whose accounts survive) is Cicero, who mentions Flaminius and his Tribunate on no fewer than five occasions. He squarely places Flaminius as being the predecessor of the last Republican Tribunes:

> Caius Flaminius, who as Consul met with great disasters in the Second Punic War, when he was tribune of the people, proposed, in a very

seditious manner, an agrarian law to the people, against the consent of the Senate, and altogether against the will of all the nobles. While he was holding an assembly of the people, his own father dragged him from the temple. He is impeached of treason. The charge is "You attacked the majesty of the people in dragging down a tribune of the people from the temple." The denial is "I did not attack the majesty of the people." The question is "Whether he attacked the majesty of the people or not." The argument is "I only used the power which I legitimately had over my own son." The denial of this argument is "But a man who, by the power belonging to him as a father, that is to say, as a private individual, attacks the power of a tribune of the people, that is to say, the power of the people itself, attacks the majesty of the people." The question for the judges is "Whether a man attacks the majesty of the people who uses his power as a father in opposition to the power of a Tribune."[11]

Following Cicero, we have a mention by Livy, but only in passing; the only other surviving source is Valerius Maximus, who, as is common, adds more colour to the incident:

As Tribune of the Plebs he had promulgated a law to distribute the Gallic territory individually against the will and resistance of the Senate, vehemently opposing its entreaties and threats and undeterred even by the levying of an army against him should he persist in the same purpose. But when his father placed a hand on him as he was already on the rostra putting the law to vote, overborne by private authority he came down from the platform.[12]

Thus, as the centuries pass, the more detail is added to the story, from a passing reference to the law in Cato through to the sensationalism of Valerius Maximus. We do not know how much of the additional details come from earlier lost sources, especially Fabius Pictor. At the heart of the matter seems to have been Senatorial opposition to Flaminius' law which he rode roughshod over, much of which has echoes of later events.

Technically, the Senate had no power of legislation and no power to veto legislation which the Tribunes wished to place before the assemblies (Rome's law-making bodies). In practice, however, by this point of the Republic, it was custom that the Senate vet all proposed laws before they were placed before the people. On this occasion it seems that when they did vet the proposal, they objected to it. On the face of it the proposed law seems sound enough, especially when taken in the context of preparations to strengthen Rome's Gallic border. The land in question had been confiscated from the Senones following the war of the 280s BC and had been designated Public Land (*ager publicus*). Many arguments have been presented as to why the Senate, or elements of the Senate, objected to this proposal, from personal greed to fear of provoking the Gauls, or possible jealously that Flaminius' popularity and powerbase would increase. Ultimately, with the source material we have, we will never know.[13]

What is clear is that, against recent custom, Flaminius appears to have asserted the rights of the office to propose any legislation he wanted to the people, regardless of the Senate's opinion. The law was proposed and apparently passed, and citizens were sent from Rome to Picenum to establish fresh colonies on the border. What is unclear is why none of Flaminius' nine Tribunician colleagues exercised their right of veto over the proposal (*ius intercessio*) as was within their rights to do so.

We have to judge what effect this had on Roman domestic politics and the evolution of the Tribunate of the Plebs. For Flaminius personally, it seemed to have done him no harm standing up to the Senate, and he was elected Praetor (the first for Sicily, as seen in Chapter Two) for 227 BC and Consul for 223 BC (as seen in Chapter Nine). But as the events of 222 BC unfolded it seems that many in the Senate welcomed an opportunity to undermine him. A second Consulship followed in 217 BC, culminating in his defeat and death at the hands of Hannibal at the Battle of Lake Trasimene.

In terms of Roman domestic politics, we know too little about other events to categorically state that this incident broke fresh ground. On the face of it, Flaminius had demonstrated that the office of Tribune could override the opinion of the Senate and propose legislation to the people without their blessing. He also showed that even though the office had no physical powers outside of the city of Rome, Tribunes could propose and see through legislation that affected matters far outside of the city, and in subjects that traditionally lay with the Senate; such as land distribution and colonization, as well as impact on matters of foreign policy and defence (within Italy in this example). He also showed the benefits of gaining a high profile domestically whilst holding what had then become a junior office, him being the first of his family to ascend to high office and the Consulship.

Appendix IV

Polybius and Roman Manpower – An Overview

I n his narrative detailing the preparations for the Gallic invasion of
225 BC, Polybius not only details how many soldiers the Romans were able
to mobilize, but also how much available manpower the Romans could
draw on throughout Italy. In preparation of the expected Gallic invasion (as
seen in Chapter Six), the Romans apparently conducted a special survey to
see how much available manpower they could muster, should it be necessary.
This was as a result of the now century-old system of alliances between
Rome and each of the defeated peoples of Italy, all of which required them
to send soldiers and cavalry to fight as part of Rome's armies. This system
of alliances gave Rome the ability to utilize the whole available manpower of
the Italian peninsula to supplement their own citizen forces.

It is only here in Polybius that we see the full extent of this system, in
what has become one of the most famous and key passages in the study of
the Roman military system:

> The lists of men able to bear arms that had been returned were as
> follows:
>
> Latins eighty thousand foot and five thousand horse,
> Samnites seventy thousand foot and seven thousand horse,
> Iapygians and Messapians fifty thousand foot and sixteen thousand
> horse in all,
> Lucanians thirty thousand foot and three thousand horse,
> Marsi, Marrucini, Frentani, and Vestini twenty thousand foot and four
> thousand horse.
> In Sicily and Tarentum were two reserve legions, each consisting of
> about four thousand two hundred foot and two hundred horse.
> Of Romans and Campanians there were on the roll two hundred and
> fifty thousand foot and twenty-three thousand horse;

so that the total number of Romans and allies able to bear arms was more than seven hundred thousand foot and seventy thousand horse.[1]

Not only is Polybius, testimony the earliest surviving account we have of the Roman manpower system, but his account is said to be based on the works of Fabius Pictor (as seen in Appendix I), who was not only Rome's first native historian, but actually fought in the Gallic Wars of the 220s himself.[2] Erdkamp summarizes the value of this passage to ancient historians best when he says: 'The manpower figures of Rome and its Italian allies, as preserved by Polybius, are unique, and not repeated in the extant historiography on ancient Rome.'[3]

These same figures can also be found being quoted in the works of Diodorus and Pliny, whilst Eutropius and Orosius both have rounded figures of 800,000.[4] For at least the last 400 years scholars have been debating the accuracy of these figures and what they mean for those studying Roman military manpower.[5] De Ligt presents one of the latest and most succinct summaries of their arguments.[6] Historians have highlighted various issues with the exact ratios between the various groups identified by Polybius and his tendency to group races together under an overarching heading. There is also a problem in reconciling this figure to the last census figure we have, which was from 234 BC and registered 270,713 Roman citizens.

Polybius' figures are fundamental to any study of the population of Italy during this period, with numerous modern scholars extrapolating the size of the total population from the number of men eligible for military service (aged between 17 and 45)[7]. Such estimates have become their own specialist industry within academic circles, with the total estimates produced varying widely depending on the scholar. Put crudely, most commentators in this area can be found in one of two camps; those who interpret the figures to produce a high estimate of the total population of Italy (the High Count) and those who favour a low estimate (the Low Count). Brunt estimated that the free population of Italy at this time was around four and a half million, with an additional half a million slaves, producing a total population of Italy of five million.[8] Other scholars have produced vastly different figures.[9]

Modern scholars will never agree on the accuracy of the figures reported by Polybius, though De Ligt does offer a stout defence of their basic accuracy.[10] Despite the modern arguments and objections, according to Polybius (Pictor), Rome at this time had a manpower reserve of 700,000 infantry and 70,000 cavalry. Even if we accept these figures, in practice it would have been impossible for Rome ever to mobilize that many men at one time. Such an attempt would have a devastating effect on Roman agriculture, with that many able bodied men being taken off their farms (Italy at this time not having developed a widespread slave culture).

Nevertheless, it does show the depth of Roman manpower resources and the numbers that Rome could keep drawing on, time after time. This not only allowed Rome to field multiple large armies at any one time, in various theatres of operation, but also to sustain losses which would have crippled any other ancient state; the losses being spread throughout the peoples of Italy.

Thus, even if we question the high numbers which Polybius (Pictor) claims were eligible for military service, we can still see the success of that key Roman policy, introduced in the fourth century BC (and detailed in Chapter One), which bound each defeated state to Rome by individual treaty and called upon them to submit soldiers to fight in Rome's wars.[11] Even if Rome only mobilized a fraction of the total available manpower of Italy, they were still able to field multiple armies each and every year should they so choose and sustain heavy losses, yet still continue to fight the war. This gave Rome and the Roman elite military resources that no other ancient state possessed at this time which when combined with a political, economic and social system which extolled the benefits of warfare, gave Rome the potential for significant expansion.

It is interesting to note the high percentage of Roman citizens (and Campanians) in these figures; 250,000, which, if we take the figures as given, also show the success of another of Rome's key policies in Italy, the spread of Roman citizenship. Here we can see the successful evolution of Roman citizenship away from being one purely based on ethnicity to embracing more tribes in Italy and binding them to Roman hegemony.

Thus we can see the key building blocks on which Rome's military domination of the Mediterranean were built on, and all thanks to policies introduced in the late fourth century BC.

Appendix V

Consequences

Even though the coverage of this period ends in 218 BC with the outbreak of the Second Punic War, Rome fought a further series of wars, in the East, northern Italy and Sicily, as a consequence of the events of this time.

The East

First Macedonian War (214–205 BC)

The most immediate war, which broke out just three years later in 215 BC, was not against the Illyrians but against Macedon itself; one of the 'big three' Hellenistic powers. A Roman protectorate in Illyria was a clear challenge to Macedonian hegemony in the region, and Rome's two Illyrian Wars had both occurred at times when Macedon was engaged in different theatres of conflict. In 219 BC, Philip V, the young king of Macedon, was fighting in the Social War in mainland Greece. By 217 BC this war had ended and Philip made moves towards Illyria, albeit the non-Roman regions. In 216 BC a Macedonian fleet approached the Adriatic, perhaps intent on restoring Demetrius; only the dispatch of a Roman naval force turned them back. By 215 BC with the Carthaginians on the ascendency in Italy, Philip and Hannibal opened negotiations and formed an anti-Roman alliance, aided by Demetrius of Pharos. In return for his help against the Romans, Philip was promised control of the Roman protectorate of Illyria and thus expansion of the Macedonian Empire to the Adriatic. In 214 BC, Rome found herself simultaneously at war with the two major rival powers of the western and central Mediterranean. [1]

However, the war which was to follow was not the epic clash between superpowers which many would have expected. Rome's attention was focused on the war with Carthage, both in Spain and Italy. Rome sought

Greek allies against Macedon and created an anti-Macedonian coalition, making alliances with the Aetolian League and the kingdom of Pergamum. Rome's Greek allies fought or harried Philip by land, whilst the navies of Rome and Pergamum kept control of the seas.[2] Years of inconclusive warfare by proxy followed, which was only brought to a conclusion by Rome's Greek allies making peace with Philip in 206 BC.[3] Although Rome in 206 was then in a far stronger position than ten years earlier, the war with Carthage still remained its priority and so the Romans made peace with Philip in 205 BC.[4]

Such an inconclusive ending solved none of the existing tensions between the two superpowers, and war broke out again within a year of the end of the Punic War. This time Roman and Macedonian forces did clash directly, culminating in the Battle of Cynoscephalae in 196 BC, which ended with a Roman victory. Further war followed in 172–167 BC, which saw another Roman victory at the Battle of Pydna in 168 BC. A final war broke out in 149/148 BC, ending with Rome annexing Macedon as its first eastern province.

Third Illyrian War (168–167 BC)

Although Rome had fought two Illyrian Wars in a decade, there were no further wars between Rome and the Ardiaei for nearly sixty years.[5] Following the Second Illyrian War, Pinnes, son of Agron and Teuta, was reaffirmed as King of the Ardiaei, under the regency of his uncle, Scerdilaïdas. However, Scerdilaïdas usurped the throne soon after and ruled, with the tacit approval of Rome, until c. 207 BC, and was succeeded by his son, Pleuratus II, who again ruled as an ally of Rome until c. 182 BC. He in turn was succeeded by his son, Genthius, who broke with recent tradition and allied with Perseus, King of Macedon (179–168 BC), against Rome during the Third Macedonian War. Rome dispatched a fleet and an army commanded by the Praetor L. Ancius Gallus and defeated Genthius within a matter of weeks. Rome responded by abolishing the Ardiaean monarchy and dividing the kingdom up into three protectorates (at the same time as abolishing the kingdom of Macedon). [6]

The Destruction of Epirus (167 BC)

Pyrrhus' old kingdom of Epirus also had the misfortune to back the losing side in the Third Macedonian War. In retaliation for their support of King Perseus, Rome sent the Proconsul L. Aemilius Paullus and his army into Epirus on a punitive expedition. What followed was not a war but a massacre, as Rome destroyed every major settlement and took over 150,000 (estimated to be half the population) as slaves. In effect, the Epirote civilization was destroyed and commentators some centuries later were still noting the desolation of the lands.[7]

Sicily

Syracusan War (215–211 BC)

Under the Tyranny of Hiero II, Syracuse remained a staunch Roman ally and maintained its independence, despite its precarious position. When the Second Punic War broke out, Hiero naturally went to war on Rome's side. He died in 215 BC and was succeeded by his grandson, Hieronymus, who continued this policy. When Hieronymus took the throne, Rome's position looked a far weaker one, following the defeats at Trebia, Trasimene and especially Cannae, and he soon made overtures to the Carthaginians and formed an alliance with both them and Philip V of Macedon. However, this change of policy resulted in a conspiracy being formed of Syracusan nobles who assassinated Hieronymus in the street in 214 BC. There followed a power struggle in Syracuse, which saw an anti-Roman faction take charge.

Rome duly dispatched an army under the command of M. Claudius Marcellus, who laid siege to Syracuse. Despite its fortifications and the ingenuity of the inventor Archimedes, the city fell and was sacked in 212 BC. The following year, Rome abolished the independent kingdom of Syracuse and added it to the Province of Sicily, becoming its capital.

Northern Italy

Despite having established their military hegemony over the Gauls of northern Italy in the Gallic War of the 220s BC, the Romans continued to fight wars in northern Italy against rebelling tribes.

Gallic and Ligurian War 201–172 BC

Hostilities with Rome's traditional Gallic enemies seem to have picked up as the Punic War was concluding and saw Rome fight a decade-long further war. In 201 BC, the Consul L. Aelius Paetus invaded Boian territory in retaliation for Boian raids on pro-Roman tribes. After initial success, one of his legates was ambushed and lost 7,000 men. The next year saw a larger Gallic uprising, comprising not only Rome's traditional enemies the Boii and Insubres but also their ally the Cenomani. They also found allies amongst a number of the Ligurian tribes. The Roman colony at Placentia was sacked and that Cremona laid siege to. Again a Consul, C. Aurelius Cotta, was dispatched to northern Italy. As it turns out it was a Praetor, L. Furius Purpurio, who defeated a Gallic and Ligurian army at Cremona that year and celebrated a Triumph.

The following year (199 BC) a Praetor, Cn. Baebius Tamphilus, invaded the lands of the Insubres but was again ambushed and lost another 7,000 men. Once again a Consul was dispatched, but he took little action. 198 BC also saw Cisalpine Gaul named a Consular province but again we hear little of any positive Roman action. The following year saw both Consuls assigned to Cisalpine Gaul, which shows the seriousness of the campaign, with C. Cornelius Cethegus winning a victory over the Insubres and Cenomani, and his colleague Q. Minucius Rufus defeating the Boii and rebellious Ligurian tribes. The next year saw a similar pattern with both Consuls again assigned to Gaul, continuing the fight against the Insubres, Boii and Ligurians. Only one Consul was assigned to northern Italy in 195 BC, but the fighting continued against the Gauls and Ligurians.

By 194 BC however both Consuls were again fighting in northern Italy, and this was again the case the following two years (193 and 192 BC), with neither the Gauls nor Ligurians letting up. In 191 BC, one Consul had to be dispatched to Greece to fight Antiochus III whilst the other continued the war in northern Italy, a pattern which was repeated the following year. The year 190 BC seems to have marked the key year in the war, with the Roman Proconsul Q. Minucius Rufus reporting that the Ligurians had been pacified, whilst P. Cornelius Scipio Nasica cleared the Boii out of lands taken from them. By 189 BC the situation was secure enough for both Consuls to be dispatched to Greece, though we do hear of a Praetor, L. Baebius Dives, being killed fighting in Liguria.

The years 188–179 BC saw continued fighting requiring both Consuls each year, though by 186 BC onwards the focus had shifted to Liguria, which was increasingly pacified and brought under direct Roman rule. The campaign was widened in 178 BC when the Consul A. Manlius Vulso invade Istria, the submission of which was completed the following year. Fighting in Liguria continued in 176 BC, which saw the Consul Q. Petillius Spurinus killed in battle, and throughout 175 BC. After a lull in 174 BC, both Consuls were again dispatched to Liguria in 173 and 172 BC. It is only the outbreak of the Third Macedonian War in 172 BC which saw Rome turn its attention fully on Greece and away from northern Italy.

Thus we can see that the post-Punic War period saw a renewed and sustained period of warfare in northern Italy. It seems to have been initiated by a Gallic and Ligurian revolt (including traditional Roman allies), and mutated into a war of conquest in Liguria. This almost continuous period of warfare coincided with the Roman invasion of Greece and the defeats of Philip V and Antiochus III, leaders of two of the three great Hellenistic powers. These superpowers of the ancient world were defeated far more quickly than the tribes of northern Italy, reflecting the different nature of the warfare; set piece battle followed by treaty, as opposed to guerrilla warfare against a tribal enemy.

Three key points can be taken from this period. Firstly, despite the warfare of the 220s BC, the Gauls of northern Italy were still able to oppose the Romans militarily. Secondly, we must note that these conflicts were focussed on the Gallic and Ligurian home territories and were not posing a threat to Italy and Rome, as they had done in the 220s. Thirdly, the Romans used these wars to finally extend full military control over the tribes of this region, beginning the process of Romanization which saw these regions becoming more integrated into the Roman system and steadily losing their tribal nature. These wars form an interesting postscript to the life or death struggle of the 220s BC and remind us that, even in the second century BC, northern Italy was still not firmly under Roman rule.

Bibliography

Anderson, E. (2015). 'The Rise of the Sons of Mars', *History Today* 65.3, 11–17.

Anson, E. and Troncoso, V. (2012). *After Alexander: The Time of the Diadochi (323–281 BC)* (London).

Astin. A. (1967). 'Saguntum and the Origins of the Second Punic War', *Latomus* 26, 577–596.

Badian, E. (1952). 'Notes on Roman Policy in Illyria (230-201 BC), *Papers of the British School at Rome* 20, 72–93.

——. (1958). *Foreign Clientelae (264–70 BC)* (Oxford).

——. (1996). 'Tribuni Plebis and Res Publica', in J. Linderski (ed.) *Imperium Sine Fine: T. Robert, S. Broughton and the Roman Republic* (Stuttgart), 187–214.

Bagnall, N. (1990). *The Punic Wars* (London).

Balsdon, J. (1954). 'Rome and Macedon 205–200 BC', *Journal of Roman Studies* 44, 30–42.

Barfield, L. (1971). *Northern Italy before Rome* (London).

Baronowski, D. (1993). 'Roman Military Forces in 225 BC (Polybius 2.23–4)', *Historia* 42, 181-202.

Beaumont, R. (1936). 'Greek Influence in the Adriatic Sea before the Fourth Century BC', *Journal of Hellenic Studies* 56, 159-204.

——. (1939). 'The Date of the First Treaty between Rome and Carthage', *Journal of Roman Studies* 29, 74–86.

Bender, P. (1997). 'Rom, Karthago und die Kelten' *Klio* 79, 87–106.

Bouffier, S. & Garcia, D. (2012). 'Greeks, Celts and Ligurians in South–East Gaul: Ethnicity and Archaeology', in A. Hermary & G. Tsetskhladze (eds.) *From the Pillars of Hercules to the Footsteps of the Argonauts* (Leuven), 21–36.

Brennan, T. (1996). 'Triumphus in Monte Albano', in R. Wallace & E. Harris (eds.). *Transitions to Empire. Essays in Greco–Roman History 360–146 BC, in Honour of E. Badian* (Oklahoma), 315–337.

——. (2000). *The Praetorship in the Roman Republic Volume 1* (Oxford).

Bridgman, T. (2005). 'Keltoi, Galatai, Galli: Were They All One People?', *Proceedings of the Harvard Celtic Colloquium* 24/25, 155–162.

Broughton, T. (1952). *The Magistrates of the Roman Republic Volumes 1&2* (New York).

——. (1960). *The Magistrates of the Roman Republic; Supplement* (New York).

——. (1986). *The Magistrates of the Roman Republic Volume 3, Supplement* (Atlanta).

Brunt, P. (1971). *Italian Manpower 225 BC–AD 14* (Oxford).

Cary, M. (1919). 'A Forgotten Treaty between Rome and Carthage', *Journal of Roman Studies* 9, 67–77.

Casule, N. (2012). 'In Part a Roman Sea': Rome and the Adriatic in the Third Century BC; in C. Smith & L. Yarrow (eds.). *Imperialism, Cultural Politics, and Polybius* (Oxford), 205–229.

Caven, B. (1980). *The Punic Wars* (London).

Champion, C. (1996). 'Polybius, Aetolia and the Gallic Attack on Delphi (279 BC)', *Historia* 45, 315–328.

——. (2000). 'Romans as Βαρβαροι: Three Polybian Speeches and the Politics and Cultural Indeterminacy', *Classical Philology* 95, 425–444.

——. (2000b), 'Histories 12.4b.1–c.1: An Overlooked Key to Polybios' Views on Rome', *Histos* 4, 1–5.

Champion, J. (2009). *Pyrrhus of Epirus* (Barnsley).

——. (2010). *The Tyrants of Syracuse. War in Ancient Sicily Volume I: 480–367 BC* (Barnsley).

——. (2012). *The Tyrants of Syracuse. War in Ancient Sicily Volume II: 367–211 BC* (Barnsley).

Coppola, A. (1993). *Demetrio di Faro* (Rome).

Corbett, J. (1970). 'L. Metellus (Cos 251, 247), Agrarian Commissioner', *Classical Quarterly* 20, 7–8.

Cornell, T. (1986). 'Review: The Annals of Quintus Ennius', *Journal of Roman Studies* 76, 244–250.

——. (1996). *The Beginnings of Rome* (London).

——. (2013). *The Fragments of the Roman Historians Volumes 1–3* (Oxford).

Cowan, R. (2009). *Roman Conquests: Italy* (Barnsley).

Curchin, L. (1991). *Roman Spain. Conquest and Assimilation* (London).

Daly, G. (2002). *Cannae* (London).

David, J–M. (1996). *The Roman Conquest of Italy* (Oxford).

DeBrohun, J. (2007). 'The Gates of War (and Peace): Roman Literary Perspectives', in K. Raaflaub (ed.). *War and Peace in the Ancient World*, 256–278.

De Ligt. L. (2012). *Peasants, Citizens and Soldiers. Studies in the Demographic History of Roman Italy 225 BC–AD 100* (Cambridge).

De Ligt, L. & Northwood, S. (2008). *People, Land, and Politics: Demographic Developments and the Transformation of Roman Italy, 300 BC–AD 14* (Leiden).

Dell, H. (1967). 'Antigonus III and Rome', *Classical Philology* 62, 94–103.

——. (1967b). 'The Origin and Nature of Illyrian Piracy', *Historia* 16, 344–358.

——. (1970). 'Demetrius of Pharos and the Istrian War', *Historia* 19, 30–38.

Derow, P. (1979). 'Polybius, Rome and the East', *Journal of Roman Studies* 69, 1–15.

——. (1991). 'Pharos and Rome', *Zeitschrift für Papyrologie und Epigraphik* 88, 261–270.

Destani, B. (ed.). (2006). *Ancient Illyria. An Archaeological Exploration by Arthur J. Evans* (London).

DeWitt, N. (1940). 'Massilia and Rome', *Transactions and Proceedings of the American Philological Association* 71, 605–615.

Develin, R. (1976). 'C. Flaminius in 232 BC', *L'Antiquité Classique* 45, 638–643.

——. (1978) 'Religion and Politics at Rome during the Third Century BC', *Journal of Religious History* 10, 3–19.

——. (1979). 'The Political Position of C. Flaminius', *Rheinisches Museum für Philologie* 122, 268–277.

Dillery, J. (2002). 'Quintus Fabius Pictor and Greco–Roman Historiography at Rome', in J. Miller, C. Damon & K. Myers (eds.). *Vertis in Usum. Studies in Honour of Edward Courtney* (Munchen), 1–23.

Dimond, A. (forthcoming). *Sparta's Last Stand* (Barnsley).

Dorey, T. (1959). 'The Treaty with Saguntum', *Humanitas* 11, 1–10.

Drummond. A. (1978). 'The Dictator Years', *Historia* 27, 550–572.

Dyson, S. (1985). *The Creation of the Roman Frontier* (Princeton).

Dzino, D. (2005). 'Late Republican Illyrian Policy of Rome 167–60 BC: the Bifocal Approach', *Studies in Latin Literature and Roman History* 12 (Brussels), 48–73.

——. (2006). 'Welcome to the Mediterranean Semi-Periphery: The place of Illyricum in book 7 of Strabo', *Živa Antika* 56, 113–128.

——. (2007). 'The Celts in Illyricum – Whoever they may be: The Hybridization and Construction of Identities in Southeastern Europe in the Fourth and Third Centuries BC', *Opuscula archaeologica*, 31, 93–112.

——. (2008). 'The People who are Illyrians and Celts: Strabo and the identities of the 'barbarians' from Illyricum', *Arheoloski vestnik* 59, 415–424.

——. (2008b). 'Strabo 7.5 and Imaginary Illyricum', *Athenaeum* 96, 173–192.

——. (2010). *Illyricum in Roman Politics 229 BC–AD 68* (Cambridge).

Eckstein, A. (1982). 'Human Sacrifice and Fear of Military Disaster in Republican Rome', *American Journal of Ancient History* 7, 69–95.

——. (1983). 'Two Notes on the Outbreak of the Hannibalic War', *Rheinisches Museum für Philologie* 126, 255–272.

——. (1984). 'Rome, Saguntum and the Ebro Treaty', *Emerita* 52, 51–68.

——. (1985). 'Polybius, Syracuse and the Politics of Accommodation', *Greek, Roman and Byzantine Studies* 26, 265–282.

——. (1987). *Senate and General. Individual Decision Making and Roman Foreign Relations 264–194 BC* (Berkeley).

——. (1989). 'Hannibal at New Carthage: Polybius 3.15 and the Power of Irrationality', *Classical Philology* 84, 1–15.

——. (1994). 'Polybius, Demetrius of Pharus, and the Origins of the Second Illyrian War', *Classical Philology* 89, 46–59.

——. (1999). 'Pharos and the Question of Roman Treaties of Alliance in the Greek East in the Third Century BC', *Classical Philology* 94, 395–418.

———. (2006). *Mediterranean Anarchy, Interstate War and the Rise of Rome* (Berkeley).

———. (2008). *Rome Enters the Greek East* (Oxford).

———. (2012). 'Polybius, the Gallic Crisis, and the Ebro Treaty', *Classical Philology* 107, 206–229.

———. (2012b). 'Hegemony and Annexation Beyond the Adriatic 230-146 BC', in D. Hoyos (ed.). *A Companion to Roman Imperialism* (Leiden), 79–97.

———. (2013). 'Polybius, Phylarchus, and Historiographical Criticism', *Classical Philology* 108, 314–338.

Ellis, P. (1998). *Celt and Roman. The Celts in Italy* (London).

Erdkamp, P. (2008). 'Polybius II. 24: Roman Manpower and Greek Propaganda', *Ancient Society* 38, 137–152.

———. (2009). 'Polybius, the Ebro Treaty, and the Gallic Invasion of 225 BCE.', *Classical Philology* 104, 495–510.

———. (2012). 'Polybius and Livy on the Allies in the Roman Army', in L. Blois & E. Lo Cascio (eds.) *The Impact of the Roman Army (200 BC–AD 476)* (Leiden), 47–74.

Errington, R. (1970). 'Rome and Spain before the Second Punic War', *Latomus* 29, 25–57.

———. (1971). *The Dawn of Empire. Rome's Rise to World Power* (London).

Erskine, A. (2013). 'The View from the East', in J. Prag & J Quinn (eds.). *The Hellenistic West. Rethinking the Ancient Mediterranean* (Cambridge), 14–43.

Evans, A. (1880). 'On Some Recent Discoveries of Illyrian Coins', *The Numismatic Chronicle and Journal of the Numismatic Society* 20, 26–302.

———. (1884). 'Antiquarian Researches in Illyricum', *Archaeologia* 48, 1–105.

———. (2006). *Ancient Illyria: An Archaeological Exploration* (London).

Ewins, U. (1952). 'The Early Colonisation of Cisalpine Gaul', *Papers of the British School at Rome*, 54–71.

Feig Vishnia, R. (1996). *State, Society, and Popular Leaders in Mid-Republican Rome 241–167 BC* (London).

———. (1996b). 'Cicero "De Senectute" 11 and the Date of Flaminius' Tribunate', *Phoenix* 50, 138–145.

Fine, J. (1936). 'Macedon, Illyria, and Rome, 220–219 BC', *Journal of Roman Studies* 26, 24–39.

Frank, T. (1910). 'Commercialism and Roman Territorial Expansion', *Classical Journal* 5, 99–110.

———. (1913). 'Mercantilism and Rome's Foreign Policy', *American Historical Review* 18, 233–252.

———. (1914). *Roman Imperialism* (London).

———. (1930). 'Roman Census Statistics from 508 to 225 BC', *American Journal of Philology* 51, 313–324.

Gibson, B. & Harrison, T. (2013). *Polybius and his World. Essays in Memory of F.W. Walbank* (Oxford).

Goldsworthy, A. (2000). *The Punic Wars* (London).

Grimal, P. (1968). *Hellenism and the Rise of Rome* (London).

Gruen, E. (1984). *The Hellenistic World and the Coming of Rome* (Berkeley).

Hammond, N. (1966). 'The Kingdoms in Illyria circa 400–167 BC', *Annual of the British School at Athens* 61, 239–253.

——. (1968). 'Illyris, Rome and Macedon in 229–205 BC', *Journal of Roman Studies* 58, 1–21.

——. (1989). 'The Illyrian Atintani, the Epirotic Atintanes and the Roman Protectorate', *Journal of Roman Studies* 79, 11–25.

Harris, W. (1984). 'Current Directions in the Study of Roman Imperialism', in W. Harris (ed.). *The Imperialism of Mid-Republican Rome* (Rome), 13–31.

——. (1990b). 'Roman Warfare in the Economic and Social Context of the Fourth Century BC', in W. Eder (ed.). *Staat und Staatlichkeit in der frühen römischen Republik* (Stuttgart), 494–540.

Harris, W. (1971). *Rome in Etruria and Umbria* (Oxford).

——. (1979). *War and Imperialism in Republican Rome 327–70 BC* (Oxford).

Heichelheim, F. (1954). 'New Evidence on the Ebro Treaty', *Historia* 3, 211–219.

Holleaux, M. (1921). *Rome, la Grece et les monarchies hellenistiques au IIIe siècle avant J-C* (273–205) (Paris).

Holloway, R. (2008). 'Who were the Tribuni Militum Consulari Potestate?', *L'Antiquité Classique* 77, 107–125.

Howarth, R. (2006). *The Origins of Roman Citizenship* (New York).

——. (1984). 'The Roman–Punic Pact of 279 BC: Its Problems and Its Purpose', *Historia* 33, 402–439.

Hoyos, D. (1985). 'The Rise of Hiero II: Chronology and Campaigns 275–264 BC', *Antichton* 19, 32–56.

——. (1994). 'Barcid Proconsuls and Punic Politics, 237–218 BC' *Rheinisches Museum für Philologie* 137, 246–274.

——. (1997). *Unplanned Wars: Origins of the First and Second Punic Wars* (Berlin).

——. (2000). 'Towards a Chronology of the 'Truceless War', 241–237 BC', *Rheinisches Museum für Philologie* 143, 369–380.

——. (2003). *Hannibal's Dynasty* (London).

——. (2007). *Truceless War: Carthage's Fight for Survival, 241 to 237 BC* (Leiden).

——. (2011). (ed.) *A Companion to the Punic Wars* (Oxford).

——. (2015). *Mastering the West. Rome and Carthage at War* (Oxford).

Husband, R. (1911). 'Kelts and Ligurians', *Classical Philology* 6, 385–401.

Jashjemski, W. (1950). *The Origins and History of the Proconsular and the Propraetorian Imperium to 27 BC* (Chicago).

Kramer, F. (1948). 'Massilian Diplomacy before the Second Punic War', *American Journal of Philology* 69, 1–26.

Larsen, J. (1975). 'The Aetolian–Achaean Alliance of ca. 238–220 BC', *Classical Philology* 70, 159–172.

Lazenby, J. (1978). *Hannibal's War. A Military History of the Second Punic War* (Warminster).

———. (1996). *The First Punic War* (London).

Lo Cascio, E. (2001). 'Recruitment and the size of the Roman Population from the Third to the First Century BC', in W. Scheidel (ed.). *Debating Roman Demography* (Leiden), 111–137.

Lomas, K. (1993). *Rome and the Western Greeks, 350 BC–AD 200: Conquest and Acculturation in Southern Italy* (London).

Loreto, L. (2007). *La grande strategia di Roma nell'età della prima guerra punica 273–229 a.C.* (Napoli).

———. (2011). 'Roman Politics and Expansion, 241–219', in D. Hoyos (ed.). *A Companion to the Punic Wars* (Oxford), 184–203.

Matyszak, P. (2009). *Roman Conquests. Macedonia and Greece* (Barnsley).

May, J. (1946). 'Macedonia and Illyria (217–167 BC)', *Journal of Roman Studies* 36, 48–56.

McCall, J. (2012). *The Sword of Rome. A Biography of Marcus Claudius Marcellus* (Barnsley)

McGing, B. (2010). *Polybius' Histories* (Oxford).

Miles, R. (2010). *Carthage Must Be Destroyed* (London).

Millar, F. (1987). 'Polybius between Greece and Rome', in J. Koumoulides (ed.). *Greek Connections: Essay on Culture and Diplomacy* (Bloomington), 1–18.

Mitchell, R. (1971). 'Roman–Carthaginian Treaties: 306 and 279/8 BC', *Historia* 20, 633–655.

———. (2010). 'The Role of Maritime Colonies in Roman Expansion', in R. Howarth (ed.). *Hearsay, History, and Heresy, Collected Essays on the Roman Republic by Richard E. Mitchell* (Piscataway), 333–344.

Momigliano, A. (1977) 'Did Fabius Pictor Lie', in *Essays in Ancient and Modern Historiography* (Oxford), 99–105.

———. (1990). 'Fabius Pictor and the Origins of National History', *The Classical Foundations of Modern Historiography* (Berkeley), 80–108.

Morley, N. (2001). 'The Transformation of Italy, 225–28 BC', *Journal of Roman Studies* 91, 50–62.

Mouritsen, H. (2007). 'The Civitas Sine Suffragio: Ancient Concepts and Modern Ideology', *Historia* 56, 141–158.

Neatby, L. (1950). 'Romano–Egyptian Relations during the Third Century BC', *Transactions and Proceedings of the American Philological Association* 81, 89–98.

Nilsson, M. (1929). 'The Introduction of Hoplite Tactics at Rome: Its Date and Its Consequences', *Journal of Roman Studies* 19, 1–11.

Northwood, S. (2007). 'Q. Fabius Pictor: was he an Annalist?', in N. Sekunda (ed.). *Corolla Cosmo Rodewald* (Gdansk), 97–114.

Oost, S. (1954). *Roman Policy in Epirus and Acarnania in the Age of the Roman Conquest of Greece* (Dallas).

———. (1976). 'The Tyrant Kings of Syracuse', *Classical Philology* 71, 224–236.

Palmer, R. (1997). *Rome and Carthage at Peace* (Stuttgart).

Pelgrom, J. (2008). 'Settlement Organization and Land Distribution in Latin Colonies Before the Second Punic War', in L. De Ligt. & S. Northwood. (2008). *People, Land, and Politics: Demographic Developments and the Transformation of Roman Italy, 300 BC–AD 14* (Leiden), 333–372.

Petzold, K.E. (1971). 'Rom und Illyrien: Ein Beitrag zur römischen Außenpolitik im 3. Jahrhundert', *Historia* 20, 199–223.

Peyre, C. (1979). *La Cisalpine gauloise du IIIe au Ier siècle avant J.–C.* (Paris).

Pittenger, M. (2008). *Contested Triumphs* (Berkeley).

Potter, D. (2012). 'Old and New in Roman Foreign Affairs: The Case of 197', in in C. Smith & L. Yarrow (eds.), *Imperialism, Cultural Politics, and Polybius* (Oxford), 134–151.

Prag, J. (2007).' Roman Magistrates in Sicily, 227– 49 BC', in J. Dubouloz & S. Pittia (eds.). *La Sicile de Ciceron, Lectures des Verrines* (Besancon), 287–310.

———. (2010). 'Tyrannizing Sicily: The Despots who Cried Carthage!', in A. Turner, K. Chong-Gossard, F. Vervaet. (eds.) *Private and Public Lies: The Discourse of Despotism and Deceit in the Graeco–Roman World* (Leiden), 51–74.

———. (2011). 'Provincia Sicilia: between Roman and Local in the Third Century BC', in E. Riaza (ed.). *De fronteras a provincias. Interacción e integración en Occidente (ss. III–I a.C.)* (Mallorca), 83–96.

———. (2012). 'Sicily and Sardinia–Corsica: The First Provinces', in D. Hoyos (ed.). *A Companion to Roman Imperialism* (Leiden), 53–65.

Purcell, N. (1990). 'The Creation of Provincial Landscape; the Roman Impact on Cisalpine Gaul', in T. Blagg & M. Millett (eds.). *The Early Roman Empire in the West* (Oxford).

Raaflaub, K. (1986). 'The Integration of Plebeians into the Political Order After 366 BC', in K. Raaflaub (ed.). *Social Struggles in Archaic Rome* (Berkeley), 327–352.

———. (1996). 'Born to Be Wolves? Origins of Roman Imperialism', in R. Wallace & E. Harris (eds.). *Transitions to Empire. Essays in Greco–Roman History 360–146 BC, in Honour of E. Badian* (Oklahoma), 273–314.

Rankin, D. (1987). *Celts and the Classical World* (London).

Reid, J. (1913). 'Problems of the Second Punic War', *Journal of Roman Studies* 3, 175–196.

———. (1915). 'Problems of the Second Punic War III: Rome and Her Italian Allies', *Journal of Roman Studies* 5, 87–124.

Rich, J. (1996). 'The Origins of the Second Punic War', in T. Cornell, B. Rankov & P. Sabin (eds.). *The Second Punic War; A Reappraisal* (London), 1–37.

Rich, J. & Shipley, G. (1993). *War and Society in the Roman World* (London).

Richardson, J. *Hispaniae. Spain and the Development of Roman Imperialism 218–82 BC* (Cambridge).

Richardson, J. (2012). *The Fabii and the Gauls: Studies in Historical Thought and Historiography in Republican Rome* (Stuttgart).

Roberts, L. (1918). 'The Gallic Fire and Roman Archives', *Memoirs of the American Academy in Rome* 2, 55–65.

Robson, D. (1934).' The Samnites in the Po Valley', *Classical Journal* 29, 599–608.

Roselaar, S. (2010). *Public Land in the Roman Republic* (Oxford).

Rosenberger, V. (2003). 'The Gallic Disaster', *Classical World* 96, 365–373

Rosenstein, N. (2012). *Rome and the Mediterranean 290 to 146 BC: The Imperial Republic* (Edinburgh).

Sage, M. (1978). 'The De Viris Illustribus: Chronology and Structure', *Transactions of the American Philological Association* 108, 217–241.

Salmon, E. (1935). 'Rome's Battle with Etruscans and Gauls in 284–282 BC', *Classical Philology* 30, 23–31.

——. (1953). 'Rome and the Latins: I', *Phoenix* 7, 93–104.

——. (1953b). 'Rome and the Latins: II', *Phoenix* 7, 123–135.

——. (1955). 'Roman Expansion and Roman Colonization in Italy', *Phoenix* 9, 63–75.

——. (1967). *Samnium and the Samnites* (Cambridge).

——. (1969). *Roman Colonization Under the Republic* (London).

——. (1982). *The Making of Roman Italy* (London).

Sampson. G. (2005). *A re-examination of the office of the Tribunate of the Plebs in the Roman Republic (494–23 BC)* (Unpublished Thesis).

Sandberg, K. (2000). 'Tribunician and Non-Tribunician Legislation in Mid-Republican Rome', in C. Bruun (ed.). *The Roman Middle Republic* (Rome), 121–140.

Scullard, H. (1952). 'Rome's Declaration of War in Carthage in 218 BC', *Rheinisches Museum für Philologie*, 95, 209–216.

Serrati, J. (2006). 'Neptune's Altars; The Treaties Between Rome and Carthage (509–226 BC), *Classical Quarterly* 56, 113–134.

Sherwin-White, A. (1973). *The Roman Citizenship, Second Edition* (Oxford).

Skutch, O. (1953). 'The Fall of the Capitol', *Journal of Roman Studies* 43, 77–78.

——. (1978). 'The Fall of the Capitol Again: Tacitus, Ann. II. 23', *Journal of Roman Studies* 68, 93–94.

Steinby, C. (2014). *Rome versus Carthage: The War at Sea* (Barnsley).

Stone, M. (2012). 'The Genesis of Roman Imperialism', in D. Hoyos (ed.). *A Companion to Roman Imperialism* (Leiden), 23–38.

Sumner, G. (1966). 'The Chronology of the Outbreak of the Second Punic War', *Proceedings of the African Classical Association* 9, 5–30.

——. (1968). 'Roman Policy in Spain before the Hannibalic War', *Harvard Studies in Classical Philology* 72, 205–246.

——. (1972). 'Rome, Spain and the Outbreak of the Second Punic War: Some Clarifications', *Latomus* 31, 469–480.

Taylor, L. (1962). 'Forerunners of the Gracchi', *Journal of Roman Studies* 52, 19–27.

Thorne, J. (2012). 'Rivals for Empire: Carthage, Macedon, the Seleucids', in D. Hoyos (ed.). *A Companion to Roman Imperialism* (Leiden), 113–125.

Twyman, B. (1987). 'Polybius and the Annalists on the Outbreak and Early Years of the Second Punic War', *Athenaeum* 75, 67–80.

——. (1986). 'The Founders of Placentia and Cremona', *Studies in Latin Literature and Roman History* IV (Bruxelles), 109–119.

Várhelyi, Z. (2007). 'The Spectres of Roman Imperialism: The Live Burials of Gauls and Greeks at Rome', *Classical Antiquity* 26, 277–304.

Walbank, F. (1945). 'Polybius, Philinus, and the First Punic War', *Classical Quarterly* 39, 1–18.

——. (1949). 'Roman Declaration of War in the Third and Second Centuries', *Classical Philology* 44, 15–19.

——. (1957). *A Historical Commentary on Polybius Volume 1; Commentary on Books I–VI* (Oxford).

——. (1963). 'Polybius and Rome's Eastern Policy', *Journal of Roman Studies* 53, 1–13.

Wallace, J. (1998). 'A (Hi)story of Illyria', *Greece & Rome* 45, 213–225.

Wallace, R. (1990). 'Hellenization and Roman Society in the Late Fourth Century BC', in W. Eder (ed.) *Staat und Staatlichkeit in der frühen römischen Republik* (Stuttgart), 278–292.

Waterfield, R. (2014). *Taken at the Flood. The Roman Conquest of Greece* (Oxford).

Whittaker, C. (1978). 'Carthaginian Imperialism in the Fifth and Fourth Centuries', in P. Garnsey & C. Whittaker (eds). *Imperialism in the Ancient World* (Cambridge), 59–90.

Wilkes, J. (1992). *The Illyrians* (Oxford).

Williams, J. (2001). *Beyond the Rubicon. Romans and Gauls in Republican Italy* (Oxford).

Wilson, R. (2013). 'Hellenistic Sicily, c.270–100 BC', in J. Prag & J. Quinn (eds.). *The Hellenistic West. Rethinking the Ancient Mediterranean* (Cambridge), 79–119.

Wiseman, F. (1956). *Roman Spain* (London).

Yavetz, Z. (1962). 'The Policy of C. Flaminius and the Plebiscitum Claudianum', *Athenaeum* 40, 325–344.

Zambon, E. (2004). 'Notes on Tyrannies in Sicily between the Death of Agathocles and the Coming of Pyrrhus (289–279 BC)', in J. Lomas (ed.). *Greek Identity in the Western Mediterranean* (Leiden), 457–474.

Zhmodikov, A. (2000). 'Roman Republican Heavy Infantrymen in Battle (IV–II Centuries BC), *Historia* 49, 67–78.

Ziolkowski, A. (1986). 'The Plundering of Epirus in 167 BC: Economic Considerations', *Papers of the British School at Rome* 54, 69–80.

Notes and References

Chapter 1

1. See T. Cornell. (1996). *The Beginnings of Rome* (London), pp.347–352.
2. Liv. 8.14
3. See A. Sherwin–White. (1973). *The Roman Citizenship, Second Edition* (Oxford) and R. Howarth. (2006). *The Origins of Roman Citizenship* (New York).
4. T. Cornell. (1996), p.351.
5. The first being 343–341 BC.
6. See T. Cornell. (1996). pp.354 & 435.
7. See J. Champion. (2010). *The Tyrants of Syracuse. War in Ancient Sicily Volume I: 480–367 BC* (Barnsley) and (2012). *The Tyrants of Syracuse. War in Ancient Sicily Volume II: 367–211 BC* (Barnsley).
8. J. Champion. (2009). *Pyrrhus of Epirus* (Barnsley).
9. Men of Mamers; their name for Mars, the God of War. See J. Lazenby (1996). *The First Punic War* (London), pp.35–36, and E. Anderson. (2015). 'The Rise of the Sons of Mars', *History Today* 65.3, pp.11–17.
10. D. Hoyos. (1985). 'The Rise of Hiero II: Chronology and Campaigns 275–264 BC', *Antichton* 19, pp.32–56.
11. Polyb. 1.11.1
12. T. Champion. (2010), pp.203–212. Syracuse's control of southern Italy lasted until the 350s/340s BC.
13. The exact amount differs depending on the ancient sources; see F. Walbank. (1957). *A Historical Commentary on Polybius Volume 1; Commentary on Books I–VI* (Oxford), p.127.
14. Zon. 8.18
15. Eutrop. 2.28
16. Polyb. 1.65.2
17. Liv. *Per.* 20
18. Oros. 4.10
19. D. Hoyos. (2000). 'Towards a Chronology of the 'Truceless War', 241–237 BC', *Rheinisches Museum für Philologie* 143, pp.369–380, (2007). *Truceless War: Carthage's Fight for Survival, 241 to 237 BC* (Leiden).
20. The extent of Carthage's Spanish possessions in this period is difficult to ascertain from the surviving evidence. Polybius (1.10.5) stated that they controlled a large part of Spain, but this may have been a Roman exaggeration, perhaps based on later events. See F. Walbank (1957), p.59.

21. See J. Serrati, J. (2006). 'Neptune's Altars; The Treaties Between Rome and Carthage (509–226 BC), *Classical Quarterly* 56, pp.113–134.

Chapter 2
1. R. Wilson. (2013). 'Hellenistic Sicily, c.270–100 BC', in J. Prag & J. Quinn (eds.). *The Hellenistic West. Rethinking the Ancient Mediterranean* (Cambridge), pp.79–119.
2. D. Kagan. (1991). *The Peace of Nicias and the Sicilian Expedition* (Cornell), P. Matyszak. (2012). *Expedition to Disaster* (Barnsley).
3. See J. Champion (2010) and (2012).
4. Zon. 8.17
5. J. Prag. (2007). 'Roman Magistrates in Sicily, 227– 49 BC', in J. Dubouloz & S. Pittia (eds.). *La Sicile de Ciceron Lectures des Verrines* (Besancon), pp.287–310, (2011). 'Provincia Sicilia: between Roman and Local in the Third Century BC', in E. Riaza (ed.). *De fronteras a provincias. Interacción e integración en Occidente (ss. III–I a.C.)* (Mallorca), pp.83–96 and (2012). 'Sicily and Sardinia–Corsica: The First Provinces', in D. Hoyos (ed.). *A Companion to Roman Imperialism* (Leiden), pp.53–65.
6. Liv. *Per.* 20, Justin. *Dig.* 1.2.2.32
7. See T. Brennan. (2000). *The Praetorship in the Roman Republic Volume 1* (Oxford), pp.91–93.
8. There is evidence to suggest that Rome's earliest Republican magistracy was in fact the Praetorship (Praetor Maximus) not the Consulship, seen through the language Livy uses. See T. Cornell. (1996), pp.227–230.
9. T. Brennan (2000). 1, pp.85–89.
10. We only know of his holding the office thanks to a reference in Solinus (5.1). Also see Liv. 33.42.8. See T. Broughton. (1952). 1, p.229.
11. Polyb. 2.24.13
12. See J. Champion (2010) and (2012).
13. Referred to by modern historians as Hieron II or Hiero II.
14. J. Champion. (2012), pp.161–162.
15. Eutrop. 3.1.2 & 3.2.1
16. A. Eckstein. (1985). 'Polybius, Syracuse and the Politics of Accommodation', *Greek, Roman and Byzantine Studies* 26, pp.265–282.
17. Polyb. 1.79.1–7
18. Polyb. 1.88.8–10
19. Polyb. 3.27.7
20. App. *Hisp.* 4, Eutrop. 3.2.1, Orosius. 4.12.2–3 actually places this in the year 235 BC.
21. App. *Pun.* 5, Zon. 8.18
22. Strabo. 5.225
23. Zon. 8.18
24. Dio. *fr.* 45.1
25. Val. Max. 6.3.3. Ammianus also refers to the story (Ammian. 14.11.32) some 600 years later.
26. Zon. 8.18
27. Vell. 2.38.2, also mentioned in Livy (23.34.15), Eutrop. 3.3.1 and Oros. 4.12.2

28. Aug. *ResGest.* 13; *de vir ill.* 79.6, Eutrop. 3.3.1, Flor. 1.19.1, 2.33.64, Liv. 1.19.3, Plut. *Num.* 20.2, *Mor.* 322B, Oros. 4.12.4–13, Varro. *LL.* 5.165, Vell. 2.38.3

29. Zon. 8.18

30. Ibid

31. Zon. 8.18

32. T. Brennan. (1996). 'Triumphus in Monte Albano', in R. Wallace & E. Harris (eds.). *Transitions to Empire. Essays in Greco–Roman History 360–146 BC, in Honour of E. Badian* (Oklahoma), pp.315–337.

Chapter 3

1. In the period 390–386 BC, the chronology is unclear. See. T. Cornell. (1996), pp.399–402 and A. Drummond. (1978). 'The Dictator Years', *Historia* 27, pp.550–572.

2. J. Williams. (2001). *Beyond the Rubicon. Romans and Gauls in Republican Italy* (Oxford).

3. Liv. 5.34–35. Similar versions of this can be found in Polyb. 2.17, Dion. Hal. 13.10–11 and Plut. *Cam.* 15. See T. Cornell (1996), pp.313–318.

4. Liv. 5.34.9

5. See T. Cornell. (1996), p.314.

6. See T. Bridgman. (2005). 'Keltoi, Galatai, Galli: Were They All One People?', *Proceedings of the Harvard Celtic Colloquium* 24/25, pp.155–162.

7. See J. Williams. (2001), pp.18–67.

8. L. Barfield. (1971). *Northern Italy before Rome* (London), pp.146–159.

9. C. Champion. (1996). 'Polybius, Aetolia and the Gallic Attack on Delphi (279 BC)', *Historia* 45, pp.315–328.

10. P. Ellis. (1998). *Celt and Roman. The Celts in Italy* (London), pp.86–103.

11. Traditional Roman chronology (Varronian) places this event in 390 BC. Parallel events given by Polybius (1.6.1) place it in c.387/386 BC. See. T. Cornell. (1996), pp.313–314 & 399–402.

12. T. Cornell. (1996), p.316.

13. Justin. 20.5.1–6

14. Diod. 14.117.7. Also see Strabo. 5.2.3

15. Liv. 5.38.3–10

16. At this time the highest office of Rome was the Military Tribunate with Consular power (*tribuni militum consulari potestate*) as opposed to the Consulship.

17. V. Rosenberger. (2003). 'The Gallic Disaster', *Classical World* 96, pp.365–373.

18. See O. Skutch (1953). 'The Fall of the Capitol', *Journal of Roman Studies* 43, pp.77–78, (1978). 'The Fall of the Capitol Again: Tacitus, Ann. II. 23', *Journal of Roman Studies* 68, pp.93–94 and T. Cornell. (1986). 'Review: The Annals of Quintus Ennius' *Journal of Roman Studies* 76, pp.244–250.

19. Liv. 6.13. See L. Roberts. (1918). 'The Gallic Fire and Roman Archives', *Memoirs of the American Academy in Rome* 2, pp.55–65.

20. T. Cornell. (1996), pp.317–318.

21. Liv. 6.42.5.–8

22. F. Walbank (1957), pp.185–186.

23. Liv. 7.11.4

24. Liv. 7.12.3
25. P. Ellis. (1998), pp.127–128.
26. Polyb. 2.18.9
27. Liv. 10.26.7–11
28. T. Cornell. (1996), p.361.
29. Ibid. p.362.
30. Polyb. 2.19.9
31. App. *Sam.* 6.12, *Gall.* 11.1–2
32. Liv. *Per.* 12
33. Oros. 2.19.5–9
34. See T. Cornell. (1996), p.362 and F. Walbank (1957), p.188. Broughton, however, favours a date of 283 BC; T. Broughton (1952). 1, p.188.
35. See W. Harris. (1971). *Rome in Etruria and Umbria* (Oxford), pp.78–84 and E. Salmon. (1935). 'Rome's Battle with Etruscans and Gauls in 284–282 BC', *Classical Philology* 30, pp.23–31.
36. Polyb. 2.20.1–3
37. U. Ewins. (1952). 'The Early Colonisation of Cisalpine Gaul', *Papers of the British School at Rome*, pp.54–71.
38. See Frontin. *Str.* 3.16.2–3, Diod. 23.8.3, Zon. 8.10 & 16
39. Polyb. 2.7.8–9
40. Polyb. 2.7.10
41. Oros. 4.7.12, Zon. 8.11
42. Liv. *Per.* 20
43. Polyb. 2.21.1–6. See F. Walbank. (1957), pp.191–192.
44. S. Dyson. (1985). *The Creation of the Roman Frontier* (Princeton), pp.27–28.
45. Zon. 8.18
46. Oros. 4.12.1
47. Zon. 8.18
48. Oros. 4.12.1
49. Ibid
50. Zon. 8.18
51. Ibid
52. See R. Husband. (1911). 'Kelts and Ligurians', *Classical Philology* 6, pp.385–401.
53. S. Dyson. (1985), pp.87–94.
54. Herod. 7.165
55. Zon. 8.18
56. Ibid.
57. Zon. 8.18
58. Plut. *Fab.* 2.1. The victory is also referred to in the *de viris illustribus* (43.1).
59. There is some dispute over the date of his Tribunate. Polybius places it in 232 BC, in the year of Lepidus' Consulship, but Cicero places it in Fabius' second Consulship in 228 BC. Both Niccolini and Broughton argue for a date of 232 BC and this is the most commonly accepted date. See F. Garofalo. (1889). *I fasti dei tribuni della plebe della repubblica romana* (Catania), p. 67, G. Niccolini, *I fasti dei tribuni della plebe* (Milan),

pp.87– 89, T. Broughton. (1952). 1, p. 225, G. Sampson. (2005). *A re–examination of the office of the Tribunate of the Plebs in the Roman Republic* (494–23 BC) (Unpublished Thesis), p.84. Also see R. Feig Vishnia. (1996). 'Cicero "De *Senectute" 11.* and the Date of Flaminius' Tribunate', *Phoenix* 50, pp.138–145.

60. There is also a fragment of Cato (*fr.* 43) on this topic.
61. T. Cornell. (1996), pp.267–271.
62. Also see R. Develin. (1976). 'C. Flaminius in 232 BC', *L'Antiquité Classique* 45, pp.638–643, (1979). 'The Political Position of C. Flaminius', *Rheinisches Museum für Philologie* 122, pp.268–277 and R. Feig Vishnia. (1996a). *State, Society, and Popular Leaders in Mid–Republican Rome 241–167 BC* (London), pp.11–48.
63. J. Corbett. (1970). 'L. Metellus (Cos 251, 247), Agrarian Commissioner', *Classical Quarterly* 20, pp. 7–8.
64. See P. Erdkamp. (2009). 'Polybius, the Ebro Treaty, and the Gallic Invasion of 225 BCE', *Classical Philology* 104, pp. 495–510 and A. Eckstein. (2012). 'Polybius, the Gallic Crisis, and the Ebro Treaty', *Classical Philology* 107, pp.206–229.
65. R. Develin. (1976), p.642.
66. Zon. 8.18.
67. Ibid.
68. Polyb. 2.22.7–8

Chapter 4

1. See T. Cornell. (1996). pp.86–92.
2. See K. Lomas. (1993). *Rome and the Western Greeks, 350 BC–AD 200: Conquest and Acculturation in Southern Italy* (London).
3. See M. Nilsson. (1929). 'The Introduction of Hoplite Tactics at Rome: Its Date and Its Consequences', *Journal of Roman Studies* 19, pp.1–11, A. Snodgrass. (1965). 'The Hoplite Reform and History', *Journal of Hellenic Studies* 85, pp.110–122 and T. Cornell. (1996), pp.183–185.
4. See D. Kagan. (1991) and P. Matyszak. (2012).
5. See J. Champion. (2010), pp. 203–212.
6. J. Champion. (2012), p.128.
7. Diod. 16.62–63
8. Liv. 8.17.8–10
9. Liv. 8.24.1
10. E. Anson. and V. Troncoso. (2012). *After Alexander: The Time of the Diadochi (323–281 BC)* (London).
11. Liv. 9.17–19
12. Liv. 10.2.1–3. Also see Diod. 20.104
13. G. Forsythe (1999). *Livy and Early Rome* (Stuttgart).
14. Diod. 21.3–4
15. Diod. 21.8
16. J. Prag. (2010). 'Tyrannizing Sicily: The Despots who Cried Carthage!', in A. Turner, K. Chong–Gossard, F. Vervaet (eds.), *Private and Public Lies: The Discourse of Despotism and Deceit in the Graeco–Roman World* (Leiden), pp.51–74, E. Zambon. (2004). 'Notes

on Tyrannies in Sicily between the Death of Agathocles and the Coming of Pyrrhus (289–279 BC)', in J. Lomas (ed.). *Greek Identity in the Western Mediterranean* (Leiden), pp.457–474.

17. J. Champion. (2009).

18. L. Neatby. (1950). 'Romano–Egyptian Relations during the Third Century BC', *Transactions and Proceedings of the American Philological Association* 81, pp.89–98.

19. Dion. Hal. 20.14.1–2, Eutrop. 2.15.1, Dio. *fr.* 41.1, Zon. 8.6, Val. Max. 4.3.9, Liv. *Per.* 14, Just. 18.2.8–9

20. Val. Max. 6.6.5. Also see Liv. *Per.* 15, Dio. *fr.* 42.1, Zon. 8.7

21. Suet. *Claud.* 25.3

22. A. Eckstein. (2008). *Rome Enters the Greek East* (Oxford), p.31.

23. Just. 28.1.5–28.2.14

24. Just. 28.2.14

25. See J. Wilkes. (1992). *The Illyrians* (Oxford), A. Evans. (2006) *Ancient Illyria: An Archaeological Exploration* (London) and D. Dzino. (2006). 'Welcome to the Mediterranean Semi–Periphery: The place of Illyricum in book 7 of Strabo', *Živa Antika* 56, pp.113–128, (2007). 'The Celts in Illyricum – Whoever they may be: The Hybridization and Construction of Identities in Southeastern Europe in the Fourth and Third Centuries BC', *Opuscula archaeologica*, 31, pp.93–112, (2008). 'The People who are Illyrians and Celts: Strabo and the identities of the 'barbarians' from Illyricum', *Arheoloski vestnik* 59, pp.415–424, (2008b). 'Strabo 7.5 and Imaginary Illyricum', *Athenaeum* 96, pp.173–192 and J. Wallace. (1998). 'A (Hi)story of Illyria', *Greece & Rome* 45, pp.213–225.

26. D. Dzino. (2010). *Illyricum in Roman Politics 229 BC–AD 68* (Cambridge), pp.46–47.

27. See N. Hammond. (1966). 'The Kingdoms in Illyria circa 400–167 BC', *Annual of the British School at Athens* 61, pp.239–253.

28. D. Dzino. (2010), pp.46–47 and E. Badian. (1952). 'Notes on Roman Policy in Illyria (230–201 BC), *Papers of the British School at Rome* 20, pp.72–93.

29. D. Dzino. (2010), pp.46–47. Also see J. Wilkes. (1992), pp.139–140.

30. Polyb. 2.2.4

31. Polyb. 2.3–5

32. Polyb. 2.8.1–4

33. App. *Ill.* 7

34. Dio. *fr.* 49.1

35. Zon. 8.19

36. See H. Dell. (1967b). 'The Origin and Nature of Illyrian Piracy', *Historia* 16, pp.344–358.

37. The Lex Claudia, which was the law restricting Senators and their immediate families from engaging in trade, interestingly did not come into force until 218 BC. See Z. Yavetz. (1962). 'The Policy of C. Flaminius and the Plebiscitum Claudianum', *Athenaeum* 40, pp.325–344.

38. As well as winning a Triumph over the Volsinii and Vulci, he was also appointed Dictator in 246 BC to hold elections in Rome.

39. Polyb. 2.8.6–13

40. See also App. *Ill.* 7, Dio. *fr.* 49.2–4, Zon. 8.19, Oros. 4.13.2, Liv. *Per.* 20, Flor. 1.21.1–3, Plin. *NH.* 34.24. Dio adds that the other was imprisoned. Pliny has the murdered man as Ti. Coruncanius, who, as with Roman custom, received a statue in the Forum, as a mark of respect.
41. See L. Loreto. (2011). 'Roman Politics and Expansion, 241–219', in D. Hoyos (ed.). *A Companion to the Punic Wars* (Oxford), pp.186–192.
42. Other sources refer to undated attacks on Apollonia (Val. Max. 1.5.e.2) and Mothone (Paus. 4.35.6–7), which are commonly assigned to this period.
43. S. Oost. (1954). *Roman Policy in Epirus and Acarnania in the Age of the Roman Conquest of Greece* (Dallas), pp.4–5.
44. Polyb. 2.11.1–4
45. Zon. 8.19, Dio. *fr.* 49.7
46. Ibid
47. Polyb. 2.11.7
48. Zon. 8.19, Dio. *fr.* 49
49. Polyb. 2.11.10
50. Polyb. 2.11.11. See N. Hammond. (1989). 'The Illyrian Atintani, the Epirotic Atintanes and the Roman Protectorate', *Journal of Roman Studies* 79, pp.11–25.
51. Polyb. 2.11.12
52. Polyb. 2.11.15
53. F. Walbank. (1957), p.164.
54. Polyb. 2.11.13
55. Hammond provides an excellent description of the geography of the region and its coastline; see N. Hammond. (1968). 'Illyris, Rome and Macedon in 229–205 BC', *Journal of Roman Studies* 58, pp.1–21.
56. N. Bagnall. (1990), p.137.
57. Polyb. 2.11.13
58. Polyb. 2.11.14 Dio. *fr.* 49.6, Zon. 8.19
59. Dio. *fr.* 49.7
60. Polyb. 2.11.16
61. A. Evans. (2006). *Ancient Illyria: An Archaeological Exploration* (London), p.40. Also see F. Walbank. (1957), p.164.
62. Polyb. 2.11.17–2.12.2
63. Fulvius on his return was awarded a Triumph for his naval victories, which he celebrated in 228 BC.
64. W. Jashjemski. (1950). *The Origins and History of the Proconsular and the Propraetorian Imperium to 27 BC* (Chicago).
65. Dio. *fr.* 49.7
66. Polyb. 2.12.3
67. App. *Ill.* 7
68. Dio. *fr.* 53
69. App. *Ill.* 7
70. See P. Derow. (1991). 'Pharos and Rome', *Zeitschrift für Papyrologie und Epigraphik* 88, pp.261–270, A. Eckstein. (1999). 'Pharos and the Question of Roman Treaties of

Alliance in the Greek East in the Third Century BC', *Classical Philology* 94, pp.395–418. N. Hammond. (1968), pp.1–21.

71. App. *Ill.* 7
72. Polyb. 2.12.4–6
73. App. *Ill.* 8
74. Zon. 8.19
75. Polyb. 2.12.8, Zon. 8.19
76. See. A Dimond. (forthcoming) *Sparta's Last Stand* (Barnsley).
77. See N. Hammond. (1968). pp.1–21, who argues that the lack of an embassy to Macedon was a direct snub.

Chapter 5
1. Just. 44.2.4
2. R. Miles. (2010). *Carthage Must Be Destroyed* (London), pp.74–76.
3. D. Hoyos. 'Barcid Proconsuls and Punic Politics, 237–218 BC' *Rheinisches Museum für Philologie* 137, pp.246–274.
4. Cornelius Nepos wrote a very short life of Hamilcar, but covered the Spanish campaign in just a few sentences.
5. Polyb. 2.1.5
6. D. Hoyos, D. (2003). *Hannibal's Dynasty* (London), p.55.
7. Ibid, pp. 55–72.
8. Diod. 25.10.1–2
9. App. *Hann.* 2
10. Diod. 25.10 .14
11. Ibid.
12. Diod. 25.10.3
13. App. *Hisp.* 5
14. Nepos. 22.4
15. Dio. *fr.* 48
16. The location is not clear, see D. Hoyos. (2003), p.68.
17. Diod. 25.10.15–18. See also Polyb. 3.14.10, Nepos. 22, Strab. 3.151, App. *Hisp.* 5, *Hann.* 5, Ampel. 36.2
18. Zon. 8.19
19. Frontin. 2.4.17
20. Diod. 25.12
21. Strab. 3.4.6
22. See F. Kramer. (1948). 'Massilian Diplomacy before the Second Punic War', *American Journal of Philology* 69, pp.1–26.
23. Erdkamp argues against this view: see P. Erdkamp. (2009). 'Polybius, the Ebro Treaty, and the Gallic Invasion of 225 BCE', *Classical Philology* 104, pp.495–510.
24. For an overview of all of the treaties between the two powers, see J. Serrati. (2006). 'Neptune's Altars; The Treaties Between Rome and Carthage (509–226 BC), *Classical Quarterly* 56, pp.113–134.
25. Polyb. 2.13.3–7

26. Polyb. 2.13.3–7, 2.22.9–11, 3.27.9, 3.30.3, Liv. 21.2.7, 21.18.9, 34.13.7, Strab. 3.159, Sil. Ital. 1.479–480, Flor. 1.22.4, App. *Hisp.* 7, *Hann.* 2, *Pun.* 6, Zon. 8.21. Also see L. Loreto. (2011), pp.193–196.
27. Which ended the First Punic War.
28. Liv. 21.19
29. Liv. 21.2
30. App. *Hisp.* 7
31. See A. Astin. (1967). 'Saguntum and the Origins of the Second Punic War', *Latomus* 26, pp.577–596, T. Dorey. (1959). 'The Treaty with Saguntum', *Humanitas* 11, 1–10, A. Eckstein. (1984). 'Rome, Saguntum and the Ebro Treaty', *Emerita* 52, pp.51–68. (2012). 'Polybius, the Gallic Crisis, and the Ebro Treaty', *Classical Philology* 107, pp.206–229, P. Erdkamp. (2009), pp.495–510 and L. Loreto. (2011), pp.193–196, J. Serrati. (2006), pp.113–134.
32. Liv. 21.2
33. See F. Kramer. (1948), pp.1–26 and N. DeWitt. (1940). 'Massillia and Rome', *Transactions and Proceedings of the American Philological Association* 71, pp.605–615
34. A. Eckstein. (1984), pp.51–68.
35. App. *Hisp.* 10
36. See note 227.
37. F. Heichelheim. (1954). 'New Evidence on the Ebro Treaty', *Historia* 3, pp.211–219.

Chapter 6
1. T. Bridgman. (2005). 'Keltoi, Galatai, Galli: Were They All One People?', *Proceedings of the Harvard Celtic Colloquium* 24/25, p.159.
2. Polyb. 2.22.1–5
3. Zon. 8.20, Plut. *Marc.* 3
4. Polyb. 2.15.8.–9
5. Also see A. Eckstein. (1982). 'Human Sacrifice and Fear of Military Disaster in Republican Rome', *American Journal of Ancient History* 7, pp.69–95 and Z. Várhelyi. (2007). 'The Spectres of Roman Imperialism: The Live Burials of Gauls and Greeks at Rome', *Classical Antiquity* 26, pp.277–304.
6. Zon. 8.20
7. Plut. *Marc.* 3. Also see Plut. *Mor.* 283F and Oros. 4.13.3
8. Erdkamp argues that this was also related to a scandal involving the Vestal Virgins; P. Erdkamp. (2009) pp.495–510. This linkage is dismissed by Eckstein though, who also highlights a parallel to a human sacrifice made by the Romans in 280 BC (Zon. 8.3); A. Eckstein. (2012), pp.206–229.
9. Dio. *fr.* 50.2
10. Liv. *Per.* 20, Justin. *Digest.* 1.2.2.32
11. T. Brennan. (2000), pp.91–95.
12. A. Eckstein. (2012), p.218.
13. Polyb. 2.22.7–8
14. Polyb. 2.22.11
15. Polyb. 2.23.2

16. Polyb. 2.24.13
17. Loreto argues differently and believes that the Romans made extensive preparations to counter a feared Carthaginian invasion by sea. See. L. Loreto. (2011), pp.97–201.
18. Polyb. 2.23.1
19. Polyb. 2.24.3–9. See. F. Walbank. (1957), pp.196–199.
20. P. Brunt. (1971). *Italian Manpower 225 BC–AD 14* (Oxford), pp.44–45, L. De Ligt. (2012). *Peasants, Citizens and Soldiers. Studies in the Demographic History of Roman Italy 225 BC–AD 100.* (Cambridge), p.41.
21. Mommsen identified the Aemilius who was Dictator in 321 BC as a Papus, but this has been disputed. See T. Broughton. (1952). 1, pp.151–152.
22. Polyb. 2.23.4
23. Diod. 25.13.1
24. Polyb. 2.23.5, Zon. 8.20
25. Polyb. 2.23.5
26. Dio. *fr.* 50.4
27. Polyb. 2.25.1–3
28. Polyb. 2.25.4–8
29. Polyb. 2.25.8–11
30. Polyb. 2.26.2
31. Polyb. 2.26.6
32. Polyb. 2.26.8

Chapter 7
1. Polyb. 2.27.2–4
2. Polyb. 2.27. 4–6
3. Polyb. 2.27.6
4. Polyb. 2.27.7
5. Polyb. 2.28.1
6. Polyb. 2.28.3
7. Polyb. 2.28.9
8. Polyb. 2.28.11–29.9
9. Polyb. 2.30.1–30.5
10. Polyb. 2.30.6–30.8
11. Polyb. 2.30.9
12. Polyb. 2.31.1, Diod. 25.13.1, Eutrop. 3.5.1, Oros. 4.13.10
13. Diod. 25.13
14. Oros. 4.8
15. Ibid. 4.10
16. Eutrop. 3.5.1
17. Flor. 1.20.4
18. Plin. *NH.* 1.138
19. Plut. *Marc.* 4.1
20. Jer. 137.4. Though he places it in the wrong Olympiad.
21. Dio. 50.2

22. Zon. 8.20
23. Polyb. 2.31.4
24. Diodorus seems to be mistaken in assigning him a Proconsulship. Not only does Polybius (and Zonaras) state that the Boian campaign took place in the same year as Telamon, but the *Fasti Triumphales* states that he Triumphed as Consul not Proconsul.
25. Dio *fr.* 50.4, Zon. 8.20, Flor. 1.20.4
26. The *Decemviri Sacris Faciundis*, see T. Broughton (1952). 1, pp. 414–415.
27. A Legate in 211 BC and again in 210 BC. See T. Broughton (1952). 2, p.534.

Chapter 8
1. Only one is recorded between 241 and 219 BC; Cn. Fulvius Centumalus in 228 BC in Illyria, see W. Jashjemski. (1950), p.100.
2. It must be pointed out that they had to abdicate the Censorship due to a flaw in their election. See T. Broughton. (1952). 1, p. 226.
3. Polyb. 2.31.8–10
4. Oros. 4.3.11
5. Zon. 8.20
6. Liv. *Per.* 20. The dating of this to 224 BC rather than 223 BC is uncertain.
7. Polyb. 2.31.8
8. Polyb. 2.31.9, Zon. 8.20
9. Polyb. 2.31.10
10. Oros. 4.3.11
11. F. Walbank. (1957), p.207.
12. Plin. *NH.* 7.139
13. Polyb. 2.32.1–3
14. F. Walbank. (1957), pp.207–208.
15. Walbank raises the possibility that both the defeat and agreement were fictitious; made up by a hostile Senatorial source, based on an argument by De Sanctis. See F. Walbank, (1957), p.208.
16. Polyb. 2.32.4–5
17. Polyb. 2.32.6–11
18. Polyb. 2.33.1–4
19. F. Walbank. (1957), p.209.
20. Ibid
21. Polyb. 2.33.5–9
22. Oros. 4.13.14
23. 217 BC and 105 BC respectively.
24. Zon. 8.20, Plut. *Marc.* 4
25. Zon. 8.20
26. Liv. 21.63.2
27. Liv. 21.63.7, see also 21.63.12 and 22.3.4
28. Plut. *Marc.* 4
29. Sil. Ital. 4.704–706
30. Ibid. 5.107–113

31. Ibid. 5.137, also see 5.646–655 for his death at the hands of a Boian (though Livy 22.6.3 has his killer being an Insubrian).
32. Ibid.6.21
33. Plut. *Fab.* 2.4
34. Zon. 8.20
35. Ibid
36. Plut. *Marc.* 4. Also *Marc.* 6.1. See also Liv. 21.63.2, 23.14.4, Flor. 1.20.4
37. See M. Pittenger. (2008). *Contested Triumphs* (Berkeley), pp.39–40 for a discussion on how this was achieved.

Chapter 9

1. Polyb. 2.34.1
2. Zon. 8.20
3. Plut. *Marc.* 6.2
4. Polyb. 2.34.2
5. See F. Walbank. (1957), p.210. Also see Strabo. 5.4.8
6. Zon. 8.20
7. Polybius states he was an Insubrian, whereas Plutarch states it was a Gaesatae.
8. Plut. *Marc.* 6.31
9. Zon. 8.20
10. Polyb. 2.34.6–9
11. Plut. *Marc.* 6.3–7.4
12. Oros. 4.15
13. Val. Max. 3.2.5
14. Frontin. 4.5.4
15. Eutrop. 3.6.1
16. Liv. *Per.* 20. Also see Liv. 27.5.7 & 29.11.13
17. *De vir. Ill.* 45.1
18. The year was disputed in Roman times. See T. Broughton. (1954). 1, p.59.
19. Plut. *Marc.* 6.5
20. Zon. 8.20
21. Polyb. 2.34.11
22. Polyb. 2.34.11–14
23. Polyb 2.34.15
24. Zon. 8.20
25. Plut. *Marc.* 7
26. Eutrop. 3.6
27. Oros. 4.13
28. Zon. 8.20
29. Zon. 8.20
30. Eutrop. 3.7
31. Oros. 4.13.16. Also see Liv. *Per.* 20
32. See H. Dell. (1970). 'Demetrius of Pharos and the Istrian War', *Historia* 19, pp.30–38.
33. App. *Ill.* 8

34. Zon. 8.20
35. B. Twyman. (1986). 'The Founders of Placentia and Cremona', *Studies in Latin Literature and Roman History IV* (Brussels), pp.109–119.
36. Polyb. 3.40.3–5
37. U. Ewins. (1952), pp.54–71.
38. Polyb. 3.40.8–10
39. Polyb. 3.40.11–14
40. Liv. 21.25.8–14
41. Liv. 21.26.1–2
42. Liv. 21.63.15

Chapter 10
1. A. Dimond. (Forthcoming).
2. H. Dell. (1967). 'Antigonus III and Rome', *Classical Philology* 62, pp.94–103.
3. A. Dimond. (Forthcoming).
4. Polyb. 2.65.5
5. Dio. *fr.* 53
6. See A. Eckstein. (1994). 'Polybius, Demetrius of Pharus, and the Origins of the Second Illyrian War', *Classical Philology* 89, pp.46–59.
7. Polyb. 3.16.2–3
8. App. *Ill.* 3.8
9. Zon. 8.20
10. F. Walbank. (1957), pp.324–325.
11. Ibid, p. 326.
12. See. H. Dell. (1970), pp.30–38.
13. See J. Fine. (1936). 'Macedon, Illyria, and Rome, 220–219 BC', *Journal of Roman Studies* 26, pp.24–39.
14. Of apparently natural causes.
15. Polyb. 3.16.1
16. Ibid. 3.16.3
17. Dio. *fr.* 53 & Zon. 8.20
18. Polyb. 3.18.1–2
19. *de. vir. ill.* 50
20. Polyb. 3.18.3–6
21. Polyb. 3.18.7–12
22. Polyb. 3.19.1–7
23. Zon. 8.20
24. Polyb. 3.18.12
25. Polyb. 7.9.13. Also see Justin. 29.2
26. App. *Ill.* 3.8, Zon. 8.20
27. App. *Ill.* 3.8
28. Liv. *Per.* 20, Zon. 8.20, Oros. 4.13.16, Eutrop. 3.7
29. Zon. 8.20
30. Ibid

31. App. *Ill.* 8
32. Poly. 4.16.6
33. Val.Max. 2.9.6, 4.2.2, Frontin. *Str.* 4.1.45, Plut. *Fab.* 14.3; *de. vir. Ill.* 50, Liv. 22.35.3, 27.34.3–5, 29.37.9–10 & 13–14, Sil. Ital. 8.290–291, 15.594–597, 15.733–734
34. See N. Hammond. (1968), pp.1–21.
35. Polyb. 5.108.1–9

Chapter 11
1. Polyb. 2.36.1
2. Diod. 25.12.1
3. Liv. 21.2
4. App. *Hisp.* 8
5. Polyb.3.13.5–8
6. Liv. 21.5
7. Ibid
8. Polyb. 3.14.1
9. Liv. 21.5
10. Polyb. 3.14.2–8
11. Liv. 21.5
12. See A. Astin. (1967), pp.577–596, T. Dorey. (1959), pp.1–10, A. Eckstein. (1983). 'Two Notes on the Outbreak of the Hannibalic War', *Rheinisches Museum für Philologie* 126, pp.255–272, (1984), pp.51–68, (2012), pp.206–229, P. Erdkamp. (2009), pp.495–510, R. Errington. (1970). 'Rome and Spain before the Second Punic War', *Latomus* 29, pp.25–57, F. Heichelheim. (1954), pp.211–219, L. Loreto. (2011), pp.193–196, J. Rich. (1996). 'The Origins of the Second Punic War', in T. Cornell, B. Rankov & P. Sabin (eds.). *The Second Punic War; A Reappraisal* (London), pp.1–37, H. Scullard. (1952). 'Rome's Declaration of War in Carthage in 218 BC', *Rheinisches Museum für Philologie*, 95, pp.209–216, J. Serrati. (2006), pp.130–134, G. Sumner. (1966). 'The Chronology of the Outbreak of the Second Punic War', *Proceedings of the African Classical Association* 9, pp.5–30, (1968). 'Roman Policy in Spain before the Hannibalic War', *Harvard Studies in Classical Philology* 72, pp.205–246, (1972). 'Rome, Spain and the Outbreak of the Second Punic War: Some Clarifications', *Latomus* 31, pp.469–480. B. Twyman. (1987). 'Polybius and the Annalists on the Outbreak and Early Years of the Second Punic War', *Athenaeum* 75, pp.67–80.
13. Polyb. 3.15.1
14. Polyb. 3.15.2
15. See T. Broughton (1952). 1, p.237.
16. App. *Hisp.* 10
17. Polyb. 3.15.7
18. F. Walbank. (1957), p.322.
19. Polyb. 3.6.2, App. *Hisp.* 10
20. Polyb. 3.15.5
21. See A. Astin. (1967).
22. Liv. 21.7

23. Polyb. 3.17.9
24. Eutrop. 3.7.2
25. Liv. 21.7
26. Livy (21.8) provides details of the Saguntine missiles; 'The missile used by the Saguntines was the phalarica, a javelin with a shaft smooth and round up to the head, which, as in the pilum, was an iron point of square section. The shaft was wrapped in tow and then smeared with pitch; the iron head was three feet long and capable of penetrating armour and body alike.'
27. Liv. 21.9
28. Liv. 21.11
29. Liv. 21.12
30. Liv. 21.15
31. Flor.1.22.5
32. Liv. 21.10
33. A. Astin. (1967), p.596.

Conclusions
1. See L. Loreto. (2007). *La grande strategia di Roma nell'età della prima guerra punica 273–229 a.C.* (Napoli).
2. E. Luttwak. (1976).*The Grand Strategy of the Roman Empire: From the First Century AD to the Third* (Baltimore).

Appendix I
1. A. Fear. (2010). *Orosius. Seven Books of History Against the Pagans* (Liverpool).
2. M. Sage. (1978). 'The *De Viris Illustribus*: Chronology and Structure', *Transactions of the American Philological Association* 108, pp.217–241.
3. T. Cornell (ed.). (2013). *The Fragments of the Roman Historians Volumes 1–3* (Oxford).
4. See T. Cornell (ed.). (2013). *1*, pp.160–178, J. Dillery. (2002). 'Quintus Fabius Pictor and Greco–Roman Historiography at Rome', in J. Miller, C. Damon & K. Myers (eds.). *Vertis in Usum. Studies in Honour of Edward Courtney* (Munchen), pp.1–23, A. Momigliano (1977) 'Did Fabius Pictor Lie', *Essays in Ancient and Modern Historiography* (Oxford), pp.99–105, (1990). 'Fabius Pictor and the Origins of National History', *The Classical Foundations of Modern Historiography* (Berkeley), pp.80–108, S. Northwood. (2007). 'Q. Fabius Pictor: was he an Annalist?', in N. Sekunda (ed.). *Corolla Cosmo Rodewald* (Gdansk), pp.97–114.
5. See F. Walbank. (1945). 'Polybius, Philinus, and the First Punic War', *Classical Quarterly* 39, pp.1–18.
6. See D. Hoyos. (2003), pp.212–222.

Appendix II
1. See N. Hammond. (1966). pp.243–247.

Appendix III
1. T. Cornell. (1996), pp.242–271 & 327–344.
2. See G. Sampson. (2005), pp.20–36.

3. E. Staveley. (1955). 'Tribal Legislation before the Lex Hortensia', *Athenaeum* 33, pp.3–31.
4. K. Raaflaub. (1986). 'The Integration of Plebeians into the Political Order After 366 BC', in K. Raaflaub (ed.). *Social Struggles in Archaic Rome* (Berkeley), pp.327–352.
5. G. Sampson. (2005), pp.223–284.
6. K. Sandberg. (2000). 'Tribunician and Non–Tribunician Legislation in Mid–Republican Rome', in C. Bruun (ed.). *The Roman Middle Republic* (Rome), pp.121–140.
7. L. Taylor. (1962). 'Forerunners of the Gracchi', *Journal of Roman Studies* 52, pp.19–27. Also see E. Badian. (1996). 'Tribuni Plebis and Res Publica', in J. Linderski (ed.). *Imperium Sine Fine: T. Robert, S. Broughton and the Roman Republic* (Stuttgart), pp.187–214.
8. The two sources for the date of his Tribunate conflict with each other. Polybius (2.21.7–8) places it in 232 BC, whilst Cicero (*Sen.* 11) places it in 228 BC. It is most commonly assigned to 232 BC. See R. Feig Vishnia. (1996), pp.138–145.
9. Polyb. 2.21.7–8. See F. Walbank (1957), pp.192–193. The earliest surviving account is the fragment of Cato (fr. 43) but this does not mention Flaminius himself, merely the law. See T. Cornell. (2013). (ed.). *The Fragments of the Roman Historians* (Oxford). 1, pp.93 & 182–183.
10. Cic. *Inv.* 2.52. Also see *Acad.* 2.13, *Brut* 57, *Leg.* 3.20 & *Sen* 11
11. Val. Max. 5.4.5
12. S. Roselaar. (2010). *Public Land in the Roman Republic* (Oxford), pp. 56–57.

Appendix IV

1. Polyb. 2.24.10–16
2. According to the testimonies of Orosius (4.13.7) and Eutropius (3.5.1). Erdkamp provides a detailed analysis for Fabius Pictor's possible motivations for including the survey of available manpower in his own work, see P. Erdkamp. (2008). 'Polybius II. 24: Roman Manpower and Greek Propaganda', *Ancient Society* 38, pp.137–152.
3. P. Erdkamp. (2008), p.138.
4. Diod. 25.13, Plin. *NH.* 3.138, Eutrop. 3.5, Oros. 4.13.6
5. This is not the place for a full bibliography of this subject; but below are some of the most recent works; D. Baronowski. (1993). 'Roman Military Forces in 225 BC (Polybius 2.23–4)', *Historia* 42, pp.181–202, P. Brunt. (1971). *Italian Manpower 225 BC–AD 14* (Oxford), P. Erdkamp. (2008), pp.137–152.
6. L. De Ligt. (2012), pp.40–78. Also see P. Brunt. (1971).
7. L. De Ligt. & S. Northwood. (2008). *People, Land, and Politics: Demographic Developments and the Transformation of Roman Italy, 300 BC–AD 14* (Leiden).
8. P. Brunt. (1971), pp.41–60 and summarised by L. De Ligt. (2012), pp.42–44.
9. Lo Cascio argues for eight million, see L. De Ligt. (2012), pp. 44–47 for a summary of his arguments. Also see E. Lo Cascio. (2001). 'Recruitment and the Size of the Roman Population from the Third to the First Century BC', in W. Schiedel (ed.). *Debating Roman Demography* (Leiden), pp.111–137.
10. L. De Ligt. (2012), pp.63–71.

11. P. Erdkamp. (2012). 'Polybius and Livy on the Allies in the Roman Army', in L. Blois &
    E. Lo Cascio (eds.). *The Impact of the Roman Army (200 BC–AD 476)* (Leiden), pp.47–74.

Appendix V
  1. See A. Eckstein. (2006). *Mediterranean Anarchy, Interstate War and the Rise of Rome*
     (Berkeley), (2008). *Rome Enters the Greek East* (Oxford), E. Gruen. (1984). *The
     Hellenistic World and the Coming of Rome* (Berkeley) and P. Matyszak. (2009). *Roman
     Conquests. Macedonia and Greece* (Barnsley).
  2. See N. Hammond. (1968). pp.17–21
  3. See R. Waterfield. (2014). *Taken at the Flood. The Roman Conquest of Greece* (Oxford),
     pp.41–61.
  4. J. Balsdon. (1954). 'Rome and Macedon 205–200 BC', *Journal of Roman Studies* 44,
     pp.30–42.
  5. See J. May. (1946). 'Macedonia and Illyria (217–167 BC)', *Journal of Roman Studies* 36,
     pp.48–56.
  6. D. Dzino. (2005). 'Late Republican Illyrian Policy of Rome 167–60 BC: the Bifocal
     Approach', *Studies in Latin Literature and Roman History* 12 (Brussels), pp.48–73.
  7. A. Ziolkowski (1986). 'The Plundering of Epirus in 167 BC: Economic Considerations',
     Papers of the British School at Rome 54, pp. 69–80.

Index

Acerrae, 165–7, 172–3

Achaean League, 75, 88–9, 185

Acra Leuce, 96, 100–101

Adriatic, 7, 37, 44, 46, 61–2, 69–76, 80–2, 84, 86–9, 114, 119, 124, 177–8, 188, 196, 198, 200, 223, 243

Aelius Paetus, L. (Cos. 201 BC), 246

Aemilius Barbula, M. (Cos. 230 BC), 55

Aemilius Papus, L. (Cos. 225 BC), 120–2, 124, 126, 128, 142–3, 146, 148, 153, 159, 220

Aemilius Papus, L. (Pr. 205 BC), 143

Aemilius Papus, M., 143

Aemilius Papus, Q. (Cos. 282 & 278 BC), 122

Aemilius Paullus, L. (Cos. 219 & 206 BC), 198, 245

Aemilius Paullus, L. (Cos. 182 & 168 BC), 66

Aemilius Paullus, M. (Cos. 302 BC), 66

Aeneas, 63

Aequi, 6

Aetolian League, 70–3, 75, 78, 88–9, 188, 191, 224, 226, 244

Africa, 4, 7–8, 10, 12–16, 23, 62, 92–3, 97, 104, 109, 122, 214–15, 217

Agathocles, Tyrant of Syracuse (317–289 BC), 67–8

ager publicus, 237, 239

Agrigentum, 9

Agron, King of the Ardiaei (c.250–231 BC), 72–4, 85–6, 89, 199, 244

Alexander I, King of Epirus (342–331 BC), 65–6

Alexander II, King of Epirus (272–242 BC), 72

Alexander III (Great), King of Macedon (336–323 BC), 3

Anares, 153, 166

Aneroëstus, Chief of the Gaesatae, 114, 130, 138

Antigonus III, King of Macedon (229–221 BC), 185–8, 190, 199

Apollonia, 70, 77–9, 194

Apronius, Cn. (Aed. c.267 BC), 70

Apulians, 64

Arbo, 79–80

Acarnania, 70–1, 73

Archidamus III, King of Sparta (360–338 BC), 64–6

Ardiaei, 72–3, 75–6, 79–82, 85–9, 116, 186–8, 190, 197, 199, 244

Ariminum, 46, 49, 51–2, 56, 124, 144

Arretium, Battle of (283 BC), 45, 138

Arruns (of Clusium), 35–7

Athens, 63–4, 88–9, 211

Atilius Regulus, C. (Cos. 225 BC), 31, 121, 123–4, 131–2, 144–6

Atilius Regulus, M. (Cos. 227 & 217 BC), 145

Atilius Regulus, M. (Cos. 256 BC), 10, 122

Atilius Regulus, M. (Pr. 213 BC), 145

Atilius Serranus, C. (Pr. 218 BC), 180

Atintanes, 79

Atis, 49

Atyrian Hill, Battle of (229 BC), 82

Aurelius Cotta, C. (Cos. 201 BC), 246

Ausculum, Battle of (279 BC), 7, 68

Baebius Dives, L. (Pr. 189 BC), 246

Baebius Tamphilus, Cn. (Pr. 199 BC), 209, 246

Bagradas, Battle of (255 BC), 10, 14–15

Bagradas River, Battle of (240 BC), 13
Bellovesus, 36
Beneventum, Battle of (275 BC), 7, 68
Boii, 7, 26, 36, 44, 46, 48–54, 56, 58–60,
  113–14, 118, 120, 122, 124–5, 130, 134–5,
  137, 141–2, 144, 149–53, 159, 165, 175–6,
  178–81, 224, 246
Brennus, 37–9
Britomaris, 45
Brundisium, 73, 76
Bruttians, 67–8

Caecilius Metellus Denter, L. (Cos. 284, Pr.
  283?), 45
Caecilius Metellus, L., 57
Caere, 37, 64
Cannae, Battle of (216 BC), 146, 198, 245
Carthage, 8–10, 12–18, 20–5, 28, 47, 62,
  69, 86, 90–9, 101–105, 107, 109, 117–19,
  178–80, 187, 189, 202–205, 207–209,
  212–18, 222–3, 229, 243–4
Carvilius Maximus, Sp. (Cos. 234 & 228 BC),
  28–9, 85
Caudine Forks, Battle of (321 BC), 6
Cenomani, 36, 115, 118–22, 142, 150,
  153–4, 157, 175–6, 208, 219, 246
Chaeronea, Battle of (338 BC), 4
Clastidium, Battle of (222 BC), 164–76, 186,
  190, 226
Claudius Caecus, Ap. (Cens. 312 BC), 6
Claudius Caudex, Ap. (Cos. 264 BC), 8, 47
Claudius Clineas, M., 26
Claudius Marcellus, M. (Cos. 222, 215, 214,
  210, & 208 BC), 22, 159, 164–75, 226, 245
Cleomenes III, King of Sparta (235–222 BC),
  89, 185–7
Cleomenic War (229–222/1 BC), 185–6
Cleonymus, 66–8
Clusium, 35, 37, 43, 126, 128
Clusium, Battle of (295 BC), 43
Colline Gate, Battle of (360 BC), 41
Concolitanus, Chief of the Gaesatae, 114,
  138

Corcyra, 67, 73, 75–7, 79, 85–6, 88, 194
Corinth, 88–9
Cornelius, P. (Pr. 234 BC), 28
Cornelius Cethegus, C. (Cos. 197 BC), 246
Cornelius Cossus, A. (Cos. 428 BC), 170
Cornelius Dolabella, P. (Cos. 283 BC), 45
Cornelius Lentulus Caudinus, L. (Cos.
  237 BC), 51
Cornelius Lentulus Caudinus, P. (Cos.
  236 BC), 51–2, 54
Cornelius Scipio, L. (Cos. 298 BC), 43
Cornelius Scipio, P. (Cos. 218 BC), 217
Cornelius Scipio Asina. P. (Cos. 221 BC), 176
Cornelius Scipio Calvus, Cn. (Cos. 222 BC),
  164, 166, 169, 172–5
Cornelius Scipio Nasica, P. (Cos. 191 BC),
  246
Corsica, 13–14, 16–17, 19–20, 23, 25–32,
  53–6, 60, 62, 74, 86, 98, 107, 119
Coruncanius, C., 73, 75
Coruncanius, L., 73, 75
Coruncanius, Ti (Cos. 280 BC), 75
Cremona, 153, 178, 246
Croton, 67–8
Cumae, 63
Cynoscephalae, Battle of (197 BC), 244

Dardani, 89, 185
Decius Mus, P. (Cos. 295 BC), 43
Demetrius II, King of Macedon (239–
  229 BC), 72, 89, 185–6
Demetrius of Pharos, 76–7, 79, 83–4, 86–7,
  177, 187–200, 243
Diadochi, 65
Dimale, 191–5
Dionysius I, Tyrant of Syracuse
  (c.405 BC–367 BC), 9, 18, 37, 64
Dionysius II, Tyrant of Syracuse (367–357 BC
  & 346–344 BC), 64
Domitius Calvinus Maximus, Cn. (Cos.
  283 BC), 45
Drepana, 10
Duilius, C. (Cos. 260 BC), 10

Ecnomus, Battle of (256 BC), 10
Egypt, 3, 62, 67, 69, 185–6
Emporion, 62
Epidamnus, 73, 75–9, 83–6, 194
Epirus, 7–9, 17, 64–5, 67, 70–5, 78, 86, 89, 185, 199, 244–5
Etruscans, 6–7, 10, 12, 36–8, 42–6, 48, 67, 120, 123–6, 128, 130–2, 141, 173

Fabius, Q. (Aed. c.267 BC), 70
Fabius Maximus Verrucosus, Q. (Cos. 233, 228, 215, 214 & 209 BC), 55–6, 59, 85, 226
Fabius Pictor, Q., 25, 133, 139, 147, 228–9, 235, 238, 241
Falisci, 10–12, 48
Faesulae, Battle of (225 BC), 125, 127–8, 132, 141, 144, 146,
Flaminius, C. (Tr. 232/228 BC, Pr. 227 BC, Cos. 223 & 217 BC), 20, 56–7, 143, 145, 151–63, 181, 234, 237–9
Fulvius Centumalus, Cn. (Cos. 229 BC), 76–7, 80, 83–4, 88, 117
Fulvius Flaccus, M. (Cos. 264 BC), 46–7
Fulvius Flaccus, Q. (Cos. 237 & 224 BC), 51, 148–9
Furius Camillus, L. (Cos. 338, 325), 5
Furius Camillus, M. (Mil. Tr. 401, 398, 394, 386, 384, 381 BC), 39–40
Furius Philus, P. (Cos. 223 BC), 152–3, 155, 157–8, 160–3
Furius Purpurio, L. (Pr. 200 BC), 246

Gadir/Gades (Cadiz), 95
Gaesatae, 114–15, 119, 122, 125, 130, 134–8, 141, 144, 164–7, 169, 172, 174–5
Galatia, 36
Galatus, 49
Gargenus, Chieftain of the Boii, 159
Gauls, 7, 20, 35–45, 47–52, 54, 57–8, 62, 67, 89, 114–18, 122–36, 138–46, 148–9, 151, 155–7, 159–60, 163–4, 166–75, 177, 180, 185, 187, 196, 201, 216–19, 222, 237, 239, 245–7
Genthius, King of the Ardiaei (c.182–168 BC), 244

Hamilcar Barca, 13–14, 92–103, 107, 109, 202–203, 207, 225
Hannibal, 14
Hannibal (Barcid), 20, 85, 100, 108, 146, 159–60, 181, 194, 202–17, 225, 228–30, 239, 243
Hanno, 13–14, 215
Hasdrubal, 96–7, 100–105, 117, 201–203, 207, 211
Helice, 100–101
Heraclea, 63
Heraclea, Battle of (280 BC), 7, 68
Herenici, 6
Hiero II, Tyrant of Syracuse (c.275–c.216 BC), 8–9, 18, 21–2, 225, 245
Hieronymus, Tyrant of Syracuse (c.216–214 BC), 22, 245
Hippo Acra, 12

Illyrian War, First (230–228 BC), 20, 62–89, 99, 176
Illyrian War, Second (219 BC), 177, 185–200
Illyrian War, Third (168–167 BC), 244
Indortes, 94–5
Insubres, 36, 51, 59, 113–14, 118, 122, 125, 130, 134–5, 137, 141–3, 149–50, 153–4, 156–7, 162, 164–5, 169, 173–6, 178–81, 246
Issa, 73–4, 76, 79–80, 85–6, 189
Isthmian Games, 88
Istria, 176–7, 187–8, 196–7, 247
Iunius Bubulcus Brutus, C. (Dict. 302 BC), 66–7
Iunius Pera, M. (Cos. 230 BC), 55, 59

Lacinium, Cape of, 67, 229
Lake Trasimene, Battle of (217 BC), 20, 145, 157, 159–60, 181, 239
Lake Vadimon, Battle of (283 BC), 7, 44, 46, 122
Latin League, 4–5, 42
Latin War (341–338 BC), 4–5
Libui, 36
Licinius Stolo, C. (Tr. 376–367 BC), 235
Licinius Varus, C. (Cos. 236 BC), 26, 52

Ligurians, 26, 28, 48, 52–6, 58, 67, 85, 142, 148, 153, 163, 176–7, 224, 246
Lilybaeum, 10
Livius Salinator, M. (Cos. 219 & 207 BC), 191–2, 195, 198–9
Locri, 68
Longanus River, Battle of (c.269–264 BC), 22
Lucanians, 64–5, 68, 240
Lutatius Catulus, C. (Cos. 220 BC), 177–9
Lutatius Cerco, Q. (Cos. 241 BC), 11, 18–19, 21, 105

Macedon, 3–4, 62, 65–7, 71–2, 89, 119, 185–91, 194–200, 216–17, 222–3, 229
Macedonian War, First (214–205 BC), 243–4
Macedonian War, Third (172–167 BC), 244, 247
Magna Graecia, 63, 67, 219
Mamertines, 8–9, 22
Manduria, Battle of (338 BC), 64
Manlius, T. (Cos. 347, 344, 340 BC), 40
Manlius Torquatus, T. (Cos. 235 & 224 BC), 27, 148–9
Manlius Torquatus Atticus, A. (Cos. 241 BC), 11–12
Manlius (Vulso), L. (Pr. 218 BC), 179–81
Manlius Vulso, A. (Cos. 178 BC), 247
Manlius Vulso Longus, L. (Cos. 256 BC), 10
Marcius, C. (Tr. 311 BC), 6
Marsi, 6, 240
Massilia, 62, 103, 107, 109, 153, 208, 221
Mediolanum, 172–4
Melpum, 173
Mercenary War (240–237 BC), 16, 23–4, 92, 222
Messana, 8–9, 15, 18, 22, 47
Messapians, 240
Minucius Rufus, M. (Cos. 221 BC), 176
Minucius Rufus, Q. (Cos. 197 BC), 246
Mutina, 179–80
Mylae, Battle of (260 BC), 10

New Carthage, 101–103, 204, 209, 213–15
Nutria, Battle of (229 BC), 81

Orissi, 100–102, 107

Papirius Maso, C. (Cos. 231 BC), 30, 98
Parthini, 79, 194
Peisistratids, Tyrants of Athens, 63
Peloponnesian War, 63
Persian Empire, 62
Petillius Spurinus, Q. (Cos. 176 BC), 247
Pharos, 76, 79–81, 83, 186–7, 191–200, 243
Philip II, King of Macedon (359–336 BC), 4
Philip V, King of Macedon (221–179 BC), 89, 185, 188, 191, 194–7, 199–200, 229, 243–7
Phoenice, 73–4
Pinnes, King of the Ardiaei (231–217 BC), 85–7, 186–7, 197, 199
Pisa, 132, 134
Placentia, 153, 178, 246
Pleuratus, King of the Ardiaei (c.260–c.250 BC), 72
Pleuratus II, King of the Ardiaei (c.207–c.182 BC), 244
Pomponius Matho, M. (Cos. 233 BC), 29
Pomponius Matho, M. (Cos. 231 BC), 29–30, 98
Postumius Albinus, L. (Cos. 234 & 229 BC), 28, 55, 76–7, 83–5, 88
Praeneste, Battle of (358 BC), 41
Ptolemy, King of Epirus (c.237–234 BC), 72
Ptolemy I, King of Egypt (323–283 BC), 67
Ptolemy II, King of Egypt (283–246 BC), 69
Ptolemy III, King of Egypt (246–222 BC), 186
Pydna, Battle of (168 BC), 195, 244
Pyrgi, 37, 64
Pyrrhus, King of Epirus (306–302 & 297–272 BC), 44, 46, 64–9, 71–2, 74–5, 77, 244
Pyrrhus II, King of Epirus (255–237 BC), 72

Rhegium, 9, 63, 68
Rhizon, 82
River Allia, Battle of (c.390–386 BC), 38
River Anio, Battle of (c.361 BC), 40
River Clusius, Battle of (224 BC), 154, 161–3
River Oglio, 153

River Po, 148–50, 153, 163, 177–8, 187, 196, 219
Romulus, 170

Sack of Rome, 38–40, 218–19
Salui, 36
Samnite War, Second (326–304 BC), 6
Samnite War, Third (298–290 BC), 7, 43, 67–8
Samnites, 6–7, 42–4, 47, 65–7, 240
Sardinia, 12, 14, 16–17, 19–20, 23–32, 53–6, 60, 62, 74, 85–6, 90, 92, 98, 107, 116, 119, 123–6, 131–3, 145, 148, 199, 221–3
Saw, Battle of (238 BC), 13
Scerdilaïdas, Regent/King of the Ardiaei (c.218–c.207 BC) 198, 244
Sellasia, Battle of (222 BC), 186, 190
Seleucus II, King of Seleucid Empire (246–225 BC), 70
Seleucid Empire, 3, 70
Sempronius Gracchus, Ti. (Cos. 238 BC), 24, 53–4, 57
Sempronius Gracchus, Ti. (Tr. 133 BC), 24, 236–7
Sempronius Longus, Ti. (Cos. 218 BC), 217
Senate, Carthaginian, 10, 97, 101, 202–203, 209–10, 214–15
Senate, Roman, 8, 15, 18, 20, 23, 26–9, 31–2, 39, 47, 50, 52, 57–8, 60, 69–70, 73–5, 85, 87, 89, 98–9, 103–106, 108–109, 116–17, 119, 122, 145, 148, 152, 157–65, 176, 178, 180, 189–91, 201–202, 209, 214–17, 222–3, 234–6, 238–9
Senones, 7, 36–40, 42–6, 49, 56–7, 234, 237, 239
Sentinum, Battle of (295 BC), 7, 43
Sextius Sextinus Lateranus, L. (Tr. 376–367 BC), 235
Sicily, 7–10, 12–23, 27, 31–2, 47, 62–3, 67–70, 75, 86, 90, 92, 107, 116, 119, 121, 152, 199, 208, 217, 221–2, 225, 229–30, 239–40, 243, 245

Social War (220–217 BC), 188, 243
Spain, 3, 14, 16, 56, 62, 90–109, 117, 179–80, 189–91, 195, 198–217, 222–3, 225, 243
Sparta, 10, 64, 66, 69, 89, 185–6, 188, 230
Spoletium, 48
Sulpicius Longus, Q. (Mil. Trib. c.390 BC), 38
Syracuse, 8–9, 15, 17–18, 21–2, 37, 62–4, 67–9, 107, 223, 225, 245

Tarentum, 21, 63–4, 66–9, 119, 121, 240
Tartessians, 94–5
Taurisci, 114–15, 122, 134–5, 137, 141
Telamon, Battle of (225 BC), 114–15, 118, 132–47, 149–50, 152–3, 172, 201, 220, 223–4, 226
Teuta, Regent of the Ardiaei (231–229 BC), 73, 75–8, 80–6, 88, 186–8, 199, 244
Thermopylae, Battle of (279 BC), 36
Thurri, 63
Tibur, 40–1
Tribunate of the Plebs, 56, 152, 158, 224, 234–9
Triteuta, 86, 186
Tunis, 12, 14

Umbrians, 7, 42, 67, 120
Utica, 12–15

Valerius Falto, P. (Cos. 238), 50–1
Valerius Flaccus, P. (Cos. 227 BC), 209
Valerius (Laevinus), M. (Pr. 227 BC), 31
Veii, 4, 11, 32, 38–9
Veneti, 67, 118–22, 142, 150, 175–7, 208
Veturius Philo, L. (Cos. 220 BC), 177–8
Virdomarus, Gallic Chieftain, 169–70
Volsinii, 46

Xanthippus, 10